TURNIPS'

EDIBLE ALMANAC

APRIL

Ardour kiwi from Landes / Pitahaya (dragon fruit) / Queen Victoria pineapples / Strawberries – Gariguette, Mara des Bois / Raspberries – Panach' Golden, Portuguese Tulameen / Spanish avocados / Wild garlic buds / Brittany herbs / Dill / Fennel herb / Italian mixed herbs / Marjoram / Moroccan mint / Norfolk marsh samphire / Oregano / Provence mint / Sorrel / Thai lemongrass / Courgette (zucchini) flowers / Tomatoes – Datterini, Early Provence, San Marzano, Sicilian / Baby mixed leaves Campania / Baby spinach / Chalke Valley watercress / Italian wild rocket (arugula) / Mizuna and Tatsoi leaf / Red and white Belgian chicory / Endives – Pis-en-lit (dandelion), Summer fine frisée / Feuille de chêne (oak leaf lettuce) / Red and green Butterhead lettuce / Salanova salad / Surrey Little Gems / Breakfast radish / Italian celery / Ridge cucumbers / Surrey Downs spring onions / Sicilian peppers / Beans – Borlotti, Italian broad (fava), Yellow / Asparagus – Les Landes white, Norfolk, Pertius green / Brittany cauliflower / Chinese bok choy / Young Italian spinach / Artichokes – Roman Mammole globe, Violet baby artichokes from Apuli / Aubergines (eggplants) – Pale Italian, Tiger / Courgettes – French round, Tromba / Wet garlic / Mushrooms – Mousseron, St George / Tropea onions / Young French leeks / Potatoes – Cornish "earlies", Ile de Ré, Jersey Royal "earlies" / Essex young beetroot / Italian fennel / Nantes carrots / Radishes – Black mooli, Red and white long French / Turnips – Tokyo, Young

MAY

Alphonso mangoes / French Charentais melon / Greek Torpedo watermelon / Iranian Cantaloupe melon / Pitahaya (dragon fruit) / Queen Victoria pineapples / Tunisian Cantaloupe melon / Panach' blackberries / Panach' blueberries / Raspberries – Panach' Golden, Portuguese Tulameen / Strawberries – Gariguette, Mara'des Bois / French apricots / Iranian yellow dates / Elderflower / Wild garlic flowers / Brittany herbs / Dill / French basil / Kentish mint – many varieties / Marjoram / Norfolk marsh samphire / Oregano / Provence mint / Rock samphire / Sea purslane / Sorrel / Tomatoes – Early Provence, Italian summer varieties / Baby mixed leaves Campania / Chalke Valley watercress / Italian wild rocket (arugula) / Mizuna and Tatsoi leaf / Red and white Belgian chicory / Endives – Pis-en-lit (dandelion), Summer fine frisée / Feuille de chêne (oak leaf lettuce) / Red and green Butterhead lettuce / Salanova salad / Surrey Little Gems / Breakfast radish / Italian celery / Cucumbers – Italian, Ridge / Surrey Downs spring onions / Sicilian peppers / Beans – Italian broad (fava), Extra fine French / Yorkshire peas / Asparagus – Les Landes white, Norfolk asparagus / Brittany cauliflower / Chinese bok choy / Young Italian spinach / Artichokes – Camus globe, Violet baby artichokes from Apuli / Pale Italian aubergines (eggplants) / Courgettes (zucchini) – French round, Tromba / Wet garlic / Mushrooms – Chicken of the Woods, Horse, St George / Young French leeks / Potatoes – Cornish "earlies", Ile de Ré / Essex young beetroot / Italian fennel / Nantes carrots / Radishes – Black mooli, Red and white long French, Kent varieties / Young turnips

JUNE

Alphonso mangoes / French Charentais melon / Greek Torpedo watermelon / Iranian Cantaloupe melon / Israeli Galia melon / Italian Cantaloupe melons / Italian Torpedo watermelon / Kent gooseberries / Panach' blackberries / Panach' blueberries / Panach' gooseberries / Raspberries – French Tulameen, Panach' Golden / Strawberries – Gariguette, Mara des Bois / Bing cherries / French apricots / Iranian yellow dates / Pêche blanche and pêche jaune / Kentish wild strawberries / Dill / French basil / Kentish mint – many varieties / Lemon verbena / Marjoram / Norfolk marsh samphire / Oregano / Rock samphire / Sea purslane / Sorrel / Sussex courgette (zucchini) flowers / Fresh almonds / Tomatoes – Early Provence, Italian summer varieties, Outdoor varieties / Baby mixed leaves Campania / Chalke Valley watercress / Italian wild rocket (arugula) / Mizuna and Tatsoi leaf / Endives – Pis-en-lit (dandelion), Summer fine frisée / Feuille de chêne (oak leaf lettuce) / Italian Cos / Red and green Butterhead lettuce / Salanova salad / Surrey Little Gems / Webb's Wonder / Breakfast radish / Italian celery / Italian Cucumbers / Surrey Downs spring onions / Bell peppers / Padrón peppers / Pimiento Asado del Bierzo / Sicilian peppers / Beans – Broad (fava) from Worcester, Extra fine French, Kent Bobby, Runner from Worcester / Yorkshire peas / Norfolk asparagus / Brittany cauliflower / Young Italian spinach / Chinese bok choy / Artichokes – Camus globe, Violet baby artichokes from Apuli / Courgettes – French round, Tromba / Mushrooms – Cauliflower, Chicken of the Woods, Horse, Puffball / Young French leeks / Potatoes – Cornish "earlies", Ile de Ré, Noirmoutier / Baby veg – Essex beetroot, carrots, fennel, and turnips / Italian fennel / Nantes carrots / Radishes – Kent varieties, Red and white long French, Kent varieties

The week-by-week
guide to cooking with
seasonal ingredients

TURNIPS'

EDIBLE ALMANAC

FRED FOSTER

Contents

Foreword by Jeff Galvin

I remember the first words I heard from Fred Foster's lips: "Oy! Oy!" This was not the kind of introduction a new supplier normally gave to a senior member of a three-Michelin-starred kitchen team.

Chez Nico at 90 Park Lane was one of only four restaurants to hold the ultimate three Michelin stars in Great Britain. The Chef Patron Nico Ladenis had said that Fred was now going to be our only supplier of fruit and vegetables (down from five), which for a restaurant of this standing we thought was ludicrous. We were all left with the feeling that this guy didn't know an apple from a pear!

It was a good lesson for us because the Chef Patron had spotted the passion and desire in a man whose main purpose and thrill in life is to seek out the best-tasting seasonal produce bar none.

I have enjoyed a career working with Fred, visiting the markets and the growers of much of the amazing produce we used in our restaurant kitchens.

After 30 years, Fred remains a constant source of information and inspiration, as well as being a dear friend.

Introduction

What should we be eating this week? We all want to eat seasonal and delicious fresh produce, but how do we know what that is, and what does "seasonal" really mean anyway?

Turnips' Edible Almanac is a fruit-and-vegetable reference book for home cooks, chefs or the culinary-interested, with 52 chapters: one for every week of the year. For each week I highlight one, sometimes two fresh products that are at their best in that week. At the top of every product essay, I include a weekly shopping list of everything that you should be looking out for while you're out in the market or at your greengrocer that week. The lists group together produce according to those that are fruit, then foraged, herbs, nuts, salads, and vegetables, and they always start with those that are the most perfect of all for that moment in time. These lists are created from decades of my experience working with and selling world-class fresh fruit and vegetables to restaurants, chefs and home cooks. All the featured fruits and vegetables are outdoor-grown and of world-class quality. (It's easier than you think to avoid anything glasshouse-grown for a full 52 weeks.) Each week, there are also two recipes designed to best showcase the highlighted ingredient. Most of these recipes are written by Tomas Lidakevicius, our head chef at Turnips Restaurant and Lithuania's answer to Eminem.

When it's appropriate, Tomas has included a preserving recipe for the star ingredient each week. Jams, pickles, ferments and infusions are a perfect way to enjoy produce when it is no longer available fresh. And his recipes will enliven your cooking and give untold joy when you open your larder or fridge and see memories of seasons past neatly lined up.

I believe that for fruit and vegetables to be seasonal, they must be grown outdoors in fields, orchards and forests, or in weather-protected sheds or under cloches, and in soil from the region. This is extremely important because regions each have a unique terroir that imparts distinct flavour to what grows there. And, after all, flavour is king.

This almanac is created primarily with a British audience in mind, with London being the hub. Our capital city is the nucleus of where my food seasonality begins. Your food journey starts wherever you live and includes your foraging spots, local farms, farmers' markets and independent retailers – they all complete your world-class food adventure. This food journey is like dropping a pebble into water and watching the concentric ripples radiate outward, with your location being in the middle. This practice is especially easy if you live in a diverse city like London or an agricultural hotspot like Sicily; less so if you live in the Sahara Desert.

Turnips is based in London and our nearest farming regions are Kent, Essex and Surrey, but we are closer to France than we are to Scotland, so it wouldn't make sense to be dogmatically British-only in my quest for the best produce.

The home counties of Kent, Essex and Surrey produce incredible salads, orchard fruits, brassicas and tomatoes, as well as foraged goods in abundance, but for some other produce we need to go further afield for better quality. This is a standard approach in the rest of Europe. If you go to Rungis Market in Paris, which is the biggest produce market Europe has to offer, you will not find French rhubarb during the Yorkshire forced rhubarb season because those Parisian traders know that Yorkshire rhubarb is better.

We look first at the UK before moving on to Europe, then the northern hemisphere and finally the rest of the world. For produce like mangoes and pineapples, which we can't grow in this country, this is especially important.

How far you need to reach out from your local area to find exceptional fresh produce, depends on the bounty available on your doorstep. This is where soil types and climate play a vital role, not just for which fruit and veg are grown locally, but also what specific seed varieties best thrive in the area. A Jubilee strawberry grown in Kent is a thing of beauty and the Gariguette strawberry thrives in Provençal soil, but neither fares so well in the other's region.

If I believe a certain British product is world-class standard, I consider the time that product is ready for harvesting as the start of its British season. However, if there is a better product of the same variety grown elsewhere in the world, then that is when the Turnips' season starts.

As you read the chapters, you will notice that the four seasons in this book are not clear-cut and easily defined and have been re-worked slightly into Winter–Spring (Weeks 1–13), Spring–Summer (14–25), Summer–Autumn (26–39) and Autumn–Winter (40–52). Often what's thought of as, say, a spring vegetable or summer fruit actually starts in the previous season. But seasons and farming are at the mercy of the weather so we all need to adopt some flexibility, and some produce can be earlier or later depending on what the weather decides to send us.

I don't believe in mediocrity and that includes in food – I have spent a lifetime seeking out stellar produce for my customers, both on the market stand and for my restaurant clients. I don't limit that search to British grown, but when we do grow something truly unbeatable on our own shores, like the mighty Yorkshire pea (see page 133) or Bing cherries from Herefordshire (page 162), this book will champion and celebrate that product and the dedicated and highly skilled farmers who grow it.

Fruit and veg are often considered an afterthought or a supporting act to a "main" course. Top chefs will know that the grouse season starts in August on the "glorious twelfth", but few have an in-depth knowledge of the seasonality of our fruit and vegetables. It's all the wrong way round.

Campaigns like British Tomato Fortnight, in May, although a step in the right direction, don't help, adding only confusion: outdoor-grown British tomatoes are a late-summer product, not an early one. I want to put the record straight.

Most outdoor-grown produce has, roughly, a six-week season. Within that season, you will get early, mid and late/main-crop varieties. Blood oranges are a perfect example of this. If you've ever complained that your blood oranges aren't red and "bloody" enough, that's because more than likely you are eating Tarocco, an early season variety and my personal favourite. The Tarocco barely blushes, but it is sweet and juicy. If you wait until the middle of the season for the Sanguinello, you'll get your precious crimson fruit, but, wait even longer and you'll find the bloodiest Moro oranges.

You can also extend the season for some produce by a few extra weeks by sourcing from other countries, but only when they are exceptional quality – this does not apply to your run-of-the-mill, bog-standard fare. Using my seasonality, tomatoes have nearly a nine-month season starting in January/ February in Sicily, moving through France, back to Italy and ending with the Marmonde from Essex in September.

Glasshouse farming means we no longer have to wait for much in the way of produce, and traditional seasons have sadly become blurred or lost. Sure, you can get Peruvian asparagus in the supermarkets all year round, but those spears are nothing compared to asparagus from Norfolk, which arrives toward the end of April and is around for a few short weeks. We should wait for the outdoor-grown seasons of our favourite fruits and vegetables and, when they are over, we should move on to the new joy that follows. Having the same things available all year round takes away the adventure in cooking and eating.

I want to encourage people to embrace the anticipation, the excitement of counting down to the arrival of a long-awaited fruit or vegetable.

It's important to note that however long I've been considered an expert in my field, flavour and taste can only ever be subjective. There can never be a truly definitive list of the best of the best when it comes to regions and varieties – local loyalties and subjectivity always get in the way. But isn't that half the fun? This book is the Turnips' and Fred Foster list, based on our judgment and the feedback from our customers since 1980.

Food is central to my life and work, and I love to eat. At Turnips we sell to many customers – from those who pop in for a box of wild mushrooms, to those doing their weekly shop, to others who buy a Sugarloaf pineapple out of curiosity and the wholesale business that supplies restaurants at all levels.

The Fred Foster Turnips' story

I am the co-director of Turnips of Borough Market, a family business with over 40 years of experience in the trade. I'm a fourth-generation costermonger, who started out in this business on my dad's salad stall, Jas Foster & Sons, at Tachbrook Street Market, in Pimlico.

I'm not going to tell you some sentimental tale about how my old man sparked a passion in me for fruit and veg. It's a tall order to expect a boy, barely out of short trousers, to get excited about salads. Especially when he's been dragged out of bed at the crack of dawn only for ice-cold water to cascade down his back off a tarpaulin in the middle of winter. Oh, the memories! But Turnips is, in a sense, the legacy of that small boy's life, working with and learning from his dad. And the Turnips' story certainly begins in Pimlico.

Some time after I was out of short trousers, Caroline (then my soon-to-be-wife) and I bought a stall in Tachbrook Street Market from my cousin Uncle Johnny (I called him my uncle owing to the huge age gap between us). Aged just 24, we decided to create a niche in the market and provide something new for our customers. Then, every town and city had a bustling market, which was the hub of the community and wonderfully egalitarian. People would join the end of the queue and wait to be served. Only the fish and meat purveyors were in bricks-and-mortar shops. Us fruit-and-veg people were a hardy bunch and we put up with weather of all kinds – rain or shine, it was a steep learning curve. Markets then were amazing places, made up of predominantly fruit, vegetable, salad and flower stalls. Each was separate from another: fruit never mixed with veg, and salads were similarly separate. Interestingly, the fruit, vegetable and salad stalls were equal in number and outnumbered the flower stalls three to one. In those days the Pimlico market had three veg stalls, three fruit stalls, two salad stalls and just one selling flowers.

Taking on Uncle Johnny's vegetable stall was a whole new experience for Caroline and me. To give ourselves an edge, we looked at what the restaurants were buying and supplied those products, as well as the staples for our commercial and market customers. We started selling mangetout and sugar snap peas, which were a delicacy back then. We even stocked truffles. One very smartly dressed lady paid for the first truffle we ever sold with a Coutts & Co cheque. We offered a free delivery service to local restaurants, something unheard of at the time – and something I was castigated for.

Caroline's family were in retail, so with her selling skills and my buying skills, we've made the perfect marriage, in both life and work. Without Caroline's input, there wouldn't be a Turnips today – of that I have no doubt.

My dad passed away when I was 11. He was and still is my hero. The day I started supplying my produce to Selfridges, on Oxford Street, I stepped through the doors of the amazing store, glanced up and thought about my dad looking down at me and feeling proud.

After Selfridges, we started supplying Harrods and some of London's finest restaurants, and in 1990 we moved from Tachbrook Street to Borough Market, which at the time was a tiny, failing wholesale space. We changed our name from Fosters of Pimlico – we wanted a name that was catchy and humorous. I'm a huge football fan and, at the time, Graham Taylor, the resident English football manager, was portrayed by the tabloids as a turnip head. We wanted to emphasize that we were a distributor of fresh produce but also maintain our sense of fun, so we became Turnips Distributing Ltd, which we later shortened simply to Turnips.

We were a pioneer in Borough Market's retail renaissance. Until the late 1990s, Borough Market had only ever operated as a wholesale trading ground and the site made more money as a car park than from selling food. Along with Neal's Yard Dairy and Brindisa, in 1998 we began opening our doors to the public for occasional warehouse sales.

Fast forward 25 years and Borough today is a cornucopia of diverse seasonal, artisanal and world-class ingredients all set within a vibrant, forward-thinking community that champions sustainability, provenance and quality.

Included in the Turnips empire is now our much-acclaimed restaurant, headed up by my son Charlie, with Tomas Lidakevicius at the helm in the kitchen. The restaurant began as a pop-up in 2020 as London was emerging from the Covid pandemic with menus centred on the best available seasonal produce.

Like many businesses in 2020, we were forced to adapt. Opening a restaurant, pop-up or otherwise, in the middle of a pandemic was a huge risk, but two years later the pop-up has evolved into a remarkable fine-dining operation under the railway bridges of Borough Market.

Charlie had joined the family firm straight after finishing university. His introduction to the company was to wear as many hats as possible: wholesale delivery driver, retail display artist, night packer and sales manager, and eventually he became one of the directors.

Tomas is Lithuanian but honed his culinary skills here in the UK, climbing the ladder and working for many top chefs until he became head chef at Jason Atherton's City Social. Tomas embraced our philosophy of championing fruit and vegetables and enhanced it with his skill and creativity. Clearly a man of many talents, Tomas was a music rapper back home in Lithuania and has adapted his style of cooking in a similar vein. He has an ability to ad lib when confronted with produce, such as Grumolo (see page 34), he has never worked with before and creates amazing dishes. But above all, he truly shares our belief that only magnificent produce can deliver truly unparalleled flavour.

Throughout our time in the fruit-and-veg business, we have sourced our beautiful produce from hard-working UK and European farmers both through agents and directly. Initially, we would buy produce from the wholesale markets around London, but when our chef clients started to ask for produce that was not available at these markets, we sourced directly from the producers and farmers themselves. Back in the early days, a chef from a very famous restaurant in Mayfair wanted a unique type of cabbage leaf. I was given the phone number of our cabbage farmer to see if he could help, but was warned that "He's a really grumpy fella." The "grumpy" farmer jumped at the challenge and went on to grow wonderful baby Hispi petal cabbages for us. The chef was delighted and our relationship with that farmer blossomed.

Partnerships that chime

Melo Laudani supplies us with lemons and blood oranges. Along with his family, he is someone whose farming practices and ethos sit perfectly with ours at Turnips. His story, in his own words, is the perfect example of how we like to do business.

"The story of the Laudani family in Sicily starts a long time ago, back when having a piece of land was the privilege of the very few and the very rich. My great-grandfather, Antonino, farmed land that he did not own, but he worked hard all year and split the yield from his crops with his landlord. Over time, and with the shifting generations, my grandfather no longer had to split his harvest with his landlord. He was able to work hard and save enough money from selling his watermelons to buy his own plot of land, on which he planted blood-orange trees. When he retired at 80 years old, my grandfather gave his sons several hectares of land that produced different varieties of fruit, but mainly citrus. The success of our wonderful blood oranges is largely down to the mineral-rich soil around Mount Etna and the peculiar climate of our geographic area, which has particular and unique properties.

All my farming knowledge has been passed down from Antonino, through the generations and eventually via my own father. We work in close contact with Nature, farming in the most natural ways possible, always changing for the better and using technology to enhance our environmental practices, but never replace them. For example, an innovative watering system and solar panels enable us to save water, energy and natural resources.

There is plenty that has not changed: we keep our farming methods simple and traditional; we avoid using chemicals on our plants and wax and preservatives on our fruits; we keep our plants healthy and clean by releasing friendly insects into the fields every spring, which help us fight parasites and diseases that might negatively affect our crops. The most important that thing my family has given me, though, is a passion for this land and the treasures it can give us if we treat it with respect."

This book is a year-long celebration of fruit, vegetables, producers, farmers, cooks and chefs – and it's a never-ending journey of joy!

Fred Foster, 2022

Useful Trimmings

Throughout the book, I refer to various accreditations that the fruits and vegetables we supply have achieved. These are marks of quality and provenance and none is achieved without enormous amounts of dedication, skill, expertise and hard work. It's also useful to know a bit more about the preserving process, which Tomas uses in many of his recipes. Feel free to refer back here if you need a reminder of the basics on your culinary adventure.

Appellation d'Origine Contrôlée (AOC)

The French AOC was set up to classify and protect specific wine-growing regions and the quality of their wines. In 1937, Châteauneuf-du-Pape became the first wine region to become accredited. Since then, over 350 wines and 100 food products have been given the official AOC seal. Many other countries and regions have their own organizations to govern and protect their produce in a similar way. The EU has Protected Designation of Origin (PDO), whereby every part of the production, processing and preparation of a food must happen within the designated area. Italy has Denominazione di Origine Controllata (DOC) and the even higher Denominazione di Origine Controllata e Garantita (DOCG) for wines. The DOC guarantees a product of quality made using traditional methods, in a specific geographical zone, by designated producers and using designated ingredients. For producers, being granted the French AOC and other EU certifications is considered the highest honour.

Sterilizing and pasteurizing

Sterilizing your preserving jars is a crucial step to ensure they aren't harbouring any bacteria that can spoil the precious contents of the jar – and waste all your hard work! Here's a fail-safe method:

First, preheat the oven to 160°C/140°C fan/315°F/Gas 2–3. Wash the jars with hot soapy water and rinse them to remove any soap residue. Do not dry the jars – instead, place them in the oven for 15–20 minutes. Meanwhile, wash the lids and rubber seals (if you're using Kilner jars) and boil these in a saucepan of water over a low heat for 10 minutes. Fill the jars while they are still hot, taking care not to touch the inside or the rim (this would contaminate the jars, so you'd have to start the sterilizing process again). Cover or seal the jars while the contents are still hot and leave them to cool before labelling and storing.

Some products and sauces require pasteurization, too. Each relevant recipe contains this information, but as a summary: place the filled and lightly sealed jars in a large saucepan and pour in enough water to come halfway up the sides of the jars. Place the pan over a low–medium heat, bring the water to a boil, reduce the heat and simmer for 10–15 minutes. Remove the jars, tighten the lids, turn the jars upside down and leave to cool before storing. Inverting jars creates a vacuum and ensures that the lids are secure and airtight.

1

Apples – French Chantecler Belchard / Bergamot / Clementines / Late Valencia oranges / Japanese yuzu / Sicilian lemons / Late season British and French apples – Braeburns, Golden Rosée, Hereford Cox Orange Pippin, Russets / Pears – Comice, Conference, Williams / Pomegranate / Spanish avocados / Bay leaves / Rosemary / Winter savoury / Almonds / Hazelnuts / Walnuts / Outdoor Sicilian tomatoes / Endives – Escarole, Winter frisée / Puntarelle / *Purple sprouting broccoli / Cauliflower – orange, purple, white, Romanesque / Cime di rapa / Chard – Rainbow, Swiss / Cabbages – Brussels tops, Cavolo Nero, January King, Somerset Savoy / Jerusalem artichokes / Perigord black truffles / Onions – Calcot, Cevenne, Roscoff / Potatoes – Agria, Cyprus Spunta, Ratte / Muscade pumpkin / Delica squash / Beetroots – Candy, Cheltenham, Golden / Celeriac / Parsnips / Salsify / Turnips*

Orchard Fruit
The Apple Doesn't Fall Far from the Tree

I am a fourth-generation costermonger – a compound word where "coster" is a medieval variety of apple and "monger" is a seller, making me a person who sells fruit and vegetables. Given the semantics, then, it is only fitting to start this book talking about the most popular fruit in the world: apples.

There is DNA evidence that puts the origin of apples in Central Asia (Kazakhstan specifically) over 2,000 years ago. Closer to home (and more recently), it is said that good old King Henry VIII got his fruiterer, Richard Harris, to create the first large-scale orchard garden in Teynham, Kent, which included apple varieties he had seen growing in France. The apple, then, is a noble fruit, with a long, established and intercontinental history.

When talking about seasons, it's easy to assume that the point at which a fruit or vegetable first appears is also when it is at its best. While that might be true for the first Jersey Royal potatoes (see page 59) or the first sweet, forced Wakefield rhubarb, it is not the case with apples. There are more than 2,000 varieties of apple in the National Fruit Collection at Brogdale in Kent, and they provide the perfect example of how the seasons actually work.

Varieties create the seasons – all fruits and vegetables have early, mid and late versions. Early season apples are beautifully sweet, fresh and juicy (something that can't be said for all apple varieties, some of which might not taste nice, look nice or indeed smell nice) and are solely for eating. In the UK, the Worcester Pearmain, Discovery and Orange Pippin, among others, are outstanding in early July to August. The mid-season (from late August to mid-September) is well served with Russets and Pippins – our home-grown apples ranking right up there when it comes to *la meilleure pomme du monde*, and storing well into December. As we leave December behind, most apple varieties tend not to store well. However, the Orange Pippin remains popular up to early April and the humble Bramley holds fast as the choice for pies and crumbles, storing well until late

Mature orchard fruits kick off the New Year with the mighty Mouneyrac French apple, including varieties such as Granny Smith, Rubinette and Belchard / Chantecler BIO.

spring of the following year. But it is the French varieties that in January power to the front: the relatively modern Rubinette, the older variety Patte de Loup and the stunning Golden Rosée – all of which store brilliantly. The Belchard Chantecler is outstanding in cooking.

Possibly the most famous apple dessert is the tarte Tatin, which originated in France and begins life upside-down – allegedly the result of a mistake by the Tatin sisters. Gifted chefs around the world have defined and re-defined it. Jeff Galvin, a good friend and one half of the talented Galvin Brothers, takes it on the chin when I rib him about their annual Tarte Tatin Competition. Each year in London, during May, amateur cooks are invited to come up with the UK's best tarte Tatin recipe. Following a final in June, the winner claims a prize of free tarte Tatin for life at the Galvin Brothers' restaurants. "How can you set a competition to cook the perfect apple dessert in early summer when the best apple to use is the French variety Chantecler, which is at its best in early winter?" I ask. Of course, the brothers who have the dish on their menus all year round, opt for the Braeburn, a variety that consistently performs.

The Belchard Chantecler apple is a regional variety grown in and around Aquitaine. The French National Institute for Agricultural Research (INRA) at Angers introduced this excellent cultivar in the 1950s. A golden-yellow fruit that is a cross between Golden Delicious and Reinette Clochard, sweet and with a hint of vanilla, it is perfect for tarte Tatin as the fruit does not disintegrate into a pulp during cooking. The apples are harvested in France between July and August and improve with age. The fruit is stored in a temperature- and atmosphere-controlled environment – it's not quite fermentation, but it is definitely scientific and best left to the botanists.

Who knew that apples have seasons? They come from all over the world and can be found in shops all year round. So, what's the problem? No problem at all. If you want to cook an apple tart in June it's fine, whatever suits your fancy. The only thing I would say, and the reason you probably have not heard of any of the aforementioned French apple varieties, is that if you choose to make apple desserts throughout the year, then you are restricted in the varieties you can use. Most retailers simply offer the same few varieties all year round.

> "How can you set a competition to cook the perfect apple dessert in early summer when the best apple to use is the French variety, Chantecler, which is at its best in early winter?"

So at this time of the year, we can truly appreciate the art of storing fruits and using them in hot dishes to warm us up in the long winter months that we have here in the UK.

Apple tarte Tatin with crème Normande *Recipe by the*
Galvin Brothers

Throughout my career I have been honoured to have worked with some truly remarkable chefs and cooks, and in this book I have included some of their iconic dishes. In 2020 at Turnips, we teamed up with one of these chefs, Tomas Lidakevicius, to create our unique restaurant at our location in Borough Market. Over the page, he offers us his apple cheese. The first of our "guest" chefs, though, are the Galvin Brothers who give us their iconic tarte Tatin dish, a stunning dessert with an amazing flavour – which means I can forgive them their choice of apple variety!

Serves 4

120g (4¼oz) puff pastry (store-bought or homemade)

110g (3¾oz) salted butter, softened

130g (4¾oz) caster (superfine) sugar

7 Braeburn apples, peeled, halved and cored

For the crème Normande

120g (4¼oz) crème fraîche

40g (1½oz) icing (confectioner's) sugar

1½ tbsp Calvados liqueur

Roll the puff pastry out on a lightly floured surface to a 21cm (8¼in) round. Prick all over with a fork and rest in the fridge for 40 minutes.

Spread the butter over the bottom of a 20cm (8in) tarte Tatin mould or an ovenproof, non-stick frying pan. Sprinkle the caster sugar over in an even layer, then arrange the apple halves over the sugar, standing them on their sides, with 2 halves in the middle. Lay the pastry round over the apples, tucking the edges down the side.

Place the mould or pan over a medium heat on the hob for about 10 minutes or until the sugar starts to caramelize. Transfer it to an oven preheated to 160°C/Gas Mark 3 and bake for 1½ hours.

For the crème Normande, mix all the ingredients together in a bowl, then cover with cling film and refrigerate for 1 hour.

Remove the tart from the oven and leave to cool for at least 30 minutes. Invert the tarte Tatin on to a chopping board and cut it into 4 portions.

Serve a generous spoonful of crème Normande with each portion of the warm tarte Tatin.

Apple cheese

This isn't a cheese at all, but a delicious way to preserve late-season apples to enjoy still later in the year. It is excellent alongside an actual cheeseboard and will keep for about three months wrapped well in the fridge.

Makes 3 cheeses

3.5kg (7lb 9oz) late-season apples (any mixture will do), peeled and cored

750g (1lb 10oz) caster (superfine) sugar

½ tsp ground cinnamon

Chop the apples into 2cm (¾in) dice. Tip the pieces into a large bowl or plastic container, then add the sugar and mix well to coat. Cover the bowl or container and leave the apples overnight at room temperature for the sugar to draw out the juices.

Strain the apples over a large pan to catch the juice, then place the pan over a medium heat. Set the apple pieces aside. Bring the juice to a boil, then leave it to bubble away until reduced by half and dark and sticky. Add two thirds of the diced apples to the pan, stir to combine, then reduce the heat to low and cook, stirring occasionally to prevent them catching on the bottom of the pan, for a further 20 minutes, until softened.

Stir in the cinnamon, then cook for 20 minutes more, until the mixture is thick enough to leave a furrow when stirred with a spoon. Add the remaining apples and cook for a further 3–5 minutes, until softened.

Spoon the hot mixture into three cheese bags and shake the bags well to disperse any air bubbles. Close the bags, place them on a tray and press them down with weights. Leave for 24 hours at room temperature, until the "cheese" has set into shape.

Remove the cheeses from the bags – it will look like hard apple chutney by now. Heat the oven to its lowest setting.

Place the cheeses on a lined baking tray and place them in the warm oven for a further 2 hours, until completely dry.

Remove the cheeses from the oven, leave them to cool and wrap them in paper or store them in an airtight box in the fridge for up to 3 months. To serve, slice and enjoy!

2

Tarocco blood oranges / *Bergamot* / *Clementine* / *Late Valencia oranges* / *Japanese yuzu* / *Lemons – Cedro, Sicilian* / *Sicilian grapefruit* / *Late season British and French apples – Braeburns, French Chantecler Belchard, Golden Rosée, Hereford Cox Orange Pippin, Russet* / *Pomegranate* / *Spanish avocados* / *Bay leaves* / *Rosemary* / *Winter savoury* / *Outdoor Sicilian tomatoes* / *Endives – Escarole, Winter frisée* / *Puntarelle* / *Purple sprouting Broccoli* / *Cauliflowers – orange, purple, white, Romanesque* / *Cime di rapa* / *Chards – Rainbow, Swiss* / *Cabbages – Brussels tops, Cavolo Nero, January King, kales, Somerset Savoy* / *Jerusalem artichokes* / *Perigord black truffles* / *Onions – Calcot, Cevenne, Roscoff* / *Potatoes – Agria, Cyprus Spunta, Pink Fir* / *Muscade pumpkin* / *Delicia squash* / *Beetroots – Candy, Cheltenham, Golden* / *Celeriac* / *Parsnips* / *Salsify* / *Turnips*

Tarocco Blood Orange
Out for Blood

"There are three sides to every story: your side, my side, and the truth. And no one is lying. Memories shared serve each differently." I love this quotation coined by Robert Evans in his unique style in his memoir *The Kid Stays in the Picture*. The infamous head of production at Paramount was the genius in charge of films such as *The Godfather*, *Rosemary's Baby* and *True Grit* to name a few.

When it comes to seasonality, this quotation rings very true for me. I dare say that there is a standard definition of what seasonality means, but, in the food world it's not that simple. My truth is that seasonality in fruit and vegetables has no boundaries, therefore I introduce flavour as a measure by which to determine what is and isn't in season. This book highlights *my* seasonality, *my* truth, *my* ethos in what determines, for example, when French Morel mushrooms are in season in the UK. For me, seasons have no borders. What's *your* truth?

Robert Evans was in charge at Paramount in 1974 when *The Godfather Part II* was filmed, much of it in Sicily. The film was a bloody affair just like one of the island's most famous exports, the blood orange.

The Tarocco blood orange, the *arancia rossa di Sicilia* (the "red orange of Sicily"), is the most popular table orange in Italy. Beautifully sweet and juicy, it has a thin, orange skin that is blushed with red markings and which peels extremely easily. As a result of growing in the fertile soil near Mount Etna, the fruit has the highest vitamin-C content of any orange variety. It holds Protected Geographical Indication (PGI), a status that means it must be grown in the provinces of Catania, Enna, Ragusa and Syracuse.

At Turnips we buy our Tarocco oranges directly from a family that has been farming the same ancient groves for generations. They provide us with truly stunning oranges (as well as lemons and grapefruits), which they grow in fertile groves set in the heart of the island. "Organic" doesn't begin to describe how pure this soil is. The family believes that the amazing structures in the earth

The incredibly sweet Tarocco blood orange from Laudani Farms is an early season orange that initially has very little red flesh, but it deepens in colour as the season progresses.

of these ancient groves are the result of the fact that Mount Etna is still an active volcano. However, if you are looking for a blood red orange right at the start of the season, you will be disappointed.

Blood oranges provide a perfect example to explain early, mid- and late-season varieties. Every year chefs call me at the very start of the blood-orange season demanding redder oranges, regardless of the flavour! I will tell you, the reader (just like I tell those chefs), that the early season Sicilian Tarocco, despite having the best flavour, has virtually no colour. The mid-season Spanish Sanguinello, which ripens in February and is available until March, starts to get a little redder – but you won't get a deep, ruby-red orange until the Sicilian Moro comes in around March. And, in my humble opinion, this latest blood orange, colourful as it may be, also happens to be the least delicious of the bunch. It is the Tarocco orange that has the flavour of sugary heaven, along with the zingy citrus kick that sucks the cheeks in.

Citrus is a major flavour source throughout the winter. All over London at this time of the year, you will find blood oranges on fine-dining menus and providing a certain wow factor in fruit bowls at home. The demand for this deep red, fleshy fruit is high among restaurateurs and food lovers.

So, varieties are important for flavour, look and texture; they extend seasons owing to early, mid- and late-breed – but expect

"There are three sides to every story: your side, my side, and the truth. And no one is lying. Memories shared serve each differently."

different colour variations, shapes and sizes and, most importantly, you should learn to love each little nuance that a particular variety owns. The Tarocco might be the tastiest blood orange, but for sure the Moro is the most stunning to look at. As we all know, though, looks aren't everything.

And here's the thing: oranges are available all year round, right? But how often do you buy oranges only to be thoroughly disappointed with their lack of flavour or juiciness? Sometimes that freshly squeezed orange juice is, well, uninspiring. This is probably because you are buying fruit that is mass produced and from the other side of the world. Our European oranges are stunning, they start late November and finish around March. We source oranges from France, Italy, Spain, Cyprus and Greece – all different varieties but equally beautiful fruits and, where possible, from independent growers to provide five months of zingy joy. After this time, give the oranges a break; move on to another fruit with excellent flavour. Less is more. By limiting when you buy that orange, you will enjoy it more and anticipate the season with excitement.

In this chapter we pay homage to the members of the Laudani family, who have farmed their citrus groves in Sicily for generations. They have provided us with the most incredible organic lemons (see page 304), blood oranges and grapefruits Nature has to offer.

Blood orange and beetroot salad with sunflower seeds

You can make this fresh little recipe a day in advance. It's not super-quick, but it's worth it… . If you're feeling lazy, you can use cooked beetroots (beets) and it will be ready in a couple of minutes. This is amazing on its own if you're looking for a vegan meal, or as a side dish to a main meal.

Serves 2 as a side

2 tennis-ball-size beetroots (beets), raw or cooked

1 large thyme sprig

2 bay leaves

1 garlic bulb

pinch of caster (superfine) sugar

100g (3½oz) sunflower seeds

5 tbsp olive oil

1 blood orange

3 tbsp pomegranate molasses

1 tsp Dijon mustard

1 tsp balsamic vinegar

salt and freshly ground black pepper

If you're using raw beetroot, put them whole in a large pan with the thyme sprig, bay leaves and garlic bulb. Add the sugar and a good pinch of salt, cover with water and bring the water to a boil over a medium heat. Reduce the heat to low and simmer for about 2 hours, or until tender when tested with the point of a knife. Leave the beetroot to cool down in the cooking liquid (about 2 hours).

Tip the sunflower seeds into a frying pan. Add 2 teaspoons of the olive oil and a little salt. Fry the seeds over a low heat, stirring often, for about 1–2 minutes, until the seeds are golden. Remove the pan from the heat and leave the seeds to cool.

Drain the beetroot and peel and cut them into small cubes. Tip the cubes into a mixing bowl and set aside. (If you're using cooked beetroot, simply cut them into cubes and tip them into the bowl.)

Finely grate the zest from the orange and set aside. Using a small knife cut the skin and pith from the orange and, holding it over a bowl to catch any juice, cut the fruit into neat segments.

Add the pomegranate molasses, mustard and vinegar to the orange juice and whisk to combine. Gradually add the remaining olive oil, whisking continuously, to thicken the mixture into a dressing that will lightly coat the beetroot.

Spoon the dressing over the beetroot – you may not need it all – season with salt and pepper, then add the toasted sunflower seeds and mix to combine. Scatter over the orange segments to serve.

Spiced blood orange candied peel

You'll have your sugar cravings sorted for a while with this quantity of candied peel, which will keep in a cool, dry larder for up to a year. You can eat the peels just as they are, or try dipping them into melted chocolate for an amazing treat, or use them to decorate your desserts and cakes. Added to a morning cup of tea, a few pieces of peel make for an unusually delicious brew.

You're using only the peel here, but don't let the orange flesh and juice go to waste. Either eat the fruit, or squeeze the juice to drink. You could alternatively reduce it in a small pan, with a little butter, as a beautiful glaze for carrots or in orange beurre blanc. We generally use caster (superfine) sugar in this recipe, but you could use honey or other types of sugar – just note that the peels will be sticky rather than firm.

**Makes 1–2 jam jars or
1 medium Kilner jar**

5 blood oranges, washed and quartered

250g (9oz) caster (superfine) sugar

2 star anise

4 cloves

3 saffron stamens

1 vanilla pod, halved

¼ tsp citric acid

Peel the skin away from the orange flesh. (Eat the orange flesh or juice it.) Cut the orange peel into 1cm (½in)-wide strips and tip the strips into a medium saucepan. Cover the strips with water and bring the water to a boil over a medium heat. Reduce the heat and simmer for 2 minutes, then drain and repeat this procedure twice more, after which the orange peel will have lost any bitterness. Drain and set aside.

Now comes the fun part. Using the same pan, combine 200g (7oz) of the sugar with 400ml (14fl oz) of water and the star anise, cloves and saffron. Bring the liquid to a boil over a medium heat and simmer for 20 minutes, until the syrup is infused with spices and has reduced by half.

Add the orange peel pieces and halved vanilla pod to the syrup and cook over a low heat, stirring often, for about 30 minutes, until the syrup has almost cooked off and the peels are nicely coated.

Remove the peels from the pan one at a time and leave them to dry on a cooling rack at room temperature for 24 hours, until hardened. Combine the remaining sugar with the citric acid and toss the candied peels in the sugar mixture to coat.

Transfer the peels to an airtight box between layers of baking paper or into an airtight jar to store for up to 1 year.

3

Stockbridge Harbinger Forced Rhubarb
Rhubarb, Rhubarb, Rhubarb

Forced rhubarb is widely regarded as the sweetest and best. The variety Stockbridge Harbinger, in particular, is a godsend at this time of the year, when fresh produce is scarce. This amazing rhubarb comes out of Yorkshire, from the "Rhubarb Triangle" – an area of roughly 14.5km (9 miles) square, with Wakefield, Leeds and Bradford at its three points and in a frost pocket on the side of the Pennines. Originally found in Siberia, rhubarb favours cool, wet and damp growing conditions, making this part of Yorkshire the perfect location. In fact, no other region in the UK has successfully produced such sweet rhubarb.

To say this rhubarb is grown using traditional methods is an understatement. The roots, or "sets", are initially grown for two to three years outside, in the nitrogen-rich soils of the Pennines. The cold fields are heavily fertilized with manure, and shoddy – a natural by-product of the local woollen industry. The rhubarb roots are then carefully transferred to special, heated indoor "forcing" sheds, where they continue to grow in total darkness for six to nine weeks. There, the plants produce sweet, tall and slender stems that are bright pink to almost blood-red in colour and have compact yellow leaves. The rhubarb is then hand-harvested by candlelight, which prevents the plants photosynthesizing and instead encourages the glucose stored in the roots to stimulate growth in the stalks.

In February 2010, the EU awarded Yorkshire forced rhubarb the status of Protected Designation of Origin (PDO; see page 15). This legal safeguard gives it the same protected status as other region-specific products, such as Champagne, Parma ham and Melton Mowbray pork pies.

Rhubarb rootstock in the Rhubarb Triangle is handed down through generations. In the late 1800s, rhubarb had something of a heyday: there were about 200 growers in the area and a dedicated transport system linked them with markets in London and further afield. Now, there are fewer than 12, who are permitted to cultivate new plants only by splitting the existing rootstock in order to preserve the quality and purity of the strain. Greenhouse varieties can mimic what the people of Yorkshire have created, but they can't match the flavour of this truly world-class product. The UK should be immensely proud.

"Hurrah! This is a true success story!" I hear you cheer. Unfortunately, though, the reality is a lot more pessimistic (I can feel my first rant in the book coming on). As the numbers demonstrate, Yorkshire growers of this vegetable gold have decreased year on year. In my opinion, this is a direct result of the supermarket's influence on our lives. I have witnessed supermarkets become global entities. They have learned that profits are far greater if you can reduce the number of fresh varieties on offer and provide a longer shelf life for those that are. There has been a burst of "super-farms", which cheat the seasons, and use state-of-the-art machinery to minimize labour while maximizing yields. Varieties have been hybridized to create a fruit or vegetable that has little or no flavour, but that can sit on the shelf for far longer than Nature originally intended. The commercial greenhouse has bastardized Nature to such an extent that we now have British Tomato Fortnight in May and June, when our outdoor tomato plants have barely broken through the soil.

The processed food industry in this country has sky-rocketed. It is so much easier for supermarkets to manage products that have a long shelf life than to curate fresh fruits and vegetables that deteriorate quickly. Of course, the supermarket giants cannot completely do away with fresh produce because they are vital for our good health. So, what is the next-best thing? To reduce the number of varieties they sell and simplify the food chain.

We are all so concerned about climate change, carbon emissions, food miles and an ever-increasing supply chain. How can it be a viable option to stock the same fresh produce, wrapped up in plastics and flown by the tonnage halfway around the world, all year long and at the expense of our farmers and to the exclusion of our home-grown seasonal produce?

> "The great Yorkshire rhubarb story doesn't have to become a fable. One change in commercial directive could stop the decline of a great industry and instead rebuild a community that can go from strength to strength."

We need to recreate a regional environment. Instead of buying Dutch or Kenyan rhubarb for nine months of the year, we should wait until British forced and outdoor rhubarb comes into season and the supermarkets should positively promote our home-grown produce throughout their stores.

If we can persuade corporate entities, such as large supermarkets, to reduce the shelf space given to convenience foods, crisps and processed snacks and to increase aisles that are stocking rhubarb, then this is a win-win-win situation – a win each for our farmers, for our planet and for our health. The great Yorkshire rhubarb story doesn't have to become a fable. One change in commercial directive could stop the decline of a great industry and instead rebuild a community that can go from strength to strength. Rant over.

Fermented rhubarb ketchup

This recipe came about by accident. In the kitchen we had loads of fermented rhubarb and little chance to use it all. So, we decided to add some other ingredients to it and whizz it up. We then served it as a tangy, fermented rhubarb ketchup with an amazing dish of wild venison. You can use the ketchup with poultry dishes or with roasted vegetables to give tartness and acidity.

Makes about 250g (9oz)

500ml (17fl oz) filtered water

1 tsp fermenting or Maldon salt

10 juniper berries

2 bay leaves

1 cinnamon stick

5 garlic cloves

1kg (2lb 4oz) forced rhubarb, trimmed and cut into thumb-size lengths

4 red onions

2 tbsp olive oil

100g (3½oz) dark brown soft sugar, plus extra if needed

80ml (2½fl oz) rice wine vinegar, plus extra if needed

Pour the water into a large saucepan and add the salt. Place the pan over a high heat and bring the water to a boil. Add the juniper berries, bay leaves, cinnamon stick and 3 crushed cloves of the garlic to the brine and pour the mixture into a large fermenting jar. Leave it to cool to room temperature.

Add the rhubarb pieces to the brine, cover the surface with fermenting weights or cabbage leaves and leave the rhubarb at room temperature, out of direct sunlight, for 2 weeks. During this time the rhubarb will change colour, become pale and will turn very sour, but with an amazing smell of spices. Burp the jar by releasing and re-sealing the lid every couple of days.

Once the rhubarb has done its fermenting, start making the ketchup. Finely slice the onions and remaining 2 cloves of garlic. Tip these into a large pan, add the oil and sweat over a low–medium heat, stirring frequently, for about 10 minutes, until soft. Meanwhile strain the rhubarb from the brine, roughly chop it and add it to the pan with the softened onions and garlic.

Continue cooking for about 10–15 minutes, until the rhubarb is soft and stringy. Add the sugar and vinegar, mix to combine, then cook for about a further 30 minutes over a low heat, until all the liquid has evaporated.

Remove the pan from the heat and either using a stick blender or food processor, blitz until smooth, taste and add a splash of vinegar or sugar if needed to balance the flavours. Pass the ketchup through a fine sieve into a bowl, then leave to cool, cover and chill until needed.

Rhubarb custard with crunchy oats

For this recipe you can use any nuts you have to hand – almonds, hazelnuts or pecans work well. If you have extra-crunchy oats left over, they store well an airtight box for up to one month.

Serves 4

5 forced rhubarb stalks, trimmed and cut into 3cm (1¼in) lengths

110g (3¾oz) caster (superfine) sugar

50g (1¾oz) spiced rum

seeds of 1 vanilla pod

For the topping

250g (9oz) rolled oats

50g (1¾oz) chopped nuts (almonds, hazelnuts and so on)

2 tbsp runny honey

finely grated zest of 1 orange

finely grated zest of 1 lemon

75g (2½oz) white chocolate, chopped

For the custard

100ml (3½fl oz) double (heavy) cream

350ml (12fl oz) full-fat milk

2 egg yolks

1½ tbsp cornflour (cornstarch)

50g (1¾oz) caster (superfine) sugar

1 tsp vanilla paste

Start with the rhubarb. Preheat the oven to 180°C/160°C fan/350°F/ Gas 4. Tip the rhubarb into an ovenproof dish in an even layer. Add the sugar, rum and vanilla seeds and mix to combine. Cover the dish loosely with foil and bake the rhubarb for 15–20 minutes, until it is very soft and juicy. Leave the oven on, but remove the rhubarb and leave it to cool. Then, transfer half to a bowl in pieces and, using a stick blender, purée the remaining half until smooth.

While the rhubarb is cooling, make the topping. In a bowl combine the rolled oats with the chopped nuts, the honey, and the orange and lemon zests. Tip the mixture on to a lined baking tray and bake it in the hot oven for about 20 minutes, until golden.

Meanwhile, melt the white chocolate in a microwave in short bursts on a low setting, or in a bowl suspended over a pan of gently simmering water. Pour the melted chocolate over the baked oat mixture, mix well to combine and leave to cool.

To make the custard, bring the cream and milk to a boil in a small saucepan over a medium heat. Meanwhile, in a bowl whisk together the egg yolks, cornflour, sugar and vanilla. Pour the hot milk mixture slowly into the egg mixture, whisking continuously until smooth.

Return the mixture to the pan and cook over a low heat, stirring continuously until thickened (about 2 minutes). Remove the pan from the heat, strain the custard into a clean bowl and leave it to cool to room temperature.

To assemble, layer the rhubarb pieces, custard and rhubarb purée equally into cocktail glasses or dessert bowls and top with the crunchy white chocolate oats to serve.

4

Radicchio Grumolo Rosso
Silly Old Chef, Doesn't He Know? There's No Such Thing as a Grumolo

What's in a name? Nearly 30 years ago the legendary chef Nico Ladenis asked me to source a peppery salad leaf he'd seen in Italy. Up until then, demand for it in the UK was almost non-existent outside of the Italian community. None of the wholesalers were able to stock it as it wasn't being commercially grown in this country. Only Italian cooks in the know knew where to get their fix.

After a bit of digging (not literally), I tracked down a French supplier at Nine Elms, the main fruit-and-vegetable wholesale market in London. He came up trumps, inasmuch as he was able to source the broader leaf French variety known as round leaf or natural rocket (arugula). In no time at all, rocket went from near obscurity to becoming the salad leaf du jour.

Fast forward 25 years… . By now you would think that I would know almost all the fruits and vegetables in existence, but history repeated itself and I was asked to track down Grumolo by another chef, Dale, whose cooking was heavily influenced by Italian cuisine. I asked around and I couldn't find it for love nor money. No matter how insistent Dale became of its existence, no one had heard of Grumolo. I love a challenge, so I kept looking. Eventually, it was my son who triumphed – and with apologies to Tim, our Italian agent, it seems that our Italian pronunciation was far from perfect… *Grumolo* (correctly, groo-MOH-loh) somehow got lost in translation.

Grumolo is a variety of radicchio from the chicory (*cicoria* in Italian) family. There are many types of chicory, mostly named for the region from which they come – Treviso, Castelfranco, Chioggia… . Grumolo is a small town not far from Venice in Vicenza, northern Italy, and Grumolo radicchio are small rosettes with striking leaves varying and variegated in colour – green, yellow, pink and purple. They have a bitter flavour and stand up as well used in hot dishes such as risotto as they do in salads.

The Italian chicory-producing regions are mostly in or around the north-eastern part of the country and each region is equally passionate about its own particular variety of *cicoria*. Tardivo (from the Italian word *tardi*, meaning "late") is often called Fiore d'Inverno ("Winter Flower") and is considered the best of all radicchios. It is available from late autumn to early spring. Grown around the town of Treviso, Tardivo requires labour-intensive skill to cultivate: in November after the first frosts, growers lift the radicchio from the fields so that it can undergo *imbianchimento*, or "whitening". For this, the radicchio is stored in crates in the dark for two to three weeks, with its roots sitting in tanks of cold spring water. The outer leaves are then stripped off and the roots trimmed to reveal long, slender, burgundy-coloured, finger-like leaves with a white rib and curling tips, and a dandelion-style stem. Tardivo is a popular among chefs for winter salads or for grilling and baking.

Chioggia, on the other hand, is an early radicchio variety – appearing in summer to late autumn. This variety is round, has thinner leaves and is deep burgundy in colour with white ribbing. The leaves are not as bitter as other varieties, making Chioggia probably the most popular radicchio for home cooks, and also the most widely available. The bittersweet Treviso comes to the fore from November and lasts well into the new year. It has a more elongated, torpedo shape with tightly packed burgundy and white leaves. There are a whole host of other chicory-based salad leaves that last throughout the winter: Escarole, Winter frisée, Puntarelle and Batavia, among them. All have varying degrees of bitterness for use in both hot dishes and winter salads.

My first recollection of a winter salad leaf was Escarole. In the late 1970s and early 1980s, an Italian importer would deliver to us direct in much the same way as the French vendors would turn up on their bikes with strings of onions and garlic (see page 188). They would arrive with huge wooden crates that you needed a crowbar to open, each packed with what at first glance appeared to be substandard and past-their-best salad. After taking off the first layer, though, we would discover huge, beautiful Escarole underneath. The Italian farmers would harvest and store these salads under a blanket of snow long before they used modern glasshouse methods. The leaves provided a welcome winter salad here in the UK when nothing else was available.

> "I am not sure how you could define which chicory variety is best, but when you combine good looks with good flavour, Grumolo is right up there."

Don't worry if you can't find Grumolo – as you can see, there's an abundance of *cicoria* to choose from. However, I think sourcing ingredients is one of the great joys of cooking – the sheer satisfaction of discovering an ingredient not normally on your radar opens up new culinary experiences. (Not dissimilar to someone recommending a good book, something that you have not heard of before, only for it to open your eyes to the delights of a new author.) I am not sure how you could define which chicory variety is best, but when you combine good looks and good flavour, Grumolo is right up there.

Grumolo rosso salsa

As easy as it gets, this recipe is all about quality, freshness and, of course, seasoning. This delicious, bitter salsa is good to serve with grilled meats and fish, and is wonderful with venison.

Serves 4

2 heads of Grumolo rosso

1 tbsp chopped coriander (cilantro) leaves

1 tbsp chopped flat-leaf parsley leaves

1 banana shallot, chopped

1–2 garlic cloves, chopped

2 tbsp capers, drained

2 tbsp drained, chopped cornichons

½ red chilli, deseeded and roughly chopped

1 tsp Dijon mustard

5–6 tbsp olive oil, plus extra if needed

lemon juice, to taste

1 slice of white bread, toasted (optional)

salt and freshly ground black pepper

salad leaves, to serve (optional)

Tip the Grumolo leaves into a food processor and add the chopped herbs, shallot, garlic cloves, capers, cornichons, chilli and mustard. Whizz the mixture until nearly smooth, then add the olive oil and whizz again until the salsa is the consistency of oily pesto.

Add lemon juice to taste, then season the salsa with salt and freshly ground black pepper.

If you want more texture in your salsa, add a crumbled slice of toast and whizz it with more olive oil until you achieve the desired result. Serve topped with salad leaves, if you wish.

Balsamic-pickled Treviso tardivo

Treviso tardivo are stunning-looking salad leaves – they are curly and very tasty and are much less bitter than chicory. They are amazing in salads, but they don't hang around for ever. The best way to prolong the life of tardivo is to pickle the leaves and serve the pickle in sandwiches, as a condiment for your roast or steak, or in salads. For this recipe use balsamic vinegar – and the better quality you use, the more delicious the end result will be.

Makes 1 small jar

5 heads of Treviso tardivo, leaves chopped into bitesize pieces
200g (7oz) balsamic vinegar
100g (3½oz) granulated sugar

Place the chopped leaves into a clean jar and set aside.

Combine 300ml (10½ fl oz) of water with the balsamic and sugar in a medium saucepan. Place over a high heat and bring to a boil, then lower the heat and simmer for 1 minute.

From here you have 2 ways you can do this recipe: for a really quick pickle, add the pickling liquid to the jar of chopped tardivo, cool and serve once cold.

Alternatively, and perhaps better, is to cool the pickling liquid and then pour it over the chopped leaves. Seal the jar with the lid and leave the pickle for 24 hours for the leaves to collapse. Strain off the pickling liquor and reserve it (see below), then seal the jar again and store the pickled leaves at room temperature for 1 week to allow the flavours to develop before using. The leaves will keep unopened for 3 months in a cool, dark place; and for 2 weeks in the fridge, once opened.

Once you've made the pickled tardivo, don't waste the pickling liquid. Pour it into a pan and reduce it to a sticky glaze for vegetables and meat – such as carrots, parsnips or a juicy rib-eye steak.

5

Seville oranges / *Bergamot* / *Clementines* / *Late Valencia oranges* / *Lemons – Cedro, Sicilian* / *Sicilian grapefruit* / *Tarocco blood oranges* / *Ugli fruit* / *Giant papaya* / *Yorkshire forced rhubarb* / *Spanish avocados* / *Lampascioni wild onions* / *Bay leaves* / *Rosemary* / *Outdoor Sicilian tomatoes* / *Italian wild rocket (arugula)* / *Endives – Escarole, Winter frisée* / *Italian radicchios – Castelfranco, Grumolo, Puntarelle, Tardivo* / *Cornish spring greens* / *Purple sprouting broccoli* / *Cime di rapa* / *Chard – Rainbow, Swiss* / *Scottish Sea kale* / *Cabbages – Cavolo Nero, kales, Somerset Savoy* / *Artichokes – Jerusalem, Violet baby artichokes from Apulia* / *Perigord black truffles* / *Onions – Cevenne, Roscoff* / *Potatoes – Agria, Cyprus Spunta, Pink Fir* / *Muscade pumpkin* / *Beetroots – Candy, Cheltenham, Golden* / *Red mooli radish* / *Salsify* / *Tokyo turnips*

Seville Orange, Fresh Turmeric
The Lady of Seville Meets *An Indian Affair*

When I started to write this chapter, I came across Elizabeth Currie. She is the author of two books *The Lady of Seville* and *An Indian Affair*. While her writing is "spicy" and her surname reminiscent of one of the most influential cuisines in this country, that's where the connection ends. This chapter is all about connections, a celebration of food diversity and the story of how Seville oranges helped to create a no-waste business model at Turnips.

Citrus and spice work beautifully together. When we are in the depths of winter and we need a flavour boost, these two food groups produce stunning dishes. Mother Nature kindly provides us with these fresh products at their seasonal best at the same time – and just when they are most beneficial to us, as both have well-documented health benefits, too: oranges are not only a good source of vitamin C and fibre, but they also contain flavonoids, which may help with lowering blood pressure. Both oranges and turmeric have anti-inflammatory and antioxidant properties. A delicious and easy way to combine them is to create a warming juice to drink each morning, so that it may help in the fight against the many seasonal nasties floating around at this time of year.

> "It took two Scotsmen, a century apart, to make the first commercial marmalades."

The Seville orange is named after the province in southern Spain where the fruit was first cultivated in the 12th century. According to Sebastian, a Sevillano and one of our staff at Turnips, the Spanish do not use these oranges for culinary purposes, regarding them as inedible – too bitter (giving them their alternative name as the "bitter orange"), too pithy and with too many pips. According to his great-grandfather, the numerous Seville orange trees that line the streets of the city and fill the parks were planted because they are evergreen in winter and provide much-needed shade from the summer heat. Equally, perfumery businesses use them widely.

In the UK, we're rather more tolerant of this orange's texture and flavour. Here, Sevilles are mostly used for making marmalade – their bitter and sour characteristics and high pectin levels making them a must for preserving. We are so obsessed with marmalade, our breakfast staple, that Cumbria holds an annual Marmalade Festival in May. This is a celebration of all things marmalade and includes tastings and demonstrations. More importantly, though, it hosts a hotly contested competition in which amateur cooks from all over the world send in their homemade marmalades to be judged in up to 15 categories. Marmalade is a very British affair.

It took two Scotsmen, a century apart, to make the world's first commercial marmalades. In Dundee in the late 1700s, the captain of a storm-ravaged Spanish ship decided to sell off his cargo. Among the booty were boxes of less-than-perfect Seville oranges. James Keiller snapped up the fruit and gave them to his mother, Janet, who already had a business making jams. She turned her hand to marmalade, adding chunky strips of peel – and Dundee marmalade was born. One hundred or so years later, a certain James Robertson foolishly imported Seville oranges for sale at his grocery shop in Paisley, only to find out how bitter they were. He gave them to his wife, who cooked them into the paler, sweeter, fine-shred marmalade we know and love today.

At Turnips, we buy our oranges directly from growers in Spain with a minimum order of 80 boxes, each containing 15kg (33lb) of fruit. We easily shift two thirds of the order to turn a profit, but we have historically had trouble selling the remainder. Seeing the oranges going to waste did not sit well, so we decided to start making our own juices, marmalades, jams, chutneys and purées to sell to our wholesale and restaurant customers. There's enormous satisfaction in using a little creativity and culinary know-how to reduce food waste. Not only do you get to enjoy the fruit itself, you enjoy the fruits of your labour at a later stage in the year.

Turmeric, the "Golden Spice", comes from further afield. We source ours from all over India, which in the culinary world is considered the very best country of origin. Indian turmeric is a world-class product that history books tell us has been used for medicinal purposes for thousands of years. Although we use most spices ground, in powdered form tumeric, like its relative root ginger, takes on a different persona when we use it fresh. Peel back the skin to reveal the bright-orange flesh – which will stain your fingers, clothes and chopping board! The flavour is warm, peppery and citrussy.

Many chefs in the UK believe that turmeric, like most spices, is used purely as a flavouring. But, according to Cyrus Todiwala, chef patron of Café Spice Namaste, in London, many Indian dishes include it for its health properties as much as for anything else. Whatever your reason for using it, and whether you are using it ground or fresh, it's good to know that this remarkable spice can produce something that is both tasty and good for you.

Seville orange trifle

For me, there is nothing better than rich and creamy cold orange trifle. This one is even better because of the amazing bittersweet Seville oranges. It's quick and easy to put together, but a real showstopper at the same time. Assemble the trifle in a glass bowl (or make individual portions in glass whisky tumblers) so that you can see the layers. For an extra indulgence pour a little orange liqueur or limoncello over the top to serve.

Serves 4

10 Seville oranges
4 platinum-grade gelatine leaves
1 tablespoon caster sugar

For the custard

350ml (12fl oz) full-fat milk
300ml (10½fl oz) double (heavy) cream
2 egg yolks
1½ tbsp cornflour (cornstarch)
50g (1¾oz) caster (superfine) sugar
1 tsp vanilla paste

To assemble

6 slices of store-bought vanilla sponge cake
icing (confectioner's) sugar, for dusting
orange liqueur or limoncello, to serve

Start by juicing and segmenting the oranges. For this recipe you will need 500ml (17fl oz) orange juice, which will be the juice from about 4 of the oranges, but measure as you go. Peel the remaining oranges and cut them into neat, pith-free segments.

Soak the gelatine leaves in a bowl of cold water for 5 minutes, until soft and floppy. Heat the orange juice in a small saucepan until hot but not boiling, then remove from the heat. Drain the gelatine, squeeze out any excess water, and add the leaves to the hot orange juice with the caster sugar. Whisk until the gelatine has melted and the sugar has dissolved. Leave to cool to room temperature.

Arrange most of the orange segments equally in the glasses, saving some to decorate the finished trifles, and pour over the orange jelly to cover. Chill for at least 1 hour, until the jelly has set.

Meanwhile, make the custard. Bring the milk and 100ml (3½fl oz) of the cream to a boil in a small saucepan over a medium heat. In a bowl, whisk together the egg yolks, cornflour, caster sugar and vanilla paste. Pour the hot milk and cream slowly into the egg mixture, whisking continuously until smooth. Return the mixture to the pan and cook over a low heat, stirring until thickened. Remove from the heat, strain into a clean bowl and leave to cool to room temperature.

Preheat the oven to 170°C/150°C fan/325°F/Gas 2–3. Crumble 2 slices of the cake on to a lined baking sheet and toast the crumbs in the oven for about 5 minutes, until crisp and golden.

To assemble the trifles, whisk the remaining 200ml (7fl oz) of cream to soft peaks. Place a 1cm (½in)-thick disk of sponge cake on top of each jelly, and use half the custard to create a layer on top of each jelly. Using half of the reserved orange segments, dot these on top, then add a big dollop of whipped cream to each. Spoon over the remaining custard and oranges. Scatter over some cake crumbs and dust with icing sugar to serve. Finish with a drizzle of liqueur, if you wish.

Seville orange marmalade with curry leaves and turmeric

I'm not sure that it's possible to eat breakfast without marmalade on toast. This bittersweet marmalade has an extra warmth and spiciness from the curry leaves and turmeric, and it will brighten your day no end. It takes a bit of time to make marmalade, but it is time well spent.

Makes 3–4 jars

10 large Seville oranges, halved

2 lemons, halved

6 curry leaves

1 small piece of turmeric root, peeled and roughly chopped

1.3kg (3lb) granulated sugar

Squeeze the juice from the oranges and lemons and pour it into a large pan. Using a spoon scrape the membranes and seeds from each orange and lemon half and place these on to a square of muslin (cheesecloth). Add the curry leaves and turmeric, gather the muslin into a pouch and tie the top tightly with kitchen string.

Cut the orange peel into strips, add these to the pan and pour over 1.5 litres (52fl oz) of water. Submerge the muslin bag into the mixture but make sure that it is tied to the pan handle with a length of string to make it easy to remove later.

Bring the liquid to a boil, then reduce the heat to low and simmer the mixture for 30–45 minutes, until the peel is very soft – the timing will depend on how thickly you have cut your strips. It's very important that they are soft, as they will not cook further once you've added the sugar. Place two saucers or small plates into the freezer to cool.

Add the sugar, stir to dissolve, then simmer for a further 15 minutes. Lift the muslin bag and squeeze it tightly over the pan to extract as much flavour as you can from the curry leaves and turmeric, and the pectin from the membranes and seeds.

Increase the heat and bring the mixture to a rapid boil, stirring often to prevent the marmalade catching on the bottom of the pan. Boil for about 20 minutes, until the marmalade reaches setting point. To test for a set, drop a teaspoonful of marmalade on to a cold saucer. Leave it for 30 seconds, then push it with your fingertip. If it wrinkles, the marmalade is ready to remove from the heat. If it doesn't, continue boiling and testing every 2 minutes until it does.

Remove the pan from the heat and leave the marmalade to cool for 5 minutes – this will allow the peel strips to settle. Pour the marmalade into sterilized jars, seal with the lids and leave to cool before labelling and storing for up to 1 year unopened, or 1 month refrigerated once opened.

6

Multi-coloured carrots / *Bergamot* / *Clementines* / *Lemons – Cedro, Sicilian* / *Moro blood oranges* / *Seville oranges* / *Giant papaya* / *Yorkshire forced rhubarb* / *Spanish avocados* / *Lampascioni wild onions* / *Bay leaves* / *Rosemary* / *Outdoor Sicilian tomatoes* / *Italian wild rocket (arugula)* / *Endives – Escarole, Winter Frisée* / *Italian radicchios – Castelfranco, Grumolo, Puntarelle, Tardivo* / *Cornish spring greens* / *Purple sprouting broccoli* / *Cime di rapa* /

Chard – Rainbow, Swiss / *Scottish Sea kale* / *Cabbages – Cavolo Nero, Somerset Savoy* / *Cardoon* / *Artichokes – Jerusalem, Violet baby artichokes from Apulia* / *Perigord black truffles* / *Onions – Cevenne, Roscoff* / *Potatoes – Agria, Cyprus Spunta* / *Muscade pumpkin* / *Beetroots – Candy, Cheltenham, Golden* / *Radishes – Red meat, red mooli* / *Salsify* / *Turnips – Golden, Tokyo, Rutabaga (swede)*

The Forgotten Veg
Why We Need to Push Against Glasshouse Farming

When I first started out in the fruit-and-vegetable business, carrots were orange. And that was all that we knew: the humble carrot came in one shape and in one colour – orange. Who knew then that you could get different-coloured varieties and shapes of carrot?

It was the same story with most other vegetables: beetroots (beets), turnips, cauliflowers, kale, sprouts and potatoes... you name it. In the commercial world, each of these vegetables had one predominant colour, shape and size. Carrots were orange, cauliflowers, turnips and potatoes were white, sprouts and kale were green and beetroot was a deep, dark, purply red.

And then in 2016, a produce revolution happened in France with the launch of *Les Légumes Oubliés* ("The Forgotten Vegetables"), led by an independent farm in Brittany called La Légumière. This French revolution was a revival of old vegetable varieties that up until then were not commercially known and grown. Among them were vegetables such as crosnes, cardoon, scorsoner, salsify, parsley root and more besides. And for the farmers it was a way to survive in an increasingly competitive market that was dominated by super-farms with their miles of polytunnels and mega-glasshouses. It was a way to fight back against the commercial corporations who had for years been squeezing the profit margins of smaller, independent farmers.

"Then, in 2016 a produce revolution happened in France with the launch of *Les Légumes Oubliés* ('The Forgotten Vegetables')."

These days, these once-forgotten vegetables are firmly back, along with some newer, colourful varieties – products such as red and green meat radish, rainbow chard, candy and golden beetroot, black radish and golden turnip. The relatively modern purple Cosmic carrot has a stunning, deep purple exterior with bright-orange flesh and a sweet and earthy flavour.

The re-introduction of old-fashioned varieties has quickly spread across the world – particularly in the USA, with California leading the charge. Forward-thinking independent farmers have been able to outpace global supermarkets, having the knowledge and dedicating the time to adapt to look forward to new varieties or into the past to revive those that have otherwise been lost to the history books. Supermarkets will eventually catch up, but it is much harder for companies who grow produce on a huge scale to change direction quickly – and by the time they do, the independent, more innovative farmers will already have moved on to the next new (or old) range of vegetables.

Thankfully, now we see more and more smallholdings springing up, growing different and interesting fruits and vegetables. In the world of carrots, we see orange "sand", white, red and Cosmic carrots all supplied from a co-operative of farmers in Brittany and Normandy. There, the carrots grow in sandy soil near the seashore. This soil is high in nutrients and minerals that result in carrots with a sweet and earthy flavour. The heirloom variety Nantes, from Créances, is picked by hand and sent to market still dirty rather than being washed (which can remove nutrients).

Brittany has more than 1,000km (620 miles) of coastline with many beaches and a rocky, coastal landscape that has a rich, fertile soil. The area is a vital source of vegetables that we import into the UK – the Bretagne Roscoff onion (see page 187) being perhaps the most famous. The French agricultural co-operatives have enabled niche products to exist in a very competitive marketplace, but unfortunately such enterprises do not exist here in the UK. We have a lot to thank our French neighbours for – in particular their dedication to farming and producing top-notch fruit and vegetables, and all the while surviving in a world of fierce agricultural competition.

These forgotten vegetables are now firmly back in favour and will remain so. Long live the carrot in all its glorious rainbow of colours – from orange... to yellow, purple and white.

Among the "Forgotten Veg" are these purple carrots from Brittany and Sand carrots from Normandy, each with their own unique bursts of flavour.

Crunchy Sand carrot salad with sesame seeds

Your meat roast or whole-roasted fish is only minutes away from being cooked and you don't have anything fresh and crunchy to go with it. Remember those beautiful Sand carrots you have sitting in the cupboard? Use them for this super-quick and naturally delicious side dish.

Serves 4 as a side

2 tbsp white or black sesame seeds

6 Sand carrots, peeled and coarsely grated

1 garlic clove, crushed

juice of 1 lemon

2 tbsp Dijon mustard

3 tbsp olive oil

2 tbsp vegetable oil

1 tsp sesame oil

2 tbsp chopped coriander (cilantro) leaves

1 spring onion (scallion), chopped

salt and freshly ground black pepper

Toast the sesame seeds in a dry frying pan over a low heat for about 1 minute, stirring often, until they smell aromatic. Tip the toasted seeds out of the pan and leave to cool.

Tip the carrots in a bowl, add the garlic and mix with your hands to slightly bruise the carrots.

In another bowl, whisk together the lemon juice and mustard. In a jug combine the oils and slowly add these to the lemon and mustard, whisking continuously to create an emulsion – this will coat the salad rather than be an oily dressing. Add the coriander and spring onion and season with salt and pepper.

Stir the dressing through the carrots to coat (you may not need it all), and spoon it all into a serving dish. Scatter with the toasted sesame seeds to serve.

Carrot kimchi

Having pickles or ferments on your plate is the culinary equivalent of balancing on a tightrope. If they are not on the plate, then 90 per cent of your dish won't balance. Creating something like a vegetable kimchi can elevate your food, and you can serve it alongside a main dish or eat it on its own. It is especially refreshing in summer.

Makes 2kg (4lb 8oz)

6–7 Sand carrots, peeled and sliced into buttons

4 large turnips, peeled and sliced into buttons

2 white onions, finely sliced

finely chopped cloves of 1 garlic bulb

1–4 red chillies (according to your preference for heat), finely chopped with seeds

3–4 tbsp table salt

100g (3½oz) white rice

8 tbsp fish sauce

2 bunches of spring onions (scallions), finely sliced

120g (4¼oz) fresh ginger, peeled and finely chopped or grated

150g (5½oz) beansprouts (optional)

about 100g (3½oz) Maldon salt

dried chilli flakes or Korean chilli flakes

Tip the carrots and turnips into a large bowl (you can coarsely grate the veg if you prefer). Add the onions, garlic and chilli, then sprinkle with the table salt. Mix to combine, loosely cover and leave at room temperature for 2 hours for the vegetables to soften.

Meanwhile bring a small saucepan of water to a boil. Add the rice and cook the grains until they are very soft, even overcooked (about 20 minutes, depending on the type of rice). Drain the rice and, using a food processor, blitz it until smooth.

Once the vegetables have softened, tip them into a colander. Rinse them under cold running water and drain them thoroughly. Add the fish sauce, spring onions, ginger, and beansprouts if using. Add just enough of the overcooked rice paste to coat the vegetables (this will speed up fermentation) and mix well to thoroughly combine.

Weigh the vegetable mixture and calculate 2 per cent of the total weight. Add this quantity of Maldon salt and some dried chilli flakes to taste (for a spicier kimchi), and mix to combine. Pack the mixture tightly into a plastic container or sterilized jar and press with the back of a spoon to expel any air bubbles.

Leave the kimchi in a cool, dark place in the kitchen for 2 weeks, burping the jar or container by releasing and re-sealing the lid every 2 days. After 2 weeks, taste the kimchi and if the sourness is to your liking, transfer it to the fridge to slow down the fermentation process, using it whenever you need. If you prefer a sourer flavour, leave it a little longer, tasting and burping the kimchi every 2 days, until you like what you have – then, transfer it to the fridge, as before.

7

Morel mushrooms / *Bergamot* /
Clementines / *Indian mandarins* /
Lemons – Cedro, Sicilian / *Moro blood
oranges* / *Seville oranges* / *Giant
papaya* / *Golden kiwi* / *Tongan
Sugarloaf pineapple* / *Yorkshire forced
rhubarb* / *Spanish avocados* /
Lampascioni wild onions / *Bay leaves* /
Rosemary / *Courgette (zucchini)
flowers* / *Wild edible flowers* /
*Tomatoes – Datterini, Outdoor
Sicilian, San Marzano* / *Italian wild
rocket (arugula)* / *Nettles* / *Endives
– Escarole, Winter frisée* / *Italian
radicchios – Castelfranco, Grumolo,*
Puntarelle, Tardivo / *Cornish spring
greens* / *Purple Sprouting broccoli* /
Cime di rapa / *Chard – Rainbow, Swiss
/ Scottish Sea kale* / *Cabbages – Cavolo
Nero, Somerset Savoy* / *Cardoon* /
*Artichokes – Jerusalem, Violet baby
artichokes from Apulia* / *Perigord black
truffles* / *Onions – Cevenne, Roscoff* /
Potatoes – Agria, Cyprus Spunta /
Muscade pumpkin / *Beetroots – Candy,
Cheltenham, Golden* / *Radishes – Red
meat, Red mooli* / *Salsify* / *Turnips –
Golden, Rutabaga (swede), Tokyo*

Morel Mushroom
The Morel of the Story

The Morel mushroom is an example of a truly wild product that, despite plenty of attempts, has so far proved nigh-on impossible to cultivate commercially. Cultivated mushroom varieties, such as Button, Chestnut and Flat, are widely produced all year round and have no season. The season for Morels is short – but when finally it arrives, it never fails to create a culinary buzz. There is joy in anticipation for this highly sought-after delicacy: the very specific growing conditions for this and other wild foods need to be perfect – you cannot rush the season for the Morel.

Found wild in the northern hemisphere, specifically in Turkey, Canada and France, the incredible Morel is somewhat rare. You'll find it in early springtime, in woods of spruce, ash and elm trees; and in fields and apple orchards. Morels also appear on the woodland floor after wildfires. This elusive fungus is one of the most expensive of all the wild-mushroom varieties, favouring a particular climate (including damp, cool weather) and terrain, and needing skilful foraging to find it. Dedicated mushroom hunters, with extensive knowledge of their natural environment, will hand-pick these mushrooms. We in the "veg trade" know the different Morel varieties by colour – white, black, grey and yellow. They are cone-shaped, oblong or bulbous with a honeycombed exterior and hollow middle, and you should never eat them raw. The Turkish Morel, found growing in the wooded hills and mountains of southwest regions of the country and foraged by local rural communities, is especially highly valued in European markets: it is the first of the year, making an appearance around the middle of February.

The mushroom season begins when the first Morel mushrooms arrive from Turkey. There is a real sense of excitement and a buzz surrounding the start of the "wild" season. In fact, it was Februrary when Gordon Ramsay's team, plus film crew, turned up at our market stand one day to talk all things mushroom. Ramsay commented that I could write my own mushroom encyclopedia, such is my extensive knowledge of fungi. He picked the Morel as his favourite, with its earthy, woody, almost apricotty flavour. It's a good job he turned up in February – it would not have been around later in the season. World-class Morel mushrooms begin their time with those Turkish specimens in mid-February, then month by month make their way across Europe to end in France in August. Of course, their rarity makes Morels expensive, but don't let that put you off. With a sensational mushroom less is more – you need only a few in a creamy sauce to experience fully their meaty texture and exceptional flavour. Serve them simply sautéed in butter and garlic and on toast, or with fresh pasta, in a risotto or alongside a fabulous steak.

There is great excitement and value in enjoying special ingredients that are available for only a short time each year. I believe that nowadays we miss out on the basic principle of *waiting for something*. We are so used to having anything and everything whenever we want it. But think how we look forward to celebrating memorable dates – birthdays and anniversaries, say. With the same anticipation and excitement, we should yearn for the changing seasons that bring us our favourite fruit and vegetables as Nature intended. My philosophy of seasonal eating and cooking means that there is always – from the beginning to the end of the year – something new or longed for to get excited about. But let's be clear, this is not a way of life that restricts you to never using cultivated or glasshouse-grown produce. That would be unrealistic. My philosophy is one that simply adds pleasure. In my opinion when you embrace the proper seasons, life's ebb and flow becomes significantly more enjoyable. As soon as you tune in to nature through seasonal ingredients, you'll find other aspects of your life will follow suit: flowers, drinks and even home scents can all get in step with the seasons.

> "Gordon Ramsay's team... turned up at our market stand one day to talk all things mushroom. Ramsay commented that I could write my own mushroom encyclopedia..."

Restricting yourself to outdoor-grown and seasonal produce might at first feel like you're reducing the varieties of fruits and vegetables available to you. In fact, when everything is on offer all year round, we become naturally self-limiting – there's a tendency to stick to favourites or what's familiar. The outdoor template enables you to take advantage of more varied produce throughout the year. You'll become more aware of the seasonal shifts, you'll look forward to the arrival of each product as its season comes around and your anticipation will lead to greater appreciation for our farmers, our producers, our foragers and more importantly, Mother Earth.

Beef wellingtons   *Recipe by Gordon Ramsay*

Here, chef Gordon Ramsay produces a heavenly match of pastry, beef and wild mushrooms to impress friends, family and, most importantly, the love of your life. This recipe is included in his book *Ultimate Cookery Course*, which accompanied the series on Channel 4 during which he showcased mushrooms at our retail stand in Borough Market – a broadcast that has gone viral on YouTube. He argued the beef was the star of the show; I beg to differ.

Serves 4

2 x 400g (14oz) beef fillets
olive oil, for frying
500g (1lb 2oz) mixture of wild mushrooms, cleaned
1 thyme sprig, leaves only
500g (1lb 2oz) puff pastry
8 slices of Parma ham
2 egg yolks, beaten with 1 tbsp water and a pinch of salt
sea salt and freshly ground black pepper

For the red wine sauce

2 tbsp olive oil
200g (7oz) beef trimmings (ask the butcher to reserve these when trimming the fillet)
4 large shallots, peeled and sliced
12 black peppercorns
1 bay leaf
1 thyme sprig
splash of red wine vinegar
1 x 750ml (26fl oz) bottle red wine
750ml (26fl oz) beef stock

Wrap each piece of beef tightly in a triple layer of cling film to set its shape, then chill overnight.

Remove the cling film, then quickly sear the beef fillets in a hot pan with a little olive oil for 30–60 seconds, until browned all over and rare in the middle. Remove from the pan and leave to cool.

Finely chop the mushrooms and fry in a hot pan with a little olive oil, the thyme leaves and some seasoning. When the mushrooms begin to release their juices, continue to cook over a high heat for about 10 minutes until all the excess moisture has evaporated and you are left with a mushroom paste (known as a duxelle). Remove the duxelle from the pan and leave to cool.

Cut the pastry in half, place on a lightly floured surface and roll each piece into a rectangle large enough to envelop one of the beef fillets. Chill in the refrigerator.

Lay a large sheet of cling film on a work surface and place 4 slices of Parma ham in the middle, overlapping them slightly, to create a square. Spread half the duxelle over the ham.

Season the beef fillets, then place them on top of the mushroom-covered ham. Using the cling film, roll the Parma ham over the beef, then roll and tie the cling film to get a nice, evenly thick log. Repeat this step with the other beef fillet, then chill for at least 30 minutes.

Brush the pastry with the egg wash. Remove the cling film from the beef then wrap the pastry around each ham-wrapped fillet. Trim the pastry and brush all over with the egg wash. Cover with cling film and chill for at least 30 minutes.

Continued overleaf...

Meanwhile, make the red wine sauce. Heat the oil in a large pan, then fry the beef trimmings for a few minutes until browned on all sides. Stir in the shallots with the peppercorns, bay and thyme and continue to cook for about 5 minutes, stirring frequently, until the shallots turn golden brown.

Pour in the vinegar and let it bubble for a few minutes until almost dry. Now add the wine and boil until almost completely reduced. Add the stock and bring to the boil again. Lower the heat and simmer gently for 1 hour, removing any scum from the surface of the sauce, until you have the desired consistency. Strain the liquid through a fine sieve lined with muslin (cheesecloth). Check for seasoning and set aside.

When you are ready to cook the beef wellingtons, score the pastry lightly and brush with the egg wash again, then bake at 200°C/180°C fan/400°F/Gas 6 for 15–20 minutes, until the pastry is golden brown and cooked. Rest for 10 minutes before carving.

Meanwhile, reheat the sauce. Serve the beef wellingtons sliced, with the sauce as an accompaniment.

Dried Morels

Morels are one of most amazing-looking and -tasting mushrooms and this method to preserve them for future use increases their flavour. Once you have your store of dried Morels, rehydrate them in boiling water and use them wherever you would use fresh. Use the soaking water as a delicious stock for risotto or gravy. Can we call this a recipe? It is really a fantastic method for preserving Morels for a time later in the year when these beauties are no longer available.

Serves – depends on mushroom quantity

It is very important to first wash your Morels. Fill three bowls with cold water. Tip the mushrooms into the first bowl and, using your fingers, lightly move or swish them around in the water to dislodge any dirt or bugs. Carefully transfer them to the next bowl and do the same thing and then into the third until the water is clear and the mushrooms are clean.

Drain the mushrooms and leave them to dry on kitchen paper for 1 hour. Meanwhile, set the fan oven to the lowest setting.

Place a cooling rack on a baking sheet and arrange the mushrooms on top. Transfer the rack to the oven and leave the mushrooms to dry for about 4 hours, although it can take up to 7 hours, depending on the size of the Morels. Check the mushrooms occasionally and turn the tray around from time to time.

Once the mushrooms are completely dry, remove them from the oven. Leave them to cool and then transfer them to a lidded jar or food bag and store them in dry place. How long will they keep? For ever!

8

Queen Victoria pineapples / Indian mandarins / Moro blood oranges / Lemons – Cedro, Sicilian / Golden kiwi / Mangosteen / Rambutans / Spanish avocados / Lampascioni wild onions / Bay leaves / Moroccan mint / Rosemary / Courgette (zucchini) flowers / Wild edible flowers / Tomatoes – Datterini, San Marzano / Italian wild rocket (arugula) / Nettles / Red and white Belgian chicory / Endives – Escarole, Winter frisée / Radicchios – Castelfranco, Puntarelle, Tardivo /

Feuille de chêne (oak leaf lettuce) / Cornish spring greens / Purple sprouting broccoli / Cime di rapa / Chard – Rainbow, Swiss / Cabbages – Cavolo Nero, Hispi, Somerset Savoy / Cardoon / Artichokes – Jerusalem, Violet baby artichokes from Apulia / Morel mushrooms / Perigord black truffles / Potatoes – Agria, Cyprus Spunta / Beetroots – Candy, Cheltenham, Golden / Radishes – Red meat, Red mooli / Salsify / Turnips – Golden, Rutabaga (swede), Tokyo,

Pineapple
If Every Fool Wore a Crown, We Should All Be Kings

It's important to me to give each individual product a season. So how do I determine when is the season for a product that doesn't grow in our country? The Queen Victoria pineapple is a good example. It is grown on the small, tropical, volcanic island of Réunion, a French overseas département that lies off the coast of Madagascar in the Indian Ocean.

In February, when very little is being grown on our own shores or in Europe, we need to look further afield for our produce. This French outpost is home to some of the most beautiful fruits this Earth has to offer: incomparable lychees, mangoes, bananas and coconuts, among them. However, Réunion's most famous fruit is the petite and aromatic Queen Victoria pineapple.

We can thank Christopher Columbus for encountering pineapples in South America on his expedition in 1493. He brought them back to Europe, and they gradually worked their way further across the globe, eventually flourishing in the tropics. They were first grown in Réunion some 200 years after Columbus's adventures, and have been growing there ever since.

Pineapples, then, have a long and well-travelled history. That history is also rather glamorous. These fruit were once considered a sign of considerable affluence: in the 1800s, a single fruit could command such vast sums that only the aristocracy could afford it. The aspirational hired pineapples as table centrepieces for dinners and banquets, and they were eaten by the super-rich. The rental shops did a roaring trade in supplying fruits for social events! Others rented them simply to hold under their arm while out and about in town, or while having their portrait painted – a sign to anyone who needed to know of their great prosperity.

The nobility and landed gentry were keen and innovative horticulturists, and no self-respecting country estate would be without a pinery in their walled gardens in which to cultivate pineapples under glass. It was no mean feat to produce ripe fruit in our cool climate, requiring time, vast wealth, great expertise, considerable manpower – and even larger amounts of horse manure, which provided the much-needed heat. Producing just one ripe pineapple could take years and set the grower back tens of thousands of pounds. Such was the need to demonstrate wealth through this exotic fruit that the pineapple became a motif to adorn everything from dinnerware to garden railings and rooftops. Needless to say, though, the Victorians soon realized that no matter how hard they tried and how much money they invested in their pineapple endeavours, it's impossible to reproduce here the stunning flavour of imported exotic fruits that have been grown outdoors and ripened in the tropical sun.

The volcanic soil of Réunion provides the ideal growing conditions for tropical fruits. Piton de la Fournaise stands at around 2,630m (about 8,630 feet) above sea level and is one of the most active volcanoes in the world, erupting roughly every nine months. Volcanic ash can act as a natural fertilizer – it is rich in magnesium and potassium and can help retain moisture to create fertile soil that is just right for growing pineapples.

Named after Queen Victoria (who is said to have loved them), these stunning golden pineapples are smaller than other varieties, weighing in at about 600g (21oz) and standing about 15cm (6in) tall. They have spiky leaves and a bright yellow, juicy flesh with a fragrant, tropical flavour and a soft, edible core. They were awarded a Red Label (*Label Rouge*) accreditation from the French Ministry of Agriculture in 2005 to acknowledge their superior quality (Scottish salmon was the first non-French product to obtain this standard... just saying).

We source our Queen Victoria pineapples from Philibon, a French family-owned producer of premium-quality fruit (and, as it goes, the by-word for excellence when it comes to Charentais melons, which the company grows in France, Morocco, Spain and Senegal to give year-round supply). Its pineapples grow on Réunion plantations that lie up to 600m (almost 2,000 feet) above sea level. These plantations produce fruit that surpasses all others in terms of flavour and quality (if you've never eaten a lychee grown in Réunion, prepare to be blown away, especially if you think you don't like them – there's a reason why Réunion lychees have also been awarded the *Label Rouge*). While the price of fruit from Réunion may be premium, every penny is justified for such stunning produce. I also believe that, if we are going to source and fly produce around the world, it's important that we focus on world-class produce rather than anything that might be bland or ordinary.

> "We can thank Christopher Columbus for encountering pineapples in South America on his expedition in 1493."

Diminutive Queen Victoria pineapples are available all year round in the southern hemisphere, but here in the UK we think of them as "in season" in February, to compensate for the lack of fruits grown closer to home. They are delicious eaten just as they are, but their sweet, aromatic flavour works brilliantly in cocktails, salads and preserves, too.

Grilled Queen Victoria pineapple salad with pecan nuts and chicken

Although it's still cold outside, this sweet and tangy salad will bring sunshine and joy to your table. You can serve it as a main meal – chopped avocado would be a great addition to the salad, if you like.

Serves 4

1 Queen Victoria pineapple, peeled and quartered

2 chicken breasts

1 tbsp olive oil

80g (2¾oz) pecan nuts, toasted

1 garlic clove, crushed

½ red chilli, deseeded and finely sliced

1 celery stalk, diced

½ bunch of spring onions (scallions), trimmed and sliced

4 tbsp mayonnaise

1 tbsp Dijon or wholegrain mustard

1 tbsp full-fat sour cream

1 tbsp maple syrup

juice of ½ lemon, or to taste

2 tbsp chopped coriander (cilantro) leaves

2 tbsp chopped flat-leaf parsley leaves

salt and freshly ground black pepper

baby gem leaves, to serve

a few micro leaves, such as shiso or red-stemmed radish, to garnish

Heat a griddle pan over a high heat. When hot, add the pineapple and cook it, turning often, until it's nicely caramelized all over. Your house will smell amazing at the same time!

Remove the pineapple from the griddle and set it aside. Brush the chicken breasts with the oil, season them with salt and pepper, and cook them on the hot griddle for about 4 minutes on each side, or until cooked all the way through. Remove the chicken from the heat and leave it to cool slightly.

Cut the chicken and pineapple into slices and tip the slices into a bowl. Add the pecans, garlic, chilli, celery and spring onions. Then, add the mayonnaise, mustard, sour cream, maple syrup and lemon juice. Stir through the chopped herbs, season to taste and mix to combine.

To serve (either immediately or cover it and chill it for 2 hours to allow all the flavours to mingle), arrange the baby gem leaves on a plate, top with a spoonful of salad and garnish with the micro leaves. (If you chill the salad, remove it from the fridge 20 minutes before plating.)

Queen Victoria pineapple and chilli chutney

This chutney pairs brilliantly with a cheeseboard or is delicious spooned over grilled goat's cheese. It is very easy to make and will keep very well in a jar or the freezer for up to three months.

Makes 1–2 jam jars

1 Queen Victoria pineapple (make sure it's not overripe), peeled

1 tbsp vegetable oil

2 red chillies, deseeded or not, depending on your heat preference, finely chopped

1 garlic clove, peeled and finely chopped

large thumb-size piece of fresh ginger, peeled and finely chopped

2 shallots, finely chopped

800g (1lb 12oz) jam sugar

100g (3 ½ oz) apple cider vinegar

juice and finely grated zest of 1 lemon

juice and finely grated zest of 1 lime

dried chilli flakes (optional), to taste

salt

Cut the pineapple into small dice.

Heat the oil in a frying pan over a low heat, then add the chillies, garlic, ginger and shallots and cook for about 2 minutes, until softened. Add the pineapple pieces, along with the sugar, vinegar and lemon and lime zests. Stir well to combine and dissolve the sugar. Continue to cook over a low heat for about 15 minutes, stirring occasionally, until the mixture is jammy and thickened.

Season the chutney with salt, and add lemon and lime juice to taste. If you like a real chilli kick, you might like to add some dried chilli flakes to taste.

Either spoon the hot chutney into sterilized jars and seal with the lids, or leave it to cool and then freeze it in a lidded container.

9

Jersey Royal Potato
May the Forced Be With You

You'll remember from the forced rhubarb a few weeks back that traditional methods of "forcing" vegetables produces an early crop with an enhanced flavour that can achieve accreditation across the globe. The famous Jersey Royal potato is another stunning example. Growers farm this kidney-shaped new potato in a unique micro-climate on the steep, south-facing coastal slopes, or *côtils*, of Jersey in the Channel Islands. The warm climate, mild winters and maritime breeze all contribute to producing a unique potato that provides the island's main crop and makes up half of its agricultural income. In fact, Jersey Royals (forced or otherwise) are grown here on a huge scale, producing up to 40,000 tonnes of spuds on land that has replaced Jersey's orchards of apples and market gardens. The majority of these potatoes, though, are not forced and are available for a short three- to four-month season from March to the end of June. However, the early crop of forced Jersey Royals, which make up only a small percentage of the entire crop, are available around the end of February.

The history of these distinctive potatoes is not unlike that of many niche products and came about more as an experiment or by happenstance. In around 1880, a Jersey farmer called Hugh de la Haye was given a large potato with an unusually prolific number of "eyes", or growing shoots. He duly divided the potato into 16 of these eyes and planted each one. Come spring, when the time came to harvest, he found that one plant had produced a crop of small kidney-shaped potatoes, while the potatoes from all the other plants were round. When cooked, these unusually shaped specimens had a far superior flavour – so Hugh set about producing what was initially called the Jersey Fluke. Like many success stories in the late 1800s, these spuds were given the word Royal in honour of Queen Victoria and, in this case, the suffix "Fluke" was dropped. Instead, the Jersey Royal was born.

Growers plant the early forced potatoes in December in glass sheds, then transfer them to poly tunnels, or cloches, on the *côtils* where the temperature is warmer, and the soil is light and free-draining. Owing to the steep terrain, almost all the planting and harvesting is done by hand (which protects the potatoes' delicate and distinctive skin) or by using tractors with ploughs attached to winches. The soil on the *côtils* is traditionally fertilized with vraic – seaweed that is harvested from the Jersey beaches. The addition of this local seaweed helps retain moisture in the soil, provides extra nutrients and contributes to the distinct earthy flavour of the potatoes.

These early beauties take around 11 to 12 weeks to grow and the traditional method of farming is incredibly labour intensive, but the results are more flavoursome. The potatoes are also more expensive, but don't let this put you off – buy fewer, but buy the best.

Although we expect to see most forced Jersey Royals around the end of February, sometimes they will appear in time for a Christmas treat. Once February has come and gone, they continue until the main crop of Jerseys arrives in the shops a month or so later. Stay alert and you'll notice the change in crop: the skins become darker and flakier as the season goes on, the flavour is dramatically reduced and the prices go down.

> "Growers farm this kidney-shaped new potato in a unique micro-climate on the steep, south-facing coastal slopes, or *côtils*, of Jersey in the Channel Islands."

Like Yorkshire rhubarb in 1997, Jersey Royals were awarded the EU accolade of Protected Designation of Origin (PDO) in recognition of the unique way in which the potatoes are grown and harvested in this particular region. The way to know that your greengrocer is buying true early Jerseys is that the spuds are sold in 6kg (13lb) boxes and are graded in two sizes: small (known as mids) and medium (known as wares). The price of these glorious potatoes can be up to ten times more expensive than those sold in the height of season in traditional 15kg (33lb) paper sacks with string stitching. To best enjoy their sweet, nutty flavour and creamy, firm texture, cook them simply – with their skins on. Never peel them – part of the Jersey Royal experience is the delicate, papery skin.

Some produce is especially remarkable when it first arrives
– like the Royal Kidney variety of Jersey potato. The real
McCoys sell from wooden baskets in 6kg (13lb) weights.

Jersey Royals with whipped sour cream butter

It doesn't get much better than these amazing British potatoes – they are absolutely stunning pieces of gold! Many people think a potato is merely a potato, but when you taste these little beauties, you will understand how wonderful a potato can be. This recipe is an exemplary combination that brings together Lithuanian sour cream butter and British potatoes. A little fresh mint sprinkled on top of the dish freshens it up and makes it more British. The recipe will make more sour cream butter than you need for this quantity of potatoes, but it will keep in the fridge for two to three weeks.

Serves 4

500g (1lb 2oz) Jersey Royals
5 garlic cloves, peeled
3 thyme sprigs
1 bay leaf
60g (2¼oz) unsalted butter, diced
600g (1lb 5oz) full-fat sour cream
5 mint leaves, chopped
salt and freshly ground black pepper

Wash the potatoes – usually they are quite sandy, so take your time and clean them well. Do not peel them or you will lose most of the sea flavour that is in the skins. Tip the potatoes into a medium saucepan and add 2 whole garlic cloves, along with the thyme sprigs and bay leaf. Season with a good pinch of salt. Cover the potatoes with water and place the pan over a high heat. Bring to a boil, then reduce the heat and simmer for about 20 minutes, until the potatoes are tender when tested with the point of a knife.

Meanwhile, place a metal bowl over of a pan of simmering water. Add the butter and melt it slowly, stirring it with a wooden spoon. When melted, remove the bowl from the heat and add a spoonful of the sour cream. Stir in the cream clockwise – this is important... stir only in one direction. Add another spoonful, stirring clockwise again and when the mixture starts to thicken, put the bowl back on the heat and slowly stir. Continue adding the sour cream, a tablespoon at a time, until you have a thick mixture the consistency of room-temperature butter.

Season with salt and pepper, then crush in the remaining garlic cloves, stirring to mix.

By now the potatoes should be cooked. Drain them and lightly crush them, then stir through the chopped mint, reserving a little for garnish. Spoon over the sour cream butter to serve and finish with the reserved mint.

New potato piccalilli salad *Recipe by Gordon Ramsay*

Gordon Ramsay was right when he described the Jersey Royal as "A potato with a delicate, sweet flavour." This is Gordon's second featured recipe, again from his book *Ultimate Cookery Course*, which accompanied his TV show. It pays homage to this most royal potato, and if ever there was a time to get excited about potatoes, it is now.

Serves 6

500g (1lb 2oz) new potatoes of a similar size

1 small cauliflower, cut into florets

275g (9¾oz) green beans, topped and tailed

1 carrot, peeled and grated

1 small shallot, peeled and finely sliced

3 spring onions (scallions), trimmed and finely chopped

pinch of ground turmeric

1–2 tsp English mustard powder, to taste

1 tbsp wholegrain mustard

1–2 tsp honey, to taste

3 tbsp white wine vinegar

100ml (3½fl oz) olive oil

Boil the new potatoes in salted water for about 15 minutes, until tender and cooked through. Blanch the cauliflower and green beans by dropping them into boiling salted water for 2 minutes, until their rawness has been removed but they are still crunchy. Refresh immediately in cold water.

Mix together the carrot, shallot, spring onions and turmeric and add the potatoes, cauliflower and green beans. To make the dressing, stir the mustard powder into the wholegrain mustard, making sure there are no lumps. Add the honey and vinegar, mix well, then slowly pour in the oil, stirring as you do so to thicken. Dress the salad and season with salt and pepper to taste.

10

Wild garlic / *Sicilian lemons* / *Mangosteen* / *Queen Victoria pineapples* / *Rambutans* / *Portuguese Tulameen raspberries* / *Spanish avocados* / *Lampascioni wild onions* / *Moroccan mint* / *Italian mixed herbs* / *Courgette (zucchini) flowers* / *Wild edible flowers* / *Tomatoes – Datterini, San Marzano, Provençal Coeur de Boeuf, Provençal Pineapple* / *Baby spinach* / *Chalke Valley watercress* / *Italian wild rocket (arugula)* / *Mizuna and Tatsoi leaf* / *Red and white Belgian chicory* / *Escarole* / *Castelfranco* / *Feuille de chêne (oak leaf lettuce)* / *Salanova salad* / *Breakfast radish* / *Ridge cucumbers* / *Surrey Downs spring onions* / *Borlotti beans* / *Cabbages – Cavolo Nero, Hispi, Somerset Savory* / *Artichokes – Jerusalem, Violet baby artichokes from Apulia* / *Mushrooms – Morel, Mousseron* / *Tropea onions* / *Potatoes – Agria, Jersey Royal 'earlies'* / *Beetroots – Candy, Cheltenham, Golden* / *Radishes – Red meat, Red mooli* / *Salsify* / *Turnips – Golden, Tokyo*

Wild Garlic
Now Nature Hangs Her Mantle Green

The week that ushers in March marks the start of the UK growing season and is a truly exciting time of year in my industry. Spring has finally sprung and with it comes an array of lush, new produce to enliven the palate after a long winter. All lies dormant until we see the arrival of wild garlic – alternatively known as ransoms, buckrams, bear's garlic, broad-leaved garlic and other names besides. If you're fortunate enough to find yourself in a forest or wood of deciduous trees in springtime, you'll undoubtedly at some point stumble across some, almost certainly next to a patch of bluebells (look for the flowers first, then look closer). The growing conditions for bluebells and wild garlic mimic one another.

Wild garlic leaves are up to 25cm (10in) long, lanceolate in shape and not dissimilar to those of lily of the valley – take care not to confuse the two, as lily of the valley is poisonous. Trust your sense of smell to distinguish them – wild garlic smells of... well, garlic, funnily enough. The emerald-green, glossy leaves are flat with pale green stems and grow in dense clumps, carpeting shady woodland floors. The plants produce delicate white, starburst flowers, each with six-pointed petals. These are also edible.

Whether you live in a metropolis or are surrounded by nature, think of where you live as the nucleus of your food world: adopt the same practices to go on a journey that invigorates your body, educates your mind and activates your taste buds. Wake up early in the morning (just before sunrise), pull on some wellington boots and find your nearest wood, riverbank, clearing, hedgerow, meadow or park – this is, in my view, an essential way to start to the week.

I am fortunate enough to live near woods in what I suppose you would call the suburbs of London. As this time of year rolls around, I start searching for wild garlic. It's the same scenario every year: at first it proves so elusive that I frustrate myself. But, of course, I'm being impatient: it has not yet broken ground. "Find the bluebells," I repeat to myself. A friend on a similar search a few miles away has found some and I am desperate to get the season moving. While the weather plays a major part in any growing season for any plant, wild or farmed (and for this reason the sunnier south of the country gets its plants earlier than the north), the ideal growing conditions for any wild food can be incredibly localized. This means that plants growing even in neighbouring woods can appear at different times.

"The first leaves of the season are more tender with a delicate garlic flavour that becomes more pungent as the seasons progresses."

But that is where the enjoyment lies. There is no better feeling than walking through the dappled shade of an ancient wood, turning the corner and suddenly discovering a sea of blue before you. Not only is this scene spectacular to look at, but you know the wild garlic leaf could be nearby. There is no guarantee that you'll find what you're looking for, even when a friend has had success not far away, but when you do, mark the spot where you found your treasure – and hope that no one else finds it. Tread lightly to avoid damaging surrounding wildlife, pick only small handfuls at a time from any patch (leaving plenty for others) and seek permission to forage on private land.

The first leaves of the season are more tender with a delicate garlic flavour that becomes more pungent as the season progresses. The flowers that appear toward mid-season make a beautiful edible garnish or addition to salads. Stir tender leaves and flowers through pasta or risotto or whizz them into pesto in place of basil. The leaves have a milder flavour when whole but become heightened when crushed or chopped.

Instead of buying wild garlic from shops and suppliers (even Turnips; I am aware that I'm shooting myself in the proverbial foot), go into those woods and pick for yourself... become a forager! Wild garlic heralds the start of an incredible adventure – an adventure that sees you source beautiful plant products for yourself to enjoy in your cooking.

Wild garlic pesto

If you pick the wild garlic yourself, a tub of this quick pesto will give you multiple meals at little cost. The flavour of the pesto will depend on how young or old your wild garlic leaves are. When they are young, the garlic flavour will be milder; the older the leaves, the more kick. You could add a little crushed regular garlic to make them more punchy, if you wish. Serve it with freshly cooked pasta, risotto or eggs on toast, or drizzled over a whole plateful of large tomatoes... the options are never-ending.

Fills a 250g (9oz) jar

125g (4½oz) wild garlic leaves

50g (1¾oz) pine nuts, toasted

140ml (4½fl oz) vegetable or rapeseed (canola) oil

50g (1¾oz) Parmesan, finely grated

finely grated zest and juice of 1 lemon, to taste

salt and freshly ground black pepper

Put the garlic leaves and pine nuts into a food processor and blitz until roughly chopped. Slowly add the oil, whizzing continuously, as you trickle it in. Now you can go two ways: either finish the pesto in the food processor, using the pulse button, or finish it in a bowl. Whichever way, mix through all the Parmesan, and then add the lemon zest and juice to taste. Season as required. Transfer the pesto to a jar, seal with the lid and leave it in the fridge for up to 2 weeks.

Wild garlic capers

I am so happy to share this recipe with everyone, as I don't really think many people have tried them or made wild garlic capers at home, and very few restaurants use them. First, they are hard to get hold of and, second, they take a long time to make, but they are so worth it as they are so tasty and will be a bonus on your table.

Eat the capers with steak or roasts or as an alternative to peppercorns in a peppercorn sauce (making it a caper sauce!). You can also add them to salsas – those little buds are worth more than gold!

Makes 1 small–medium jar

250g (9oz) wild garlic flower buds (it doesn't matter if you leave a little stalk attached)

3–4 tbsp table salt

200ml (7fl oz) apple cider vinegar

100g (3½oz) caster (superfine) sugar

Rinse the buds well under cold running water. Shake off the excess water and place the buds into a lidded container and cover them with the salt. Replace the lid and chill the buds for 2–3 weeks, mixing every few days, until they soften.

Wash the softened buds under cold running water to remove the salt and transfer the buds to a clean jar.

Pour 300ml (10½fl oz) of water into a small saucepan, add the vinegar and sugar and place the pan over a medium heat. Bring the liquid to a boil, stirring to dissolve the sugar, then reduce the heat and simmer for 1 minute. Pour the pickling liquor into the jar over the capers, seal with the lid and turn the jar upside down. Leave the contents of the jar to cool.

Once cool, turn the jar the right way up and store the capers in the fridge until needed. They will keep unopened for 6 months, or 1 month in the fridge once opened.

11

Italian fennel / *Sicilian lemons* / *Mangosteen* / *Queen Victoria pineapples* / *Rambutans* / *Portuguese Tulameen raspberries* / *Spanish avocados* / *Wild garlic* / *Italian mixed herbs* / *Moroccan mint* / *Courgette (zucchini) flowers* / *Tomatoes – Datterini, Provençal Coeur de Boeuf, Provençal Pineapple, San Marzano* / *Baby mixed leaves Campania* / *Baby spinach* / *Chalke Valley watercress* / *Italian wild rocket (arugula)* / *Mizuna and Tatsoi leaf* / *Red and white Belgian chicory* / *Escarole* / *Castelfranco* / *Feuille de chêne (oak leaf lettuce)* / *Salanova salad* / *Breakfast radish* / *Ridge cucumbers* / *Surrey Downs spring onions* / *Sicilian peppers* / *Beans – Borlotti, Yellow* / *Brittany cauliflower* / *Young Italian spinach* / *Cabbages – Hispi, Somerset Savoy* / *Artichokes – Jerusalem, Violet baby artichokes from Apulia* / *Pale Italian aubergines (eggplant)* / *Mushrooms – Morel, Mousseron* / *Tropea onions* / *Young French leeks* / *Potatoes – Jersey Royal "earlies", Italian Spunta* / *Candy beetroot* / *Nantes carrots* / *Radishes – Red meat, Red mooli* / *Turnips – Golden, Tokyo*

Italian Fennel
The Fennel Countdown

This week I am highlighting Italian fennel and the importance of aniseed as a flavouring, specifically bringing Italian – or Florentine – fennel to the fore. This is the bulb variety of the familiar herb of the same name.

Wild fennel grows prolifically in the Mediterranean in dry, sandy soils where the tall perennial plants, with wispy, feathery leaves are topped with small yellow flowers – often referred to as fennel pollen in culinary circles. This wild fennel does not produce the familiar white bulbs of Italian fennel and is used only for its leaves, flowers and seeds.

The use of fennel as a medicinal plant stretches back hundreds of years, and the seeds, herb and bulbs are loaded with symbolism and folklore. For example, fennel appears in Greek mythology – Prometheus is said to have used it to steal fire from the gods; Roman soldiers and gladiators are said to have fortified themselves for combat by eating fennel seeds for courage; and the fennel flower was a Roman symbol of strength and honour. In Shakespeare's play *Hamlet*, Ophelia gives out fennel with columbine to symbolize false flattery.

At Turnips, you're more likely to hear "that's the male and that's the female" than quotes from *Hamlet*. The conversation generally centres around the arrival of aromatic Italian fennel. These large white bulbs have thick, very pale green and white stems that lead to deep green, feathery angel-hair foliage. I am convinced that the large round bulbs of Italian fennel are the male, and the thinner, more elongated fennel bulbs from France and those grown in the UK later in the season are female. But really the truth is that they are neither male nor female. The fennel plant is similar to the lemon tree: it has hermaphrodite flowers (with both male and female parts). The shape of the bulb is entirely down to variety and soil conditions. The Rondo variety produces round, bulbous fennel – roughly the size of a tennis ball; the Victoria variety produces longer, more slender bulbs and greener foliage and is more often seen growing in France and the UK.

Fennel has a slightly sweet, aniseed and mild liquorice flavour that is more pronounced in the seeds than the other parts, meaning that it can be a hit or a miss at dinner parties. The crisp bulb is in fact the overlapping bases of the stalks, and you can separate them into layers much like an onion. I have included this herby vegetable not so much for its outstanding flavour (in that respect, I do believe that the Italian fennel is the best), but because it is a nutritional powerhouse. Fennel is packed full of vitamins and minerals, making the health benefits of incorporating this in your diet numerous. Among other things, fennel can aid digestion and boost your immune system. It is also a breath freshener, palate cleanser, antioxidant and anti-inflammatory, and it is a hunger suppressant (meaning that it can help with weight loss). Wow!

Overall, then, fennel is a generous plant, because you can use every part – bulb, stems, leaves, flowers and seeds – epitomizing the Turnips' ethos of "all taste, no waste". It offers everything from the crisp bulb to shred into salads (particularly delicious with oranges and radicchio – how very seasonal) or add to hot dishes such as gratins, soups and braises; to the leaves to use as a herb in pasta and salads; and the seeds to use as a seasoning in Italian cuisine or as a spice in Indian. All the parts will bring a unique anise flavour in varying degrees. Not many vegetables live up to it.

"The seller was trimming fennel, releasing wafts of its scent into the air."

In 2015 I visited the Milanese wholesale fruit-and-vegetable market *Ortomercato Milano* with Stefano, my agent there. At the time, the 1965 building was very run down I turned to Stefano and asked if we were in the right place. He smiled. It was like opening the doors of a dilapidated pub only to find Club Tropicana inside. Lettuces, tomatoes, courgettes (zucchini), aubergines (eggplants) and Cantaloupe melons were piled as high as you could see and the atmosphere was as electric as at a car auction in Detroit. I nearly got knocked off my feet by a man on a bicycle with five wooden crates of tomatoes strapped to the back. You had to have your wits about you.

The aroma of aniseed that drew me toward one stand in particular. The seller was trimming fennel, releasing wafts of its scent into the air. The wooden boxes of it were still wet from being hosed with cold water to stave off the extreme heat of the summer nights. There must have been more than 300 boxes of those white jewels. Next to them were stacks of courgette flowers lined up neatly, 12 to a tray. I was in the proverbial sweet shop, standing there with my mouth wide open and not knowing where to look next.

That day we went for lunch at Joia, which has been serving ground-breaking food since 1989 and is, as I write, the only vegetarian restaurant in Italy to hold a Michelin star. I handed over to Stefano to choose the main course, which was a magnificent fennel dish – simple yet bursting with flavour. I devoured the food and the atmosphere and later that day left Milan feeling inspired by the pride and love that the Italians have for their food and produce.

Finally, if I've learned nothing else while researching this book, at least it has stopped me from spouting the untruth that the round bulbous Italian fennel is male. I apologize to all the females out there for this 30-year misconception.

Italian fennel is full of vitamins and minerals, making it a healthy addition to your diet. An aniseed explosion, it pairs beautifully with all fish, and bonus herby fronds, too!

Fennel and cucumber salad with toasted nuts and dill

The combination of anise flavour from the fennel (both the vegetable and the seeds), and the beautiful, aromatic fresh cucumber and dill will draw your attention and I think will become your new favourite salad combination. The cucumbers are left unpeeled to add great texture, which pairs beautifully with crisp, thinly sliced fennel and toasted nuts.

Serves 4

2 fennel bulbs

2 small ridged Italian cucumbers

1 Cevenne onion

½ lemon

3 tbsp olive oil

2 tbsp chopped dill

50g (1¾oz) flaked (slivered) almonds, toasted

50g (1¾oz) hazelnuts, toasted and roughly chopped

20g (¾oz) fennel seeds, toasted

salt and freshly ground black pepper

Trim the fennel, reserving the leafy tops and cut the bulb in half. Using a mandoline slice the fennel bulb very thinly and place the slices in a bowl of iced water for at least 10 minutes, until the slices are firm and very crisp. Roughly chop the leafy fronds.

Thinly slice the cucumber and onion using the mandoline and tip both into a large bowl.

Drain the fennel, pat the slices dry on kitchen paper and add them to the sliced cucumber and onion. Finely grate the lemon zest directly into the bowl and squeeze the juice on top. Add the olive oil, dill, fennel fronds, and toasted nuts and seeds, then season with salt and pepper and mix to combine. Serve and enjoy!

Fennel sauerkraut

In the kitchens at Turnips, we ferment almost everything – from meat to fish. Of course, though, a massive proportion of our ferments are vegetables. Sauerkraut is at the heart of Lithuanian heritage and traditionally it is made with just cabbage, but here we combine it with other amazing, crisp vegetables, including fennel, to create delicious pickles and ferments to use throughout the year. The whole process of making sauerkraut is quite simple and takes relatively little time – the hardest part is waiting! You'll need large, sterilized fermenting vessels, such as stoneware crocks or large Kilner jars, for this recipe.

Makes 4 large jars

4 fennel bulbs

2 white cabbages

about 100g (3½oz) Maldon or fermenting salt

2 onions, sliced

1 garlic bulb, cloves separated, peeled and chopped

30g (1oz) fennel seeds

30g (1oz) caraway seeds

30g (1oz) dill seeds

4 bay leaves

Wash the fennel and cabbage under cold running water and cut the fennel in half and the cabbage into quarters. Using a mandoline or food processor fitted with a shredding blade, thinly slice both vegetables, reserving 4 cabbage leaves to use to cover later.

Weigh the sliced vegetables and make a note of the total weight. Work out 2 per cent of the total weight and add this amount of salt to the veg in a bowl. Add the onion, garlic, all the seeds and then the bay leaves and mix well to thoroughly combine. Spoon the mixture into the fermenting jars, cover the surface of the vegetables with a cabbage leaf and press with a weight. Leave the vegetables at room temperature for 2 hours, until they have released enough water to cover themselves. If not, make a brine to top up: measure out enough filtered water and pour it into a saucepan. Bring it to a boil and add 2 per cent of the weight of the water in salt (for example, for every 100ml/3½fl oz of water you will need to add ¼ teaspoon of salt). Cool the brine to room temperature, then pour this over the shredded vegetables to cover them.

Cover the jars loosely with a lid and leave them in a dark place for a week, so that the vegetables ferment. Relase, mix and re-seal every 2 days to burp the sauerkraut and release the carbon monoxide from the fermenting mixture.

After a week taste the sauerkraut. If you like a light fermentation, spoon the sauerkraut into clean jars and store it in the fridge for up to 2 years unopened. If you want a more sour-tasting ferment, then leave it and taste it every couple of days until you reach your desired sourness. Once opened, use the sauerkraut within 1 month.

12

Sicilian tomatoes / *Queen Victoria pineapples* / *Raspberries – Panach' Golden, Portuguese Tulameen* / *Spanish avocados* / *Wild garlic* / *Italian mixed herbs* / *Moroccan mint* / *Courgette (zucchini) flowers* / *Tomatoes – Datterini, San Marzano* / *Baby mixed leaves Campania* / *Baby spinach* / *Chalke Valley watercress* / *Italian wild rocket (arugula)* / *Mizuna and Tatsoi leaf* / *Red and white Belgian chicory* / *Escarole* / *Feuille de chêne (oak leaf lettuce)* / *Red and green Butterhead lettuce* / *Salanova salad* / *Breakfast radish* / *Ridge cucumbers* / *Surrey Downs spring onions* / *Sicilian peppers* / *Beans – Borlotti, Yellow* / *Asparagus – Les Landes white, Pertuis green, Brittany wild* / *Brittany cauliflower* / *Young Italian spinach* / *Hispi cabbage* / *Artichokes – Jerusalem, Violet baby artichokes from Apuli* / *Pale Italian aubergines (eggplant)* / *Tromba courgettes* / *Mousseron mushrooms* / *Tropea onions* / *Young French leeks* / *Potatoes – Italian Spunta potatoes, Jersey Royal "earlies"* / *Italian fennel* / *Nantes carrots* / *Radishes – Red meat, Red mooli* / *Tokyo turnips*

Sicilian Tomato
Shooting the Breeze

This week sees the Spring Equinox and with it comes a dive into Italian winter tomatoes – but that's not before we've weaved our story via the arrival of the Three-cornered leek and the importance of correct plant identification.

The sun is coming up and off I go with Sapphire, my beautiful black Labrador, by my side, wondering what I'll find on my forage this glorious March morning. There's been a frost in the night (not exactly what you would expect on the Spring Equinox), and there is an abundance of bluebells everywhere and very little wild garlic. That said, I have managed to find enough locally to serve me well. I know that, at this time of year, another flavour from the allium family is growing wild – the Three-cornered leek, and I'm hoping to find some.

A beautiful, tender leafy plant not dissimilar to wild garlic, though with narrower, stiffer leaves and a flavour more in common with spring onions (scallions), baby leeks or chives, the Three-cornered leek is an invasive species originally from the Mediterranean regions. You are permitted to uproot the whole plant if you find it growing in the wild (that's not the case with most wild plants), but it is an offence to grow it. You should, of course, follow the rules of public foraging and remove only one plant to identify you have the right leaf. Once you have made your identification, you can freely pluck the leaves.

These have a stiff ridge on the underside and the flower stems are triangular when cut in cross-section. The nodding flowers with white petals, each with a green ridge on the outside, sit on top of each stem and have a strong garlic flavour. All parts of this plant are edible – flowers, leaves and stem, and the roots are not unlike spring onions.

For a long while I had been patting myself on the back, impressed at my foraging skills and that my early morning treks into the wilds were so fruitful. I called Martin, my trusted forager from Norfolk who supplies Turnips, proudly telling him that I'd found a great patch of ramps, another member of the allium family best described as the love-child of a spring onion and wild garlic. Martin told me that I would need to travel a lot further than the Kent countryside to find ramps, as they are found growing wild mainly in North America and Canada. Clearly, what I'd actually found was Three-cornered leeks.

By this week in the year, you would think that there would be a cavalcade of spring vegetables appearing in the markets, but in fact there is no such luck. I often think that, at this time, we are so keen for an end to winter that we look desperately for signs of spring. I have to tell myself, "Be patient, not long now." In the meantime, there is more spectacular produce from Italy to enjoy. In this chapter, then, Three-cornered leeks aside, we are focussing on winter tomatoes from Sicily and Sardinia and, in particular, the Marinda and Camone varieties.

Marinda tomatoes grow in the southernmost tip of Sicily, around Pachino, where the mineral-rich soil, warm climate and salty sea air provide the perfect environment for winter varieties. These large tomatoes are rounded, slightly flattened in shape and deeply ridged. Their skin is thick and ranges in colour from green to orange and red and with dark green patches on the shoulders when ripe. These markings are distinctive of the variety and a clear indication of quality.

The Marinda tomato is thought to originate from a French heirloom variety, Marmonde, which comes from a city of the same name in southwest France. However, Marinadas are now very much considered a Sicilian cultivar. Its flesh is firm, crisp and crunchy; it is red and green and has yellow seeds. These tomatoes have a fruity, savoury (umami) and lightly salty taste, which comes from the coastal soil in which they grow. The tomatoes are slow to mature and are grown with controlled levels of rain and salt water, which encourages the plants to absorb all the available minerals from the soil. Their flavour pairs well with fruity olive oil and creamy cheese.

The other winter tomato variety hitting its peak now is Camone, which we source from southern Sardinia. Similar to the Marinda, this tomato is hardy and slow-growing, with a thick green and red skin. It is less ribbed, smaller and rounder in shape than the Marinda, and the flavour is a little sharper, but it is equally good for winter salads. (The thicker skins of these winter tomatoes make them less suitable for cooking.)

Italians are bonkers about tomatoes and from the beginning to the end of the year, you can criss-cross the country savouring the delights of each region's specific variety of red (and green) beauties. As the seasons move on, the weather improves and the heat increases – at the same time, the tomato skins get thinner, and their flavour intensifies. This is when the Italians start celebrating tomatoes more suited to being cooked or semi-dried.

I can hear Giorgio Locatelli now: "Never, never use a San Marzano in salads, you English are crazy!" The great Italian chef was, at that time (in 1992, before owning his own restaurants) working at Olivio, a restaurant in Belgravia, London, specializing in Sardinian cuisine. Tomatoes were high up on the list of

"Never, never use a San Marzano in salads, you English are crazy!"

ingredients he used there and I was his fruit-and-vegetable supplier. I explained to him that I fully understood what he was talking about because my dad once owned a salad stall not far away in Pimlico, a stall that I was then running. My father taught me all about salad tomatoes – how they should not be deep red but should in fact have an orangey green tint to them.

My earliest memory of my time on the stall, aged ten, was being given the job of unwrapping all the tomatoes. In those days, the winter tomatoes came from the Canary Islands and every single one was wrapped in paper, packed in a nest of straw and transported in wooden boxes that we called "boats", because of their shape. In a single sitting, I would unwrap up to 20 boxes, each containing around 80 tomatoes – at the time, I thought this was seriously unfair! I now know that it was an education.

If I'm lucky enough to find some Three-cornered leeks while out foraging, I'll finely chop the leaves and mix them with some top-notch extra-virgin olive oil (Sicilian, of course) to create a lovely dressing to spoon over the winter tomatoes that are in their prime right now. This is how connections are created: a Kent-grown and -foraged allium combined with a winter tomato from Italy.

Italian winter tomatoes have a much thicker skin than their
summer cousins and a higher level of acidity. They are great
for making salads.

Sicilian marinated tomatoes

When I was a little kid, I used to go downstairs to our cellar to sneak some goodies made by my mum – often my treat would be marinated tomatoes in brine. They are a great condiment to have with steak or to add a little acidity to salads. Or, you can enjoy them in the same way as my wife, who has them on their own when she craves something sour. The marinade liquid is useful as a hangover cure, or you can use it like any full-flavoured vinegar. Try to use smaller tomatoes so that you can fit more in the jar. And feel free to tweak and adjust this recipe – add onions, celery, chillies or anything you like to add flavour.

Makes about 1 large jar

3 bay leaves

4 dill sprigs

8 black peppercorns

2 tsp dill seeds

1kg (2lb 4oz) Sicilian tomatoes, washed

4 garlic cloves, peeled

700ml (24fl oz) filtered water

1 tbsp salt

2 tbsp granulated sugar

3 tbsp apple cider vinegar

Place the herbs and spices into the bottom of the jar. Tuck the tomatoes and garlic on top, gently pressing them to fit.

Pour the water into a large saucepan and add the salt and sugar. Bring the liquid to a boil over a high heat, stirring to dissolve the salt and sugar. Boil for 1 minute, then add the vinegar and pour the liquid into the jar to cover the tomatoes.

Check the seasoning – it should taste a little vinegary. Tightly cover the jar with a lid and turn it upside down to create a vacuum. Leave the contents of the jar to cool, then turn the jar the right way up and store it either in a cool cellar or the fridge for up to 1 year. Once you've opened the jar, keep the tomatoes refrigerated and use them within 1 week.

Sicilian tomato and burrata salad

Personally, there is nothing better than fresh burrata! I'm a huge fan of soft cheeses, but this super-creamy cheese on top of lightly dressed ripe tomatoes is something special. Add a couple of pickles – whatever you have around – and it will make a truly beautiful starter.

Serves 4

5 mixed large Sicilian tomatoes

4 tbsp olive oil

3 garlic cloves, peeled and sliced

2 thyme sprigs, leaves picked

10 basil leaves

pinch of caster (superfine) sugar

1 tbsp runny honey

1 tbsp Dijon mustard

80ml (2¾ fl oz) rapeseed (canola) oil

Maldon salt, to taste

6 pickled baby onions; or ½ fresh red onion, thinly sliced

4 burrata

salt and freshly ground black pepper

toasted bread, to serve

Cut a cross on the underside of each tomato. Place the tomatoes in a bowl and cover them with the freshly boiled water. Leave them for 30 seconds to loosen the skins and then transfer them to a bowl of iced water.

Carefully peel off the skins and discard them, then slice the tomato flesh or cut it into rough dice. Tip the tomato flesh into a bowl and add the olive oil, garlic, thyme leaves and 2–3 roughly torn basil leaves. Add the pinch of sugar, and season with salt and pepper. Stir to combine, cover the bowl and leave the mixture at room temperature for 1–2 hours to marinate. If it's a sunny day, you could leave the bowl next to the window to get a little warmth.

In the meantime, make the dressing. In a bowl whisk together the honey and mustard to combine. Whisking continuously, slowly add the rapeseed oil to emulsify. If at any time the dressing looks like it is about to split, whisk in a little boiling water and it should come back together.

Remove the tomatoes from the marinade and place them into a serving bowl. Sprinkle with Maldon salt and drizzle them with the dressing. Scatter the onions around the tomatoes and top the salad with the burrata. Drizzle with a little of the tomato marinade, scatter with the remaining basil and enjoy with toasted bread.

13

Wet garlic / *Ardour kiwi from Landes* / *Queen Victoria pineapples* / *Raspberries – Panach' Golden, Portuguese Tulameen* / *Spanish avocados* / *Italian mixed herbs* / *Moroccan mint* / *Courgette (zucchini) flowers* / *Tomatoes – Datterini, San Marzano, Sicilian varieties* / *Baby mixed leaves Campania* / *Baby spinach* / *Chalke Valley watercress* / *Italian wild rocket (arugula)* / *Mizuna and Tatsoi leaf* / *Red and white Belgian chicory* / *Endives – Escarole, Summer fine frisée* / *Feuille de chêne (oak leaf lettuce)* / *Red and green Butterhead lettuce* / *Salanova salad* / *Breakfast radish* / *Italian celery* / *Ridge cucumbers* / *Surrey Downs spring onions* / *Sicilian peppers* / *Beans – Borlotti, Italian broad (fava), Yellow* / *Asparagus – Les Landes white, Pertuis green* / *Brittany cauliflower* / *Young Italian spinach* / *Hispi cabbage* / *Pale Italian aubergines (eggplant)* / *Tromba courgettes (zucchini)* / *Artichokes – Roman Mammole globe, Violet baby artichokes from Apuli* / *Mousseron mushrooms* / *Tropea onions* / *Young French leeks* / *Potatoes – Italian Spunta, Jersey Royal "earlies"* / *Italian fennel* / *Nantes carrots* / *Tokyo turnips*

Wet Garlic
Wet Behind the Ears

"Hi Turnips, what's your pleasure?"

"Hi Pete, I'll have a pallet of Agria spuds, twenty cues, ten French grass and chuck in five bunches of the wet garlic."

"Any snips?"

"No thanks."

"What the hell are they talking about?" I hear you say. This is the language of a nighttime fruit-and-veg wholesale market in London. If you were in a wholesale market in New York, Paris or Milan, I'm not sure you'd hear such colloquial terms as those echoed in the grand food halls of our capital city. It's like entering a new – but old – world with a language all of its own; one that's been in use since the time of Charles Dickens.

"What's the ecrip of those heads?"

"A rouf," Pete replied.

Okay, I'll come clean. That's not how we always talk in the markets of London, but if you didn't know the parlance or patter, you would struggle. Let me translate for you: spuds are potatoes, cues are cucumbers, grass is of course asparagus, heads are cauliflowers, and snips are parsnips. The ecrip is the price, a rouf is four... and wet garlic is not exactly wet or dry, but fresh. Easy!

Wet garlic, in fact, is the first harvest of cultivated garlic bulbs. So far our weeks have already given us garlic in a leaf form (see page 64). Now we have the bulbs. Wet garlic is similar to new potatoes. These are the first varieties to be harvested in February or March and do not store particularly well, so the season is short and sweet. They are planted in the autumn and are a larger, softer, quicker-growing plant, with a milder, sweeter flavour than the garlic varieties we see later in the season. The first wave of wet garlic comes from Egypt, but it is not until we move to the French supplies that we see a truly world-class product.

Garlic is possibly the most important flavouring in almost every cuisine in the world and to me it's impossible to think of cooking without using it. Once grown for medicinal and therapeutic purposes, garlic has a history that we can trace back to ancient civilizations in Egypt, China, India, Greece and Rome. It's said that the enslaved people who built the ancient Egyptian pyramids ate garlic during their toils; and archeologists found garlic in the tomb of King Tutankhamun in Egypt's Valley of the Kings. Throughout the centuries, people have used it to treat such ailments as indigestion, respiratory problems, and fatigue. Now we may use it to lower blood pressure and cholesterol, for its antiseptic properties and as a general immune-booster.

The arrival of the first bulbs of wet garlic heralds the only time we use garlic as a vegetable rather than as a flavouring. Similar in looks to fennel, the immature bulbs are ribbed with a single stem or thick neck (unlike fennel, which has multiple stalks, or "fingers"). You can thinly slice the bulbs and use the slices raw in salads, or drizzle them with a little olive oil, stalks and all, and roast them to use in place of leeks or spring onions (scallions) in soups and risottos.

The majority of garlic production is in the south of France, in the Tarn region where the terroir of well-draining chalky and clay soils and the warm, dry climate provide the perfect growing conditions. In France, there are more than 30 varieties of commercially grown garlic, with Parador and Vayo the most popular. These bulbs are either white or purple and are differentiated by the external stem colour: white garlic has a green stem, and purple has a green or purple stem. However, the bulbs of all garlic varieties have a white exterior – the colour of the skin appears only as a result of the drying process, when the outer layers peel off.

"If you were in a wholesale market in New York, Paris or Milan, I'm not sure you'd hear such colloquial terms as those echoed in the grand food halls of our capital city."

Widely regarded as the very best of all garlic varieties is the slower growing, deeply flavoured springtime Ail Rose de Lautrec. This variety is the only garlic to have not only a *Label Rouge* accreditation (awarded in 1966), but has it also been granted Protected Geographical Indication (PGI). Together these endorsements recognize the exemplary growing standards and ensure the provenance of each bulb. Each must be perfect: throughout growing, growers check the garlic bulbs constantly to ensure they meet the exacting standards of accreditation, so that they can wear their labels proudly when they are sold.

In most European countries, including the UK, when a regional product is given the highest accreditations, the growing area often holds an annual festival to celebrate and honour the produce. The calendar highlight for garlic is the Fête de l'Ail Rose de Lautrec, when visitors besiege the village of Lautrec for three days over the first weekend in August to take part in competitions, taste the new crop and sample all the associated garlic products.

When Charles and Camilla met Charles and Camilla

In 2013 TRH The Prince of Wales and The Duchess of Cornwall came to officially open the new market at Borough in London after it had gone through a three-year upgrade and redevelopment programme. The Trustees of the market asked me, as the longest-serving trader at the time, to meet them. I gladly agreed. My wife, Caroline, and I presented the royal couple with a fresh, "wet" purple garlic. The magnificent specimen stood about 60cm (2 feet) tall from bulb to leaf. I wanted to find out once and for all if Prince Charles's vampiric heritage was real or not – I had heard that garlic did not travel well in Transylvania where he allegedly owns vast swathes of land with a magnificent castle at its centre. I'm glad to report that he did not flinch in the slightest – although he did shoot me a curious look when I thrust the allium into his hand.

I then introduced the royal couple to my son Charles and my niece Camilla, who ran a Saturday stall selling wild mushrooms and truffles at Duke of York Square in Chelsea. Their Royal Highnesses spoke to them at length and were especially intrigued to learn from my son how dogs had replaced pigs for hunting truffles. It seems the pigs had expensive tastes – and were found eating all the bounty (see page 271).

It was a truly memorable event. I'm not sure if the royal couple left with the garlicky trophy I'd given them and I often wonder what would have happened if I had charged The Prince of Wales a "rouf". Would he have had any "quids" on him to pay me?

*Wet garlic is available only in spring and provides one of the
few opportunities we have to use garlic as a vegetable rather
than as a flavouring.*

Roasted wet garlic sauce with Parmesan

This is an amazing sauce that is delicious spread on to chargrilled bread, fish or vegetables.

Makes 1 large jar

2 wet garlic bulbs
3 banana shallots, sliced
1 tbsp olive oil
5 thyme sprigs, leaves picked
100ml (3½fl oz) white wine
200ml (7¾fl oz) chicken or vegetable stock
100ml (3½fl oz) double (heavy) cream
75g (2½oz) Parmesan, grated
freshly ground black pepper

Preheat the oven to 180°C/160°C fan/350°F/Gas 4.

Wash the garlic heads and place them on a sheet of foil. Wrap them up and roast them in the preheated oven for 25–30 minutes, until soft.

Meanwhile, tip the shallots into a small saucepan, add the olive oil and place the pan over a low–medium heat. Sweat the vegetables for about 5 minutes, until soft and translucent. Add the thyme leaves and white wine, and bring the liquid to a boil. Leave to bubble away for about 10–15 minutes, until reduced by half.

Add the stock and reduce the volume by half again. Then, add the cream.

Check the garlic. If it is soft, remove and discard the hard central stalk, and roughly chop the heads. Add these to the pan. Using a stick blender, blitz the mixture until smooth. Taste and add the Parmesan a little at a time until you get the saltiness just right (you may not need all the cheese). Season with a little black pepper.

Leave the sauce with a slightly coarse texture or pass it through a fine sieve so that it's silky smooth, if you prefer.

Wet garlic fermented in raw honey

The smell of honey with wet garlic is absolutely stunning. In this preserve you have two uses for the price of one – you can use the garlicky honey in dressings and glazes and the fermented garlic in any dish where you would use fresh. Try adding cloves or Sichuan pepper to the mixture for a hint of spice.

Makes 1 large jar

500g (1lb 2oz) wet garlic cloves, peeled

5 thyme sprigs

½ tsp cloves or Sichuan pepper (optional)

150g (5 ½ oz) raw honey

100ml (3 ½ fl oz) filtered water

Place the peeled, wet garlic inside a sterilized jar.

Add the thyme sprigs and the spices if you're using them. In a jug, mix together the honey and water and pour the mixture into the jar to completely cover and submerge the garlic – you may need to add a little more honey and water (or less) depending on the precise size of your jar.

Mix well to combine. Cover the jar with a clean muslin cloth (cheesecloth) and leave it in a dark cupboard at room temperature for about 2 months to ferment.

When the garlic has fermented, it will smell sweet and sour and the garlic will have a more subtle flavour; the honey will be little cloudy.

Once you have reached your desired level of ferment, seal the jar with the lid and store it in the fridge. Use it within 6 months, or 2 months once it is opened.

Ile de Ré potatoes / *Ardour kiwi from Landes* / *Queen Victoria pineapples* / *Raspberries – Panach' Golden, Portuguese Tulameen* / *Spanish avocados* / *Dill* / *Fennel herb* / *Italian mixed herbs* / *Moroccan mint* / *Thai lemongrass* / *Courgette (zucchini) flowers* / *Tomatoes – Datterini, San Marzano, Sicilian* / *Baby mixed leaves Campania* / *Baby spinach* / *Chalke Valley watercress* / *Italian wild rocket (arugula)* / *Mizuna and Tatsoi leaf* / *Red and white Belgian chicory* / *Summer fine frisée* / *Feuille de chêne (oak leaf lettuce)* / *Red and green Butterhead lettuce* / *Salanova salad* / *Breakfast radish* / *Italian celery* / *Ridge cucumbers* / *Surrey Downs spring onions* / *Sicilian peppers* / *Beans – Borlotti, Italian broad (fava), Yellow* / *Asparagus – Les Landes white, Pertius green* / *Brittany cauliflower* / *Chinese bok choy* / *Young Italian spinach* / *Artichokes – Roman Mammole globe, Violet baby artichokes from Apuli* / *Aubergines (eggplants) – Pale Italian, Tiger* / *Tromba courgette* / *Wet garlic* / *Mousseron mushrooms* / *Tropea onions* / *Young French leeks* / *Jersey Royal "early" potatoes* / *Italian fennel* / *Nantes carrots* / *Tokyo turnips*

Ile de Ré Potato
The World Class Standard

This week marks the move away from winter and into the spring and early summer months. It's important to realize that although we have very clearly defined seasons in the fruit-and-vegetable world, there is some overlap. Here in the UK and in the rest of Europe, at this time of year we appreciate the amazing produce that is grown on our doorstep. Generations of farmers hand down traditional skills to cultivate and harvest amazingly flavourful products. From now on in the year, it gets really exciting – asparagus, artichokes, beans and new potatoes all start to arrive to set our culinary world alight.

A month or so ago, we talked about our fabulous Jersey Royal potatoes, and now we're talking about spuds again. This time it's the Ile de Ré potato and specifically the Starlette variety. Ile de Ré is a small, picturesque island off the Atlantic coast of southwest France. It is a low-lying island some 85km² (33 square miles) and with a highest point of 20m (65 feet). A tourist hotspot, with golden, sandy beaches, delicious, locally caught seafood and a climate to rival the south of France, it is popular with the Parisian chic and with celebrities who want to get away from it all.

The island also happens to grow world-class potatoes that have been awarded Appellation d'Origine Contrôlée status (AOC, meaning "controlled designation of origin"). This French certification protects the location, terroir, cultivation techniques and quality of distinctive French produce and appears also on exceptional wine, spirits, produce and cheese (see page 15). All AOC products must comply with a set of clearly defined and closely regulated standards. Ile de Ré potatoes are the only potatoes to have been awarded this prestigious mark of quality and the criteria to achieve accreditation are strict. The potatoes can be grown only in specific areas of the island (and outdoors, not in glasshouses) and must be produced, sorted, graded and packed within that area. They must be planted between January 20 and March 31, and can be marketed as Ile de Ré potatoes only until July 31 of the same year.

The unique growing conditions on the island mean that the potatoes are ready to harvest earlier than those grown on mainland France. The strong, warm winds blowing off the Atlantic, sandy coastal soil, low rainfall in spring and abundance of sun all contribute to produce a firm-textured potato with a fine skin that comes loose with gentle scrubbing. Like Jersey Royals, these potatoes are fertilized with seaweed, in this case seaweed that is harvested on the island. The resulting potatoes are small, measuring up to 7cm (2¾in) in length, with a firm texture and slightly starchy consistency. They have a nutty, sweet and slightly mineral flavour. You can spot them easily in a market, because they are sold in wooden boat-shaped boxes with a blue marine motif and, of course, they carry the all-important AOC hallmark.

> "The island also happens to grow world-class potatoes that have been awarded Appellation d'Origine Contrôlée status."

At Turnips we really get excited when these little French potato beauties appear. We know that this marks a turning point in the year and from now on we see more products – including asparagus and soft and stone fruits – week by week. Ile de Ré potatoes are not cheap, but buy a handful, sauté them with some wild garlic and enjoy them simply as a wonderful accompaniment to your main course. Or, try them as Tomas has, showcasing one of his very popular restaurant dishes and using his great imagination for preserving.

Ile de Ré potatoes with roasted yeast sauce

Unusual as this recipe might be, you can serve it readily as a side or main. Served with Ile de Ré potatoes, the sauce, laced with the roasted yeast, really enhances the seaweed flavour of the spuds.

Serves 4

1kg (2lb 4oz) Ile de Ré potatoes

2 tbsp olive oil

4 garlic cloves, peeled

2–3 thyme sprigs

100g (3½oz) fresh yeast

knob of butter

2 banana shallots, sliced

100ml (3½fl oz) white wine

300ml (3½fl oz) double (heavy) cream

2 dill sprigs, chopped, or a few nasturtium leaves

salt and freshly ground black pepper

Preheat the oven to 180°C/160°C fan/350°F/Gas 4.

Tip the washed potatoes into a roasting tin and toss them in the olive oil. Add 3 of the garlic cloves and all the thyme sprigs and season everything with salt and pepper. Mix well. Take another smaller roasting tin, line it with baking paper and crumble the fresh yeast over the top.

Place the yeast in the oven and roast it, stirring from time to time once the yeast starts to firm up, for about 45 minutes, until golden.

About 20 minutes into the roasting time, pop the potatoes into the oven on another shelf and roast these for about 30 minutes, until tender, crisp and golden.

Meanwhile, slice the remaining garlic clove. Melt the butter in a small saucepan, add the shallots and garlic and sauté everything over a medium heat for about 5 minutes, until softened. Add the wine, bring it to a boil and let it reduce by half. Then, add the cream, bring the liquid to a boil again, then reduce the heat and simmer for 10–15 minutes, until thickened enough to generously coat the back of a spoon. Remove the sauce from the heat and, using a stick blender, whizz until smooth.

Once the yeast has roasted, set 2 teaspoons aside to serve, then add the remainder a little at a time to the sauce, whizzing continuously until the flavour is to your liking. The sauce should be a golden colour.

Remove the potatoes from the oven and discard the thyme sprigs. To serve, pour most of the sauce into a serving dish, then arrange the potatoes and garlic on top. Pour over the remaining sauce, and season with salt and freshly ground black pepper. Scatter with the reserved yeast and dill or nasturtium leaves and enjoy.

Pickled Ile de Ré potatoes

I doubt many people have tried pickled potatoes, and while these little potatoes are the best in their league and delicious fresh, pickling them means you can enjoy them later in the year, too. This recipe is a labour of love, but once you've done it, you have Ile de Rés to enjoy fried, in salads or on their own, all year round.

Makes 1kg (2lb 4oz)

1kg (2lb 4oz) small Ile de Ré potatoes

125ml (4fl oz) apple cider vinegar

2 bay leaves

1 kombu sheet

10 thyme sprigs

4 garlic cloves, peeled

100g (3 ½ oz) cipollini onions, peeled

Place the potatoes into a saucepan of salted water over a high heat. Bring to a boil, then reduce the heat and simmer until tender (about 20 minutes).

Meanwhile, prepare the pickling brine. Pour 250ml (9fl oz) of water into another saucepan. Add the vinegar, bay, kombu, thyme, garlic and onions. Place the pan over a high heat and bring the liquid to a boil, then reduce the heat and simmer for 10 minutes.

Drain the cooked potatoes and plunge them into ice-cold water to stop them cooking any further. Drain them again, then pack them into sterilized jars. Pour over the hot pickling liquor and seal in the jars with tight-fitting lids. Turn the jars upside down to create a vacuum and leave to cool.

Once the contents of the jars are cold, turn the jars the right way up and store the pickled potatoes in a cool, dry place for up to 6 months. Once opened, refrigerate and use them with a couple of weeks.

15

Gariguette strawberries / Ardour kiwi from Landes / Queen Victoria pineapples / Raspberries – Panach' Golden, Portuguese Tulameen / Spanish avocados / Brittany herbs / Dill / Fennel herb / Italian mixed herbs / Thai lemongrass / Courgette (zucchini) flowers / Tomatoes – Datterini, Early Provence, San Marzano / Baby mixed leaves Campania / Baby spinach / Chalke Valley watercress / Italian wild rocket (arugula) / Mizuna and Tatsoi leaf / Red and white Belgian chicory / Summer fine frisée / Feuille de chêne (oak leaf lettuce) / Red and green Butterhead lettuce / Salanova salad / Breakfast radish / Italian celery / Ridge cucumbers / Surrey Downs spring onions / Sicilian peppers / Beans – Borlotti, Italian broad (fava), Yellow / Asparagus – Les Landes white, Pertius green / Brittany cauliflower / Chinese bok choy / Young Italian spinach / Artichokes – Roman Mammole globe, Violet baby artichokes from Apuli / Aubergines (eggplants) – Pale Italian, Tiger / Tromba courgettes / Wet garlic / Mousseron mushrooms / Tropea onions / Young French leeks / Potatoes – Ile de Ré, Jersey Royal "earlies" / Italian fennel / Nantes carrots / Radishes – Black mooli, Red and white long French / Tokyo turnips

Gariguette Strawberry
I've Got a Soft Spot for You

A few years ago, while holidaying in the South of France, I met up with Marc, my French supplier who took me to see a local strawberry grower. After enjoying some Pernod and a spot of lunch, I asked the farmer (with the help of Marc's translation) what makes his Carpentras strawberries so much sweeter, more fragrant and more delicious than glasshouse ones? He spread his arms expansively to take in the beautiful scenery and gave a one-word answer that needed no translation: "*Nature.*"

This week puts our favourite soft fruit under the microscope, and I want to explain to you why an outdoor-grown strawberry is such a thing of beauty. Produce grown in Nature's soil, ripened by the sun and watered by the rain is a subject that I am passionate about, if you haven't already noticed. But before we start did you know that the strawberry, like rhubarb, is not actually a fruit? Rhubarb is a vegetable and strawberries are technically classed as part of the flower of the strawberry plant. The yellow seeds are actually the fruit. Hey ho! They are all beautiful fruits in my mind.

Gariguette strawberries are a perfect example of a variety that owes its intoxicating flavour to precisely the area in which it is grown. These ruby berries flourish in the beautiful hilly countryside and flower-rich meadows around the town of Carpentras. They bathe in the sunshine and grow in the warmth of a Mediterranean climate. They have been growing in this scented landscape since the 1880s. The strawberries are planted by hand in the warm soil from August to September and the berries are harvested, again by hand, in April and May.

Carpentras lies in the fertile agricultural plains of the Vaucluse region of Provence, an area that is well known for its gourmet delights. Like all good gastronomic regions, the town takes its produce very seriously and has an annual strawberry festival and even a Brotherhood of Strawberries (*Confrérie Fraise de Carpentras*), who are ambassadors for their fruits. Members of the brotherhood wear a special red-and-green costume for the parades and festivals that happen when the strawberries are blessed in the cathedral. The French are nothing if not passionate about their produce, and thankfully so.

The fruit labelled *Fraises de Carpentras* has held an Appelation d'Origine Contrôlée accreditation (AOC; see page 15) since 1997: the strawberries you buy come from a strictly controlled area around Carpentras. The Gariguette variety is a medium-size berry with an elongated shape. It is bright red in colour, and aromatic and sweet in flavour. The Gariguette represents 20 per cent of French strawberry production and is possibly the favourite variety in France.

We can grow Gariguette strawberries in the UK – but without the Provençal growing conditions, where the fruit ripen in the warm sunshine, they lack the flavour of their French counterparts. If you're looking for the best UK-grown strawberry, in my opinion you need to go for the fragrant Jubilee from my home county of Kent; or for the alpine variety Alexandria, from Scotland.

A word of warning… don't keep outdoor-grown strawberries in the fridge. Picked at maturity, they will deteriorate rapidly and must be eaten within 48 hours of harvesting. We buy our Gariguette strawberries from *Marché de Rungis* – the wholesale fruit-and-veg market on the outskirts of Paris. Our supplier Marc explains the military operation required to get this delicate product from the Provençal farms to us in London all within 24 hours: "The fruits are picked by hand early in the morning before the heat of the day comes upon them." (I love the French turn of phrase.) Then, it's a race against time. The strawberries are loaded into transport to get to Paris by early evening. Rungis opens its doors for trading at 2am, the vehicles are then packed and arrive in London for early evening. "*Et voilà*! 24 hours!"

In my opinion nothing can replace, replicate or improve on these fantastic outdoor-grown fruits, which is why I rail against technological "advancements" in farming. Strawberries are now being grown in 20m-high (66 feet) vertical farms, ripened by artificial lights and watered by computers – vast "winter farms" in regions where the climate is not conducive to berries that need to grow outside. These farms may be able to produce tonnes of fruit in smaller areas, but at what cost? Their focus is not on flavour, but on mass production, all year round. If we continue down this path, our beloved seasonal fruits will no longer have seasons at all, and our children will never get to eat a sun-ripened strawberry, grown and harvested just as Nature intended.

> "In my opinion nothing can replace, replicate or improve on these fantastic outdoor-grown fruits, which is why I rail against technological 'advancements' in farming."

Has the world gone mad? Are we seriously converting all our traditional farms first to cities of glasshouses and then to ultraviolet, hydroelectric indoor

Outdoor-grown, Gariguette strawberries give immensely better flavour than glasshouse varieties. Put away the sugar: floral notes give way to intense sweetness on the tongue.

growing spaces? Because farms these are not. The traditional methods of farming that for years have bought us superior produce are in danger of being eradicated and replaced by "advancements", in the name of technology and science. Is this the result of globalization? The world follows in the footsteps of North America, where this rapidly expanding electrical revolution in fruit-and-vegetable-growing is gathering pace.

Well, to coin the phrase of our former Prime Minister: "This man is not for turning." The fear-mongering scientists can keep their sanitized indoor arenas – I'll stick to the great outdoors, even if it means we have to go back to the horse and plough.

Unfortunately, though, here in the UK we are almost entirely producing commercial strawberries in greenhouses. Apart from the months of June through to August, when you will find some outdoor varieties in local farmers' markets, our producers have substituted varieties such as Jubilee, which have amazing flavours, with hardier, longer-life strawberries, such as the most popular Elsanta. Just like milk, which now has an extended shelf life, these fruits can be refrigerated for days after purchase without showing signs of deterioration – but neither do they have any flavour.

In this country we have an absolute love of strawberries – a love that culminates during the Wimbledon fortnight when we devour tonnes of the fruit, all served with lashings of double (heavy) cream, and washed down with Pimm's bobbing with strawberries, too. The wonderful combination of strawberries and cream is said to have been created by Thomas Wolsey in the court of King Henry VIII (a king who loved his food). If he knew what producers are doing to one of his favourite foods, Henry would be turning in his grave. And he might even have to concede that his old rivals, the French, know a thing or two about growing some mighty fine soft fruit.

Gariguette strawberry jam

Can there be anything better than opening a jar of super-sweet jam in the middle of winter that you made months ago and stored in your larder? This jam is easy to make, and you can improvise by adding spices such as cinnamon or cloves, or even lemon thyme leaves, if you wish.

Makes 2 jam jars

1kg (2lb 4oz) Gariguette strawberries, hulled and halved

375g (13oz) jam sugar

1 vanilla pod, halved

1 tsp lemon juice

Tip the strawberries into a large saucepan. Add the sugar and vanilla pod halves and place the pan over a low heat. Stir until the sugar dissolves, then bring the syrup to a boil. Stirring often, cook the jam steadily for 15–20 minutes, until the strawberries are soft and the jam has started to thicken. Taste and add the lemon juice to balance the sweetness.

Remove the vanilla pods and spoon the jam into sterilized jars, seal with the lids and leave to cool before labelling and storing for up to 6 months unopened. Once opened, refrigerate and use within 1 month.

Gariguette strawberry tart

There are strawberries and then there are Gariguettes. These pointed red little diamonds are fragrant, sweet and juicy. Strawberries were a big part of my childhood summers. Most mornings, breakfast would be crushed strawberries with fresh milk and freshly baked white bread. The flavour of Gariguettes is as close to those memories as I can find. They are delicious in this easy tart.

Serves 4 generously

For the tart base

250g (9oz/1¾cups + 2 tbsp) plain (all-purpose) flour, plus extra for rolling out

¾ tsp baking powder

60g (2oz) icing (confectioner's) sugar

pinch of salt

125g (4½oz) butter, chilled and diced

finely grated zest of ½ orange

1 egg, lightly beaten

For the filling

300g (10½oz) Gariguette jam (see page 95)

200g (7oz) Gariguette strawberries, hulled and quartered

2 tbsp chopped pistachios

whipped cream, to serve

Start by making the pastry. Sift the flour, baking powder, icing sugar and salt into a large mixing bowl. Add in the diced butter and, using your hands, rub the butter into the dry ingredients until the mixture resembles crumble and there are no pieces of butter still visible. Stir through the orange zest.

Gradually add the egg (you may not need it all) and mix the dough using a palette knife until it clumps together. Knead the dough briefly until smooth, then flatten it into a disk, cover and chill it for 30 minutes.

Roll out the pastry on a floured work surface and use it to line an 18cm (7in) tart tin. Trim off any excess, prick the base with a fork and chill the tart case while you preheat the oven to 180°C/ 160°C fan/350°F/Gas 4.

Line with pastry case with foil and fill it with baking beans (pie weights). Blind bake for 15–20 minutes, until golden brown, then remove the foil and beans and cook the pastry for a further 2–3 minutes to dry out the base. Remove from the oven and leave to cool.

Add the filling. Spoon the jam into the pastry case and spread it level.

Scatter the strawberry pieces on top of the jam and sprinkle with the chopped pistachios. Serve with whipped cream.

St George mushrooms / *Ardour kiwi from Landes* / *Queen Victoria pineapples* / *Raspberries – Panach' Golden, Portuguese Tulameen* / *Strawberries – Gariguette, Mara des Bois* / *Spanish avocados* / *Wild garlic buds* / *Brittany herbs* / *Dill* / *Fennel herb* / *Italian mixed herbs* / *Marjoram* / *Oregano* / *Provence mint* / *Thai lemongrass* / *Courgette (zucchini) flowers* / *Tomatoes – Datterini, Early Provence* / *Baby mixed leaves Campania* / *Baby spinach* / *Chalke Valley watercress* / *Italian wild rocket (arugula)* / *Mizuna and Tatsoi leaf* / *Red and white Belgian chicory* / *Summer fine frisée* / *Feuille de chêne (oak leaf lettuce)* / *Red and green Butterhead lettuce* / *Salanova salad* / *Breakfast radish* / *Italian celery* / *Ridge cucumbers* / *Surrey Downs spring onions* / *Sicilian peppers* / *Beans – Borlotti, Italian broad (fava), Yellow* / *Asparagus – Les Landes white, Pertius green* / *Brittany cauliflower* / *Chinese bok choy* / *Young Italian spinach* / *Artichokes – Roman Mammole globe, Violet baby artichokes from Apuli* / *Pale Italian aubergines (eggplants)* / *Tromba courgettes* / *Wet garlic* / *Young French leeks* / *Potatoes – Ile de Ré, Jersey Royal "earlies"* / *Italian fennel* / *Nantes carrots* / *Radishes – Black mooli, Red and white long French*

St George Mushroom
By George – I Think She's Got It!

The St George mushroom kicks off the UK mushroom season, appearing around St George's Day, which falls on April 23. You'll remember that only wild mushrooms have a season. Forageable until about the end of May, St George mushrooms are the first of five native specimens that appear throughout the year. They are followed by the Chicken of the Woods (May to August), Scottish Girolles (May until perhaps November), Giant Puffballs (July to September), and the king of them all, the one much sought-after by fine restaurants, the Penny Bun (August to October) – but more of those beauties later (see page 218). Our native mushrooms, then, cover three seasons from spring through to autumn. With Morels (see page 49) coming from Europe over the winter, we pretty much have the year covered.

St Georges and Giant Puffballs grow in grasslands and meadows and on verges near hedgerows. The other varieties are all found in ancient woodlands of deciduous trees such as beech, oak, elm, ash and sycamore and also near pine trees. The St George mushroom is easily identified by its white cap and its white gills and stems. A stout mushroom, it has a distinctive smell – once cut, the soft, white flesh has a strong "mealy" or sawdust aroma.

There's no cultivated equivalent to the St George mushroom, making it quite special. You'll find it easily if you look for a ring of lush grass – this is where these mushrooms grow, usually every year in the same place.

This book is a 12-month appreciation society of fruit and vegetables, but did you know that mushrooms fit into neither category? In a category of its own, the mushroom is the fruiting body of the fungus. So intriguing is this "kingdom" that vast numbers of books are written about mushrooms, and yet we still have much to learn.

Mushrooms obtain their nutrients in a very different way to plants. The mushroom "seed" creates millions of microscopic spores that form in the pores or gills under the mushroom cap. Animals or the wind then transport the spores, which fall on earth or wood, where they germinate and form a labyrinth of microscopic rooting connections called the mycelium. In turn, this mycelium helps to decompose plant material and return valuable nutrients to the ecosystem. The mycelium can live underground and in wood for many years and is the reason why a ring forms where St George mushrooms grow.

When you see a St George, pick it because its life above ground is fleeting and it can very quickly rot or become a food source for bugs. However, be very careful not to damage the undergrowth and don't disrupt the mushroom's hidden underground foundations, which have survived for years.

Earlier I emphasized the need to correctly identify any plant species when you're out foraging, but it is in the fungi world that we must be most careful. There are numerous poisonous varieties that can give you mild or serious health problems and several mushrooms that are deadly. The safest way to hunt for mushrooms is to go with an experienced forager.

While we are celebrating St George's Day with a feast of all that's seasonal and British, we should also honour a true expert in the world of mushrooms and, frankly, a national treasure: Roger Phillips, forager, botanist, photographer, writer, artist and gardener. Roger is the author of the foremost mushroom reference book – *Mushrooms* – with over 1,250 detailed descriptions and photographs of mushrooms and other fungi.

I first met Roger at Borough Market when he came to talk to me for a documentary. We soon got chatting about the produce I had on show. I had thought that Roger was an expert only in mushrooms, but I've since learned that he was a true botanist with a vast knowledge and love of all things grown in nature. This larger-than-life character was already in his 80s when I met him, but his enthusiasm and energy were infectious. He had agreed to do an interview with me for this book, but sadly he passed away in 2021 before we could talk further – a great loss to all who were privileged to be entertained and educated by this lovely man. His memory lives on in his amazing catalogue of books and the paintings that he created.

It is the wild mushroom varieties that attract most attention with their magical charms and mind-altering properties. Sitting and listening to Roger tell tales of his experiences with these wonderful specimens was a deep privilege for me and many, many more enlightened people.

> "This book is a 12-month appreciation society of fruit and vegetables, but did you know that mushrooms fit into neither category? In a category all of its own, the mushroom is the fruiting body of the fungus."

St George mushrooms, poached egg, preserved tomatoes

In need of a new breakfast idea? Those fresh St George mushrooms sitting in the fridge and some preserved tomatoes (see page 155) will do just the job. All you need is a slice of toast and you're sorted!

Serves 2

2 tbsp vegetable oil

1 banana shallot, finely diced

1 garlic clove, finely diced

150g (5½oz) St George mushrooms, chopped into chunky bitesize pieces

3 tbsp sour cream

½ tsp chopped dill, plus extra for serving

pinch of salt, plus extra to season

1 tsp white wine vinegar

2 eggs

2 dried Provençal tomatoes in oil (see page 155), drained and diced

freshly ground black pepper

Heat the oil in a saucepan over a medium heat. Tip in the shallot and garlic and sweat for about 5 minutes, until softened. Add the mushrooms and cook for about 3–4 minutes, until softened. Add the sour cream and dill and stir to coat the mushrooms in the cream.

Meanwhile, fill a small saucepan with water. Add the salt and the white wine vinegar, place the pan over a medium heat and bring the water to a simmer. Using a spoon, spin the water and gently crack in the eggs. Poach the eggs for about 2 minutes, or until cooked to your liking.

Using a slotted spoon, lift the eggs from the pan and drain them on kitchen paper.

Spoon the mushrooms into the middle of each plate, top each serving with the tomatoes and an egg, then season with salt and pepper, scatter with extra dill, and enjoy!

Preserved St George mushrooms

The season for St George mushrooms is short, so let's preserve them. In a few little steps, you'll have a great product to use out of season as a condiment to serve alongside roast meats, or with soups, salads and stews.

Makes 2 large jars

2kg (4lb 8oz) St George mushrooms, chopped into chunky bitesize pieces

3 tbsp salt

2 wet garlic bulbs, cloves separated, peeled and sliced

3 bay leaves

1 litre (35fl oz) filtered water

1 tbsp apple cider vinegar

4 black peppercorns

Tip the mushrooms into a large saucepan, cover them with tap water. Place the pan over a medium heat and bring the water to a boil. As soon as the water is boiling, drain the mushrooms in a colander.

Clean out the pan and return the mushrooms to it. Cover them with tap water again and bring the water to a boil. Add 2 tablespoons of the salt, along with all the garlic and bay leaves and simmer for about 20 minutes, until soft but not mushy. Drain the mushrooms and spoon them into sterilized jars, discarding the bay leaves.

Pour the filtered water into a large saucepan and add the remaining tablespoon of salt. Place the pan over a high heat and bring the liquid to a boil. Add the vinegar and peppercorns and pour the hot liquid over the mushrooms to cover. Seal the jars with tight-fitting lids and leave to cool. Store in fridge for at least 2 weeks before using, then store in the fridge and use within 3 months. Once opened, use within 1 month.

17

Norfolk asparagus / *Queen Victoria pineapples* / *Raspberries – Panach' Golden, Portuguese Tulameen* / *Strawberries – Gariguette, Mara des Bois* / *Spanish avocados* / *Wild garlic buds* / *Brittany herbs* / *Dill* / *Fennel herb* / *Marjoram* / *Norfolk marsh samphire* / *Oregano* / *Provence mint* / *Sorrel* / *Courgette (zucchini) flowers* / *Tomatoes – Datterini, Early Provence* / *Baby mixed leaves Campania* / *Baby spinach* / *Chalke Valley watercress* / *Italian wild rocket (arugula)* / *Mizuna and Tatsoi leaf* / *Red and white Belgian chicory* / *Summer fine frisée* / *Feuille de chêne (oak leaf lettuce)* / *Red and green Butterhead lettuce* / *Salanova salad* /

Surrey Little Gems / *Breakfast radish* / *Italian celery* / *Ridge cucumbers* / *Surrey Downs spring onions* / *Sicilian peppers* / *Asparagus – Les Landes white* / *Beans – Italian broad (fava), Yellow* / *Brittany cauliflower* / *Chinese bok choy* / *Young Italian spinach* / *Artichokes – Roman Mammole globe, Violet baby artichokes from Apuli* / *Pale Italian aubergines (eggplants)* / *Courgettes – French round, Tromba* / *Wet garlic* / *St George mushrooms* / *Young French leeks* / *Potatoes – Cornish "earlies", Ile de Ré, Jersey Royal "earlies"* / *Essex young beetroot* / *Italian Fennel* / *Nantes carrots* / *Radishes – Black mooli, Red and white long French*

Norfolk Asparagus
A Jolly Good Time!

I've just heard that a certain Mr Jolly is sending his first harvest of Norfolk asparagus to Turnips and my good luck has skyrocketed. I may even buy a lottery ticket. At Turnips we could easily buy some early pre-season English asparagus – the crowns that are forced in the glasshouse and under cloches – but we don't. Unlike the exquisite early forced rhubarb or early Jersey Royal potatoes (see pages 30 and 59), we don't believe that this asparagus has a better flavour than that of the first main outdoor crop. So we choose to wait.

If we are going to play around with Nature and speed up the seasons, we should make sure there is a very good reason for it. If it is possible this way to produce a better-quality, better-flavoured product, then we can justify giving a helping human hand. Likewise for produce grown and shipped from other parts of the world – if it is not as good as the produce we farm in this country or nearby in Europe, we can't justify the air miles. And that's only one part of the story – there is also fair trade to consider.

> "Thanks to some great PR and a renewed interest in and appreciation for our farmers, UK asparagus is rightly considered a premium product."

In this age of sustainability and carbon footprints, we must carefully consider shipments of perishable cargo. Supermarkets regularly stock Peruvian asparagus cheaply and at a time when our English asparagus is plentiful and in season. It is packaged, flown across the Atlantic and distributed throughout the UK and it is then sold for less than our locally grown and far superior produce. In most regions of the UK, you are rarely less than 80km (50 miles) from an asparagus grower – this one is a no-brainer... buy British.

Let's get back to the positives.... It's a long wait, but finally the outdoor asparagus is ready. Chefs and home cooks alike are chomping at the bit. Years ago, few people wanted our home-grown, wonky asparagus. Instead, they preferred dead straight, jumbo spears from the USA. Thanks to some great PR and a renewed interest in and appreciation for our farmers, UK asparagus is now rightly considered a premium product.

Growers plant the asparagus crowns in Norfolk's light sand soil, where they are allowed to grow for two years, building up energy and without being harvested. You need patience in the asparagus game. In the third year, each crown can produce eight to ten asparagus spears over an eight-week period. Each spear is selected and hand cut at the optimum time. Then, on the day of harvest, the spears are graded, bunched and packed by hand. Asparagus, like sweetcorn (see page 230), should be cooked and eaten straight after picking. The crowns remain in the ground and can produce crops of spears for up to 12 years – there aren't many vegetables that take such a long time to reach maturity and then, if the conditions are right, go on to be fruitful for so long.

The Jollys have been farming asparagus for over 30 years. They grow their produce outdoors, in tune with the seasons. Inevitably, the process can be temperamental. On warm days, the asparagus can grow quicker than on cold days, meaning long hours of delicate picking. Along the way the family has embraced some progress in farming methods but has rejected anything that might prevent them from providing asparagus of the very best flavour.

Every year at Turnips, we conduct a taste test of asparagus grown in six different counties. Over two days, we cook and serve asparagus from each county to our customers in Borough Market. In the 12 years since we've been running this taste test, Norfolk asparagus has come out top 11 times. The one time it failed was when it was pipped by spears from a farmer in Suffolk... only just over 3km (2 miles) from the Jollys' Norfolk farm.

Eat me, Petal!

A confession: the delicate micro-flowers that Turnips supplies to restaurants grow in glasshouses. In the case of herbs and flowers, I admit (for one time only) that the glasshouse produces stunning results with similar flavours to the wild, outdoor ones. Now that I've got that off my chest, here's a story...

What a sunrise! I walk out of the house and turn right with my Labrador, Sapphire. We soon reach a hillside by the edge of an ancient woodland. At the top of the hill is a beautiful, unspoilt pasture where wild flowers are in abundance – but which varieties are edible? I call Darren, my Dorset forager and an ex-marine SCUBA diver, who not only forages in the fields and woods but also skippers a boat catching some of the best fish and diver-caught scallops his county has to offer. I ask Darren what flowers I should look for. He sends me pictures of four: oxeye daisies, red clover, hawthorn and mallow. I find all but the hawthorn. They will go on the salad tonight, along with the new-season French tomatoes, crisp, leafy breakfast radishes and some peppery wild rocket (arugula). How lucky am I?

The strengths in the UK's asparagus lie in our green varieties,
while Italy and France give us outstanding purple and white,
respectively, to extend the asparagus season.

Pickled green asparagus

If you've never had pickled asparagus, then you're in for a treat. It is one of the best things you can have with your breakfast poached eggs or smoked salmon, or with a piece of grilled fish. You'll need tall jars to store the pickled asparagus in – they look fabulous all neatly lined up on a kitchen shelf.

Makes 2 tall (1 litre/35fl oz) jars

30 asparagus spears, trimmed

2 litres (70fl oz) filtered water

80g (2¾oz) salt, plus 1 tbsp

250g (9oz) apple cider or white wine vinegar

1 tbsp caster (superfine) sugar

1 tsp white mustard seeds

2 tsp dill seeds

1 onion, sliced

10 garlic cloves, sliced

1 tsp chilli flakes

2 dill sprigs

Place the trimmed asparagus into a large bowl, cover with the filtered water and add the 80g (2¾oz) of salt. Mix to dissolve the salt and leave the mixture at room temperature for 2 hours, to soften the asparagus. Drain the asparagus and rinse them under cold water.

In a large saucepan combine the vinegar, tablespoon of salt, and all the remaining pickling ingredients. Place the pan over a medium heat, bring to a boil, then reduce the heat and simmer for 1 minute.

Place the asparagus spears in the jars, tips uppermost and pour the hot vinegar mixture into the jars to cover. Seal the jars tightly with the lids.

Half fill a saucepan with water, place it over a high heat and bring the water to a boil. Place the jars in the boiling water and simmer for 10 minutes to pasteurize the contents of the jars.

Remove the jars from the water, turn them upside down to create a vacuum and leave the pickles to cool. Once cool, turn the jars the right way up again and store the pickles in a cool, dry place for at least 2 weeks before using. The pickles will store like this for up to a year unopened, and in the fridge for up to 1 week once opened.

Asparagus-topped quiche with herring roe

Lots of people said we were brave to put quiche on the menu, as it seems so ordinary – but what's wrong with something that works so well? We make this one at the start of the asparagus season. You can add other ingredients, too, if you wish – strips of bacon, mushrooms, cheese, smoked paprika...

Serves 4

For the pâte brisée

360g (12¾oz/2¾ cups) plain (all-purpose) flour, plus extra for rolling out

225g (8oz) butter, chilled and diced

5 thyme sprigs, leaves picked

120ml (4fl oz/½ cup) ice-cold water

For the filling

120ml (4fl oz) double (heavy) cream

120ml (4fl oz) full-fat milk

70g (2½oz) Parmesan, finely grated

4 eggs

1 egg yolk

salt and freshly ground black pepper

To serve

2 tbsp olive oil

1 banana shallot, finely chopped

2 garlic cloves, crushed

12 asparagus spears, trimmed

100ml (3½fl oz) vegetable stock

4 pickled asparagus spears (see page 105), drained and roughly chopped

100g (3½oz) herring roe

Start by making the pâte brisée. Tip the flour into a food processor, add the butter and thyme leaves and whizz until only tiny pieces of butter remain and the mixture looks like crumble. Add the iced water and mix again using the pulse button until the mixture starts to clump together. Tip the dough on to the work surface and knead it lightly to bring it together into a ball. Cover and chill for 1 hour.

Dust the work surface with flour. Roll out the dough into a disk and use it to line an 18–20cm (7–8in) tart tin. Prick the base with a fork, and line it with baking paper and baking beans. Chill the pastry case for 15 minutes, while you preheat the oven to 170°C/150°C fan/325°F/Gas 3.

Blind bake the pastry case for 20 minutes, until golden, then remove the paper and baking beans and bake for a further 2–3 minutes to dry out the bottom of the tart. Leave the case to cool while you prepare the filling. Reduce the oven temperature to 150°C/130°C fan/300°F/Gas 2.

In a bowl, whisk together the cream, milk and Parmesan. Add the eggs and egg yolk, and season well with salt and pepper. Whisk until smooth and thoroughly combined. Pour the mixture into the baked pastry case and bake for 20–30 minutes, until the filling is golden and set. Leave to cool to room temperature while you prepare the ingredients to serve.

Heat the oil in frying pan over a low–medium heat. Add the shallot and garlic and sweat for 5 minutes, until softened. Increase the heat to high, add the fresh asparagus and the vegetable stock, cover with a lid and steam for about 2 minutes, until the asparagus is al dente. Season with salt and pepper.

Serve the quiche in slices with the steamed and pickled asparagus and top and with spoonfuls of herring roe.

18

French apricots / Pitahaya (dragon fruit) / Queen Victoria pineapples / Raspberries – Panach' Golden, Portuguese Tulameen / Strawberries – Gariguette, Mara des Bois / Wild garlic buds / Brittany herbs / Dill / French basil / Marjoram / Norfolk marsh samphire / Oregano / Provence mint / Sorrel / Early Provence tomatoes / Baby mixed leaves Campania / Baby spinach / Chalke Valley watercress / Italian wild rocket (arugula) / Mizuna and Tatsoi leaf / Red and white chicory / Endives – Pis-en-lit (dandelion), Summer fine frisée / Feuille de chêne (oak leaf lettuce) / Red and green Butterhead lettuce / Salanova salad / Surrey Little Gems / Breakfast radish / Italian celery / Ridge cucumbers / Surrey Downs spring onions / Sicilian peppers / Yellow beans / Asparagus – Les Landes white, Norfolk / Brittany cauliflower / Chinese bok choy / Young Italian spinach / Violet baby artichokes from Apuli / Pale Italian aubergine (eggplant) / Courgettes (zucchini) – French round, Tromba / Wet garlic / St George mushrooms / Young French leeks / Potatoes – Cornish "earlies", Ile de Ré, Jersey Royal "earlies" / Essex young beetroot / Italian fennel / Nantes carrots / Radishes – Black mooli, Red and white long French / Young turnips

Corsican Apricot
Don't Waste Too Many Stones on One Bird

The stone-fruit group is one of the largest fruit groups of all. It includes apricots, peaches, nectarines, cherries, mangoes and plums. This group really does illustrate the long summer season in Europe. These edible drupaceous (I love that word) fruits arrive in spring and finish in autumn, giving us about five months of varied taste sensation. Stone fruits make excellent preserves – either whole, or as drinks, jams or chutneys, which allow us to enjoy a second season when fresh are in short supply. Drying stone fruits takes them to a new level – in some cases, creating almost a new fruit altogether. Think how plums become prunes and you'll see where I'm coming from.

That's stone fruits in general, but it's the apricot I really want to highlight this week. I think the apricot is a much misunderstood and undervalued fruit. So often people come to Turnips and walk past it without a second glance. When I approach them and ask if they don't like apricots, the usual response is that they find the fruit too tart and flavourless, either that the flesh is rock hard or that it has a strange texture and mouthfeel – rather like eating cotton wool. I reply by cutting them a slice from a Corsican apricot – the earliest stone fruit to arrive. Most people are shocked (in a good way) that the slice tastes almost peachy. I tell them that what they are tasting is truly apricot – something most people never experience.

The first of the apricots come from Corsica in late April and then we move to Roussillon in Provence. The Corsican fruits – *albicocca* (another great word) to give them their Corsican name – are big, sweet and juicy with a hint of almond and honey. The skin is orange and heavily speckled with deep pink and red.

Corsica is well known for its exceptional produce that gives wonderful flavours – something the Corsicans put down to their Mediterranean-island climate and beautiful landscape. It is particularly famous for the Corsican clementine (the only clementine grown in France), which has a PGI status (see page 24) and a uniquely underripe green look to it. Chestnuts, too, which are mainly ground into an AOC-accredited flour (yes, that old chestnut again!). There is a strong tradition of preserving and jam-making on the island: almost all the fruits become some sort of jam – often including the local honey.

It is Corsica's incredibly high-quality stone fruit – apricots, peaches and the famous Corsican nectarines – that pre-empt the mainland's fruits. Apricots have been grown in France for hundreds of years, and commercially in Provence for two centuries, having made their way along the silk route from Armenia. Their origins, though, are believed to date much further back and further East – to China, where there is evidence of them growing since 2000BCE. You'll find them growing prolifically in the Himalayan region of Hunza in Pakistan, too.

Unlike strawberries, say, apricots are less known for their varieties and more for the region in which they are grown (such as Corsica and Roussillon). That said, all French apricot varieties are superb and there are early, mid and late versions that stand out: the early Orange Red and Tom Cot from Corsica (fragrant with a musky flavour) start the season; the mid-season Rouge de Roussillon is delicate with a stunning red flush; and the late, medium-size Orange de Provence is juicy.

In 2016, the Rouge de Roussillon apricot was awarded a PDO (see page 15). The fruit flourishes in the mild spring weather of Provence and in the long, sunny days, warm climate and dry soils on the region's plains and hills. There are around five varieties grown within the

"I think the apricot is a much misunderstood and undervalued fruit. So often people come to Turnips and walk past it without a second glance."

accreditation, including Rouge de Roussillon, Aviéra, Royal Roussillon and Avikandi. They have an apricot-orange-coloured skin with vivid red speckling, a sweet flavour, soft, juicy flesh, a melt-in-the-mouth texture and a fragrant peachy aroma. They must be harvested by hand when ripe and packed in the area of growing. And – yes, you've guessed it – the region holds an annual apricot festival.

The apricot season in France is long, starting in the southernmost region of Corsica in May and then moving up the mainland from Roussillon to Gard-Crau and ending in the Rhône Valley, which goes on to produce fruit until mid-September. The French sure know the value of this exceptional fruit.

Whether poached, baked into tarts and cakes, or made into wonderful jams, apricots are perfect for cooking. Like most stone fruits, they make great preserves in sugar syrup and alcohol – amaretto liqueur being a popular choice with its almond flavour. The kernel inside the apricot stone is often added to jams and preserves to add an extra almondiness – although add it in moderation and with caution: it can be toxic if consumed in quantity.

Apricots and Greek yogurt honey cream

At Turnips, we love roasting all types of fruits to see what incredible results we can achieve with such a simple cooking method. Apricots are stunning when roasted: hard when raw and ripe, they become meltingly soft and sweet after cooking. Serve these apricots with yogurt cream as an amazing pud at the end of a light dinner.

Serves 4

800g (1lb 12oz) apricots, halved and destoned

3 large rosemary sprigs

1 vanilla pod, halved

peel of 1 orange, chopped

130ml (4½ fl oz) orange juice

3 tbsp runny honey

crushed sweet biscuits (such as amaretti, gingersnaps or digestives/graham crackers), to serve (optional)

For the yogurt honey cream

100g (3½ oz) Greek yogurt

100ml (3½ fl oz) double (heavy) cream

1 tbsp runny honey

1 tbsp icing (confectioner's) sugar

Preheat the oven to 170°C/150°C fan/325°F/Gas 3.

Place the apricots cut side up on a baking dish large enough to accommodate them in a single layer. Tuck the rosemary sprigs, one half of the vanilla pod and all the orange peel around the apricots. Pour the orange juice all over to moisten the apricots and drizzle with the 3 tablespoons of honey.

Bake the fruit for 20–25 minutes, gently shaking the baking dish from time to time to make sure the fruit doesn't burn, until softened but not completely collapsed.

Meanwhile, make the yogurt honey cream. In a bowl, combine all the ingredients with the seeds from the remaining half of the vanilla pod. Whisk until the mixture will hold soft peaks, then refrigerate until you're ready to serve.

Remove the roasted apricots from the oven and serve them hot, warm or at room temperature in bowls with the yogurt cream spooned on top and the roasting juices drizzled over. For a little crunch, you can scatter with some crushed biscuits.

Apricot compôte (drinking style)

This compôte is something I remember having every winter, especially at Christmas time when the tables were abundant with food and glasses filled to the brim. For this recipe, the apricots must be ripe but not overripe, and if you prefer you can use half granulated sugar and half muscovado sugar for a deeper flavour. Try adding whole spices, such as star anise, cardamom or cloves to the syrup, and experiment with pears, apples, cherries and plums instead of apricots – they all work well in this way.

Makes 2 large jars

5kg (11lb) apricots, halved and destoned

1kg (2lb 4oz) granulated sugar

1 tsp citric acid

1 vanilla pod or 2–3 drops of vanilla extract

This recipe is as easy as it gets – but it's most important that you have hot sterilized jars to pour your compôte into (see page 15).

Tip the halved apricots into your sterilized jars.

In a large saucepan combine the sugar with 3 litres (105fl oz) of water the citric acid and the vanilla pod or extract and place the pan over a high heat. Bring the water to a boil to dissolve the sugar, then reduce the heat and simmer for 1 minute to thicken the syrup a little. Remove the pod, if using, and pour the syrup over the fruit in the jars and leave them for 20 minutes. Then, strain the syrup back into the pan and bring it back to a boil. Once boiling, remove from the heat.

Once again, pour the hot syrup into the jars over the apricots, this time sealing the lids tightly and turning the jars upside down to create a vacuum. Leave the apricots to cool and then store them in a cool, dry place for up to 6 months. Once opened, refrigerate and eat the apricots and drink the syrup within 1 month.

19

Alphonso mangoes / Pitahaya (dragon fruit) / Queen Victoria pineapples / Panach' blackberries / Panach' blueberries / Raspberries – Panach' Golden, Portuguese Tulameen / Strawberries – Gariguette, Mara des Bois / French apricots / Wild garlic flowers / Brittany herbs / Dill / French basil / Marjoram / Norfolk marsh samphire / Oregano / Provence mint / Sorrel / Early Provence tomatoes / Baby mixed leaves Campania / Chalke Valley watercress / Italian wild rocket (arugula) / Mizuna and Tatsoi leaf / Red and white Belgian chicory / Endives – Pis-en-lit (dandelion), Summer fine frisée / Feuille de chêne (oak leaf lettuce) / Red and green Butterhead lettuce / Salanova salad / Surrey Little Gems / Breakfast radish / Italian celery / Ridge cucumbers / Surrey Downs spring onions / Sicilian peppers / Extra fine French beans / Asparagus – Les Landes white, Norfolk asparagus / Brittany cauliflower / Chinese bok choy / Young Italian spinach / Violet baby artichokes from Apuli / Pale Italian aubergines (eggplants) / Courgettes (zucchini) – French round, Tromba / Wet garlic / Mushrooms – Chicken of the Woods, Horse, St George / Young French leeks / Potatoes – Cornish "earlies", Ile de Ré / Essex young beetroot / Italian fennel / Nantes carrots / Radishes – Black mooli, Red and white long French / Young turnips

Alphonso Mango
Cometh the Hour, Cometh the Mango

So here we are at the beginning of May and farming in the UK is in full swing. We are currently enjoying lovely asparagus, new potatoes, beetroots (beets), kale, spring greens and many other vegetable delights. Our spring salads are well provided for with local spring onions (scallions), watercress and wonderful red radishes from Kent. Europe is giving us fruits such as lemons, loquats, apricots, the last of the apples and a tinkering of strawberries. Perhaps it's still a little sparse compared with how it will be, but, with "exotics" thrown into the mix, we still have world-class fruit from all over the world: pineapples, bananas, rambutans, papayas – and now mangoes from India.

We've dipped into the Indian subcontinent on our shopping lists with mandarins for our citrus kick, but it is not until we see the mangoes arrive that we really get excited. The first seasonal mango is the Alphonso. Smaller than other varieties and with a large stone and so less flesh, this mango is regarded as one of the tastiest – the flavour more than makes up for the reduced flesh.

My friend Bob Harrington runs Speciality Produce, a family-owned, fresh-produce supplier that has been working in San Diego, California, for the past 30 years. His love for and knowledge of fruit and vegetables is legendary. Here is his low-down on Alphonso mangoes.

"Alphonso mangoes are small and somewhat egg-shaped. They grow suspended from long stems on evergreen leafy trees. When immature, the soft yellow skin will retain spots of green. When fully ripe, the deeper saffron-hued skin may have a blush of red, but no green colour will remain. Alphonso mangoes have very thin skins, so many are hand-harvested to protect the fruit.

The aroma of Alphonso mangoes is intense owing to their high levels of myrcene, a kind of terpenoid, a naturally occurring chemical responsible for flavour and aroma. The Indian mangoes are sharply sweet along with more mellow tropical flavours. The flesh is non-fibrous, unlike other mango varieties.

"Grown in India, where they are known as the 'King of Mangoes' for their exceptional flavour and texture, Alphonso are a variety of *Mangifera indica*, highly praised for its sweetness. There are multiple cultivars of the Alphonso mango, some more distinct than others primarily due to growing conditions in their specific geographic regions. They grow primarily in the states of Goa and Maharashtra along the western coast of India, and only with very particular soil and weather requirements. Because of this, the variety is subject to limited availability and the occasional poor season.

> "Alphonso mangoes were introduced to India by the Portuguese military strategist Afonso de Albuquerque."

"Alphonso mangoes were introduced to India by the Portuguese military strategist Afonso de Albuquerque, who helped establish a Portuguese colony in western India during the 15th century. They have been popular in the UK ever since they were shipped to London for Queen Elizabeth's coronation in 1953 and are in high demand during the brief season in the summer.

"Like all mangoes, Alphonso contain high amounts of potassium and magnesium. In addition to being packed with many essential vitamins, mangoes contain enzymes that aid digestion."

A stunning fruit, then, that is much sought after. Although you can buy mangoes all year round from all over the southern hemisphere, the King of Mangoes is in season right now, in May. We extend our mango season with another Indian variety, King Kesar, which is a larger fruit with an equally huge depth of mango sweetness.

Finding your seasonal nucleus: a tale of two cities – London and San Diego

I consider the Alphonso mango from India to be up to my world-class standard in May, so that's when I consider the mango season to be in full swing in the UK. Mangoes do grow elsewhere, but not to the high standards I look for, which got me thinking about seasonality in other parts of the world. Would someone like my good friend Bob in San Diego also be sourcing mangoes from India in May, or will his exceptional mangoes come from closer to home? And what other similarities or differences would we find with other fruit and vegetables when comparing London, UK, to San Diego, USA?

The following tables compare and contrast the two cities, looking at the availability of the same 14 key produce groups and taking one product from each. We include the variety, the location where it is sourced and roughly how long it is in season in London or San Diego, respectively. And of course, we're mindful of the criteria that I apply to all produce (including no glasshouses!). In London, we radiate outward and do not stop our journey until we believe that we have found the best fruit, salad, nut, mushroom or vegetable, as close as possible to home. But just how different are things for Bob, thousands of kilometres away (8,929km/5,548 miles to be precise) in San Diego?

The London Seasons

Group	Name	Location	Variety	Comment
Exotic	Pineapple	Réunion	Queen	This Pacific island produces stunning fruits, some of which have gained the AOC status, including pineapples and lychees. Available all year round.
Onions	Sweet Onion	Chile	Vidalia	When main-crop European onions are unavailable (from April to early July), Chile provides us with these stunners, available there all year round.
Garlic	Wet	France	Paradour	This is the first of the bulbous garlics we supply (from mid-April). Because they are "fresh", the season is short – by mid-June they are finished.
Potatoes	Ile de Ré	Ile de Ré, France	Starlette	AOC-accredited with strict harvesting guidelines, these are the only potatoes to have this accolade. Available from April to the end of June.
Herbs	Mint	Morocco, Greater Maghreb region	*Mentha spicata* var. *crispa* 'Moroccan'	Europe's most popular mint, from throughout the Greater Maghreb region (encompassing Algeria, Libya, Tunisia, Mauritania – and Morocco). We import it from January to the end of May.
Foraged	Wild Garlic	Kent, UK	Ramsons	No need to travel far for this beauty. It grows in almost any woodland where you see bluebells, from early May to the end of June.
Brassica +	Asparagus	Norfolk, UK	Portlim	The Jolly family in Norfolk originally grew asparagus crowns from America, which gave them ten years of fruitful harvests. They now grow European varieties, which are more suited to their soils. Available from May to mid-June.
Root veg	Beetroot (Beet)	Brittany, France	Candy	In February, we go from Sussex to Brittany to get our Candy beets – the French variety stores better, lasting until the new-season Spanish in May.
Soft Fruit	Raspberry	Vendée, France	Tulameen	The farmers at Panach'Fruits grow this stunning raspberry and have extended their season by introducing glasshouses – their excellent husbandry means the flavour has not suffered. That said, we prefer to wait until their outdoor season starts, in early May (until September).
Tomatoes	Heirloom	Provence, France	Pineapple	Thin-skinned and heavy, these large "beefsteak" tomatoes are super-sweet and at their best from early May, just before the real heat of the Mediterranean cranks up, until September. They do not store well – eat them soon after purchase.

Continued overleaf...

Mushrooms	Wild	Üzümlü, Turkey	Morel	Very rare in the UK, this mushroom starts our "wild" season. Turkey has some of its finest specimens, from mid-February until the end of May.
Citrus	Mandarin	West Bengal, India	Nagpur	We travel halfway around the globe to find these delicious fruits from India, which give the last of the season's tangerines, clementines and mandarins. From March until the end of May.
Stone Fruit	Mango	India	Alphonso	This variety kicks off our mango season. The Alphonso is revered throughout Europe and you'll find it from May to the end of June.
Salad	Spring Onion (Scallion)	Surrey, UK	Green Onion	A much-undervalued salad onion, this one really enhances most salads. Avoid bulbous varieties unless you want them to repeat on you for hours! This one is yours from April to October.
Nuts, Dried	Walnut	Grenoble, France	Noix de Grenoble	Nuts really do have seasons, whether you use them fresh when first harvested in autumn or dried to appear just before Christmas and store up to July, when they lose "freshness" and their flavour deteriorates. PDO-accredited both in Grenoble and Perigord, this nut is used in many forms, walnut oil possibly being the most famous.

Now, entry by entry, compare these 14 key produce categories with what Bob does in the USA, radiating outward from his own nucleus of San Diego...

'

The San Diego Seasons

Group	Name	Location	Variety	Comment
Exotic	Pineapple	Costa Rica	Pinkglow®	Exclusive, rare, sweet and fruity pink pineapples are also known as the "Jewel of the Jungle". Pinkglow® pineapples are cultivated and hand-harvested on carbon-neutral farms in an area known for its tropical climate and fertile volcanic soil. The pineapples are sold without their crowns, which are reused to plant new crops. Pinkglow take about two years to grow in ultra-limited quantities and are available year-round.
Onions	Heirloom	Lompoc, California	Torpedo	The Italian native is known as Rossa di Tropea and is loved for its unusual shape and mildly sweet flavour. As the soil is crucial for the torpedo onion's flavour and productivity, this specialty crop is grown only in mild-climate regions of Europe, Asia, Australia and North America that are similar to its Mediterranean roots. Fortunately, it grows well in central California from January to September.
Garlic	Young Garlic	Carpinteria, California	Green	Green garlic blossomed in popularity in the USA in the 20th century. This fresh ingredient evolved from a secondary crop that was pulled early from farms simply to make room for larger plants, to become the sought-after garlicky greens we know and love today. Green garlic is now second-to-none in the early harvest and is available from January to July.
Potatoes	Fingerling	Tehachapi, California	Alaskan Fingerling	The Alaskan fingerling potato, also known as Magic Myrna, was developed in Alaska, where the state's unique and diverse climate allows for the successful growth of thousands of potato varieties from around the world. This creamy, earthy, sweet fingerling potato is also grown at Weiser Family Farms in California all year round.
Herbs	Verbena	Jamul, California	Lemon Verbena	Loved by chefs and herbalists alike, this adaptable, speciality herb is grown in temperate climates worldwide for both culinary and medicinal applications. It is loved for its robust lemony fragrance, delicate herbal sweetness, and citrussy-sour finish. Lemon verbena is available from May to July.

Continued overleaf...

Foraged	Wild Leek	Michigan, USA	Ramps	The wild ramp is considered a culinary delicacy, boasting a bold, spicy, garlicky-onion flavour. It grows wild in cool, shady areas with rich, damp soil from the Eastern USA northward into Quebec, Canada, where it is listed as a threatened species. Its heightened popularity has been met with increased concern of over-foraging. Sustainable harvesting practices have been put in place to protect this this slow-growing, short-seasoned treasure, which we enjoy responsibly in April and May.
Brassica +	Broccoli	Carpinteria, California	Spigarello	Coleman Family Farms grew this variety for over 15 years before it began trending among chefs in southern California as an unusual, locally grown green. Its full-bodied, subtly sweet yet grassy flavour brings a taste of southern Italy to the coast of California from October to June.
Root veg	Beetroot	Petaluma, California	Red Forno	This rare European heirloom variety is favoured for its uniform cylindrical shape, fine-grained flesh, and mild, earthy, sweet flavour. Native to the Mediterranean and Atlantic coasts of Europe and north Africa, it is now grown in regions with similar climates in California and graces our plates from January to May.
Soft Fruit	Peaches	Dinuba, California	Yellow	Regier Family Farms has been producing world-class, tree-ripened fruit since 1983, picked to ensure peak ripeness and sweetness. Their location in Dinuba, California, is the ultimate sweet spot with no late freezes, providing the perfect growing climate for yellow peaches. They are available from May to early September.
Tomatoes	Hybrid	Fillmore, California	Early Girl	This meaty and juicy slicing tomato is dry-farmed to produce what many have deemed to be the ideal tomato. Famous for its rich, sweet flavour, the vibrant red fruits are a welcomed sight early in the season. They are available from May to October.
Mushrooms	Wild	Midwest USA	Morel	Despite its rarity, this is the most prized edible mushroom in the USA, favoured by chefs for its unusual shape and deep, earthy, nutty flavour. Grown only in the wild, you'll find this mushroom on the edges of wooded areas, especially around oak, elm, ash, and apple trees. We eagerly await its limited appearance in late March, and it continues until May.

Citrus	Tangerine	Valley Center, California	Tom's Terrific	Exclusively grown by Polito Farms in Valley Center, California, Tom's Terrific tangerines are affectionately known as "Triple Ts". Rumour has it that their name came about when Bob and Mary Polito's son, Tom, was tasting these new tangerines for the first time and he exclaimed, "These are terrific!" The tangerines are in season from February to May, and are valued for their balanced, sweet-tart flavour.
Stone Fruit	Cherry	Bakersfield, California	GG1	Unrivalled in many ways, Murray Family Farms offers the largest selection of cherries of any commercial grower in California, and the company is the first to harvest cherries each season. The one-of-a-kind, huge, dark and exceptionally flavourful GG1 cherry is the top seller throughout the short yet sweet season in May and June.
Salad	Lettuce	Santa Ynez, California	Salanova®	Salanova® lettuce was developed by Rijk Zwaan, a family-owned company and one of the largest vegetable breeders in the world. Exceptionally appealing to chefs and farmers alike, it requires less labour to harvest and prepare, and it is prized for its small size, full flavour, long storage life, and unique core that can be removed with one cut. Available year-round.
Nuts, Dried	Date	Mecca, California	Medjool	The Medjool has earned a reputation as the "King of Dates" or the "Crown Jewel of Dates" thanks to its superior flavour, consistency, size and availability. It became popular to grow in the USA in the 1920s, particularly in Arizona and California, where it continues to rule the season from May to September.

Alphonso mango parfait

This easy parfait will happily sit in the freezer for up to a month, giving you Alphonso mango joy far beyond the fresh Alphonso season. The parfait is delicious served in slices with extra fresh mango and a wedge of lime or with white chocolate mousse.

Serves 4

3 Alphonso mangoes, peeled and destoned, plus extra diced to decorate

1 platinum-grade gelatine leaf

60g (2oz) caster (superfine) sugar

2 egg yolks

270ml (9½fl oz) whipping cream

micro lemon balm leaves, to decorate

Whizz the fruit in a food processor until smooth. Spoon out 3 tablespoons of the purée and set aside. Pour the remaining purée into a small saucepan and set it over a low–medium heat. Bring the purée to a boil, then reduce the heat and simmer for 2–3 minutes, until the purée has reduced and is thick enough to generously coat the back of a spoon.

Tip the purée into a pan and reduce by half. Place the gelatine in a bowl of cold water and leave it to soften for 4 minutes. Remove the leaf from the water and squeeze out the excess, then add the leaf to the hot purée. Stir so that the gelatine melts.

Tip the sugar into a small saucepan. Add 25ml (1fl oz) of water and place the pan over a medium heat. Leave the sugar to dissolve and come to a boil. Continue boiling until the syrup reaches 118°C/244°F on a sugar thermometer.

Tip the egg yolks into a small mixing bowl and pour over the hot syrup, whisking until thickened and the mixture holds a firm ribbon trail when you lift the whisk.

In another bowl, whip the cream to soft peaks.

Fold the reduced mango purée and the 3 tablespoons of reserved mango purée into the egg mixture until combined and then fold in the whipped cream until thoroughly combined and no streaks remain. Spoon the mixture into a lined 450g (1lb) loaf tin lined with cling film (leave plenty of overhang to help you release the parfait) or a plastic freezer box and freeze until solid (overnight is best). To serve, turn the parfait out of the tin or container and serve it in scoops or slices decorated with micro lemon balm leaves and diced mango flesh.

Mango chutney

Growing up in Lithuania, I'd never seen a mango until I was probably nine or ten, and I'd never tasted mango chutney. I discovered this delicious condiment when I started working in commercial kitchens, when we made a beautiful curry for staff meals and served the chutney alongside. Since then, it has become a firm favourite for me – and Alphonso mangoes take it to a whole new level.

Makes 1 large jar

1 tbsp vegetable oil

2 banana shallots, finely chopped

3 garlic cloves, crushed

30g (1oz) grated fresh ginger

1 red chilli, deseeded and finely chopped

1 tsp grated fresh turmeric

1 cinnamon stick

4 star anise

1 tbsp ground coriander

½ tbsp ground cumin

5 Alphonso mangoes, peeled and diced

300g (10½ oz) caster (superfine) sugar

150ml (5fl oz) rice wine vinegar

salt

Heat the oil in a medium saucepan over a low heat. Add the shallots and garlic and sweat for about 5 minutes, until soft but not coloured. Add the ginger, chilli, turmeric, cinnamon, star anise, coriander and cumin, stir to combine and cook for a further 1–2 minutes for the spices to release their flavours.

Add the mango pieces to the pan with the sugar and vinegar and cook over a low heat for about 1 hour, stirring often, until the mangoes soften considerably and become thick and jammy – you want the pulp to coat the back of a spoon but still have some texture of mango. Remove the pan from the heat and season the mango pulp with salt to taste. Remove and discard the whole spices.

Spoon the chutney into a large sterilized jar and seal with the lid. Stand the jar in a large saucepan and pour water into the pan so that it comes at least halfway up the sides of the jars. Place over a medium heat and bring the water to a boil. Reduce the heat and simmer for 10 minutes to pasteurize the contents of the jar. Remove the jar from the pan, turn it upside down and leave the chutney to cool.

Turn the jar the right way and up and store the chutney in a cool, dry place for up to 1 year. Once opened, refrigerate and use within 1 month.

20

Camus globe artichokes / Alphonso mangoes / *Greek Torpedo watermelon* / *Tunisian Cantaloupe melon* / Panach' blackberries / Panach' blueberries / Raspberries – Panach' Golden, Portuguese Tulameen / Strawberries – Gariguette, Mara des Bois / *French apricots* / Elderflower / Dill / *French basil* / Kentish mint – many varieties / Marjoram / Norfolk marsh samphire / Oregano / Sorrel / *Early Provence tomatoes* / Baby mixed leaves Campania / Chalke Valley watercress / Italian wild rocket (arugula) / Mizuna and Tatsoi leaf / Red and white Belgian chicory / Endives – Pis-en-lit (dandelion), Summer fine frisée / Feuille de chêne (oak leaf lettuce) / Red and green Butterhead lettuce / Salanova salad / Surrey Little Gems / Breakfast radish / Italian celery / Ridge cucumbers / Surrey Downs spring onions / Sicilian peppers / Extra fine French beans / Asparagus – Les Landes white, Norfolk / Brittany cauliflower / Chinese bok choy / Young Italian spinach / Violet baby artichokes from Apuli / Pale Italian aubergines (eggplants) / Courgettes (zucchini) – French round, Tromba / Wet garlic / Mushrooms – Chicken of the Woods, Horse / Young French leeks / Potatoes – Cornish "earlies", Ile de Ré / Essex young beetroot / Italian fennel / Nantes carrots / Radishes – Black mooli, Red and white long French / Young turnips

Camus Artichoke
You Must Be Choking

We're coming up to Vegetarian Week at the end of May and how better to celebrate than with the most stunning globe artichokes? The Brittany Camus variety is a large globe artichoke much revered for its beautiful, tender heart with its nutty, tangy flavour. Planted in the spring and autumn like garlic and harvested by hand in May and June and again in September and October, the Brittany Camus gives nearly a seven-month season. Globe artichokes are an edible relation of the thistle, and the Camus variety is the largest. The heavy globes are covered in spiky leaves, which are matt grey–green in colour. It's best to steam globes to eat them, removing the leaves to reveal the soft heart inside. The base of each leaf is fleshy, and delicious dipped into butter sauces or oil. You can use the hearts as a pasta filling and they are perfect gratinated with cheese or preserved in olive oil. Alternatively, steam the whole globes and then stuff and bake them to serve as a main course.

> "One of Jennifer's particular traits was to rummage around at the back of the stall to find the produce that was slightly past its best."

Our very dear friend Jennifer Paterson, one half of the "Two Fat Ladies", loved globe artichokes. She would frequent the Tachbrook Street Market in Pimlico and rummage around at the back of the stall to find the produce that was slightly past its best. One day I had removed about ten globe artichokes from the "show" at the front of the stall – their outer leaves had turned dry and were nearly black. Jennifer found them and asked me "How much?" I told her to take them – gratis. A week later she scootered up to the stall and presented me with an impressive Kilner jar filled with artichoke hearts infused in lemony olive oil. "Half for you and half for me!" And with a brilliant smile, she got back on her scooter and promptly left.

Jennifer Paterson was a regular customer at our stall. She was a larger-than-life character who never, ever took her scooter helmet off. "Frederick, dear boy, what's good today?" (She was the only person to call me Frederick other than Mrs Cotter, my primary school teacher.) At the time, Jennifer was the food columnist at *The Spectator* and starred in the hugely popular TV show *Two Fat Ladies* with Clarissa Dickson Wright. She was our number-one fan and even came to our daughter's christening. A true friend, she is sorely missed. In her memory, this chapter includes one of her recipes, which uses baby Italian artichokes.

Cordially yours...

This week is the perfect time to rummage in the hedgerows and get your hands on some elderflower. It looks like nature's answer to floral candyfloss, but elderflower cordial or champagne is definitely the grown-up choice for teetotallers everywhere.

It's the big day today. We've had three days of torrential rain followed by a nice warm spell and I noticed white flowers in abundance on the trees and in the hedgerows as I drove alongside the railway track in my hometown. Elderflower time. I pull on my wellies, clamp a wide-brimmed hat on my head to stop my eyes being plucked out, and of course I'm wearing rubber gloves. I'm not fussy what colour… .

"You're not going out dressed like that!" my wife, Caroline, blasts. "You look like you're going to clean the dishes in the Australian outback!" I inform her of the necessity of all my attire. The wellies are for getting right into those elder trees and bushes that are surrounded by stinging nettles and spiky hawthorns, the hat as I have explained, and of course the bright yellow rubber gloves for dexterity when picking. Reluctantly, she allows me to go out, dog in tow, and she's hoping that I don't run into anyone she knows.

Two hours and one large bag filled to bursting later, elderflower cordial here I come. It will be the perfect accompaniment for the artichoke salad I will make with the first of the Brittany Camus artichokes that have just arrived.

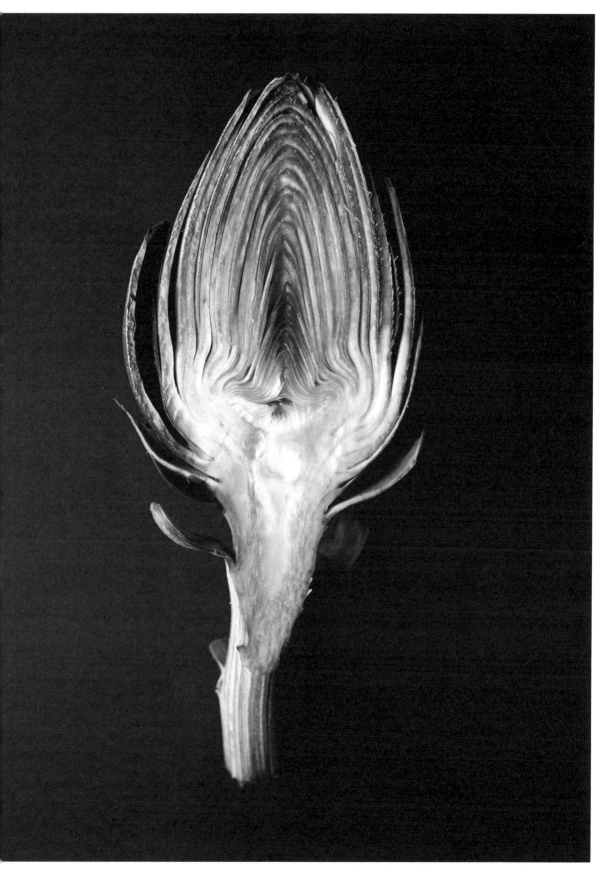

Renowned for its artichokes, Brittany, France, boasts not only the Camus variety, but also beautiful baby artichokes, which are great preserved in olive oil.

Camus artichokes in oil

The floral delicacy of artichokes in a deliciously infused oil, these preserved artichokes are absolutely amazing on a charcuterie board, or as a side dish to a fish or meat main course. I love them served with a slice of lemon for squeezing over.

Makes 1 medium–large jar

250ml (9fl oz) olive oil

250ml (9fl oz) rapeseed (canola) oil

1 bunch of thyme

4 rosemary sprigs

5 bay leaves

1 bunch of chervil

½ bunch of tarragon

6 garlic cloves, crushed

10 white peppercorns

20g (¾oz) fennel seeds

20g (¾oz) dill seeds

2 lemons

4 Camus artichokes

Start by making an infused oil. Pour both oils into a heavy-based saucepan. Reserve 2 thyme sprigs, 1 rosemary sprig and 2 bay leaves and place all the remaining herbs into the pan. Add the garlic, peppercorns and both seeds. Heat the oil over a very low heat for 1 hour – do not allow the oil to boil or the herbs and seeds will fry and make the oil bitter. Leave to infuse and cool.

Fill a large bowl with water and add the juice of one of the lemons. One at a time, trim the base of each artichoke and remove the tough outer leaves. Cut the artichoke in half and, using a spoon, scrape away the tough fibrous choke from the heart. Rinse, then place the two artichoke halves in the bowl with the lemony water. Repeat until you have prepared all the artichokes.

Bring a large pan of salted water to a boil and add the reserved herbs. Drain the artichoke halves from the lemony water and add them to the boiling water. Reduce the heat and simmer for about 20 minutes, until tender. Drain and cool.

Place the artichoke hearts in a sterilized jar and strain over the infused oil, cover and store in the fridge for about 3 days before opening and using – the longer you leave the artichokes, the more flavour the oil will have. The artichokes will keep in the sealed jar in the fridge for 3 months, or 3 weeks once opened.

Green artichoke salad *Recipe by Jennifer Paterson*

This recipe is taken from Jennifer Paterson's book, *Jennifer's Diary, By One Fat Lady*, published by *The Oldie*.

Peel the leaves off the artichokes until you come to the purple and green part. Discard the hard green leaves. Cut the artichokes into quarters and remove the chokes. Cut the remaining quarters vertically into fine slices and plunge them into a basin of cold water or they will discolour.

Fry some chopped garlic in 3 tablespoons of olive oil. Drain the artichokes, pat them dry and stir into the pan. Moisten with a glass of white wine and cook over a good heat for 10 minutes. Season. Pour into a receptacle and cool.

21

Italian cucumbers / *Alphonso mangoes* / *Greek Torpedo watermelon* / *Panach'* *blackberries* / *Panach' blueberries* / *Raspberries – Panach' Golden,* *Portuguese Tulameen* / *Strawberries –* *Gariguette, Mara des Bois* / *French* *apricots* / *Elderflower* / *Dill* / *French* *basil* / *Kentish mint – many varieties* / *Marjoram* / *Norfolk marsh samphire* / *Oregano* / *Rock samphire* / *Sea purslane* / *Sorrel* / *Early Provence tomatoes* / *Baby mixed leaves Campania* / *Chalke* *Valley watercress* / *Italian wild rocket* *(arugula)* / *Mizuna and Tatsoi leaf* / *Red* *and white Belgian chicory* / *Endives –* *Pis-en-lit (dandelion), Summer fine* *frisée* / *Feuille de chêne (oak leaf* *lettuce)* / *Red and green Butterhead* *lettuce* / *Salanova salad* / *Surrey Little* *Gems* / *Breakfast radish* / *Italian celery* / *Surrey Downs spring onions* / *Sicilian* *peppers* / *Extra fine French beans* / *Asparagus – Les Landes white, Norfolk* / *Brittany cauliflower* / *Chinese bok* *choy* / *Young Italian spinach* / *Artichokes – Camus globe, Violet* *baby artichokes from Apuli* / *Courgettes* *(zucchini) – French round, Tromba* / *Wet garlic* / *Mushrooms – Chicken of* *the Woods, Horse, St George* / *Young* *French leeks* / *Potatoes – Cornish* *"earlies", Ile de Ré* / *Essex young* *beetroot* / *Italian fennel* / *Nantes carrots* / *Radishes – Red and white long French,* *Kent varieties* / *Young turnips*

Sicilian Cucumber
An Alternative to the Greenhouse

No matter where you are in the world, there is a time of year when fruits and vegetables come together in perfect splendour and when choice is abundant and the quality of everything on offer is top notch. In the UK, that time is right now. From Coeur de Boeuf tomatoes to our most famous finger-sandwich filling, the cucumber, some of our best produce is in full swing. Nature's larder is plentiful. Or is it? Not, as it goes, if you're a Surrey cucumber.

I read an article on the internet this morning and smiled to myself. It extolled the virtues of growing glasshouse cucumbers. It said they are easy to grow, good croppers and have the added benefit of not needing to be peeled. Plus, you don't need to worry about the weather or garden pests. And there you have it: less hassle, fewer pests, less chance of disease and you don't even have to peel the horrible, tough skin.

And then I found pages waxing lyrical about another salad staple that we grow in glasshouses – the tomato. Under glass apparently means fewer bugs and pesticides and less uncertainty about what you're eating. It's baffling to me that British Tomato Fortnight runs from the end of May to early June. According to my searches on the World Wide Web, British tomatoes are everywhere right now. So, in the UK, homegrown cucumbers and tomatoes are being promoted only really just as our outdoor crops are being planted. The "cukes" apparently taste nicer, and tomatoes must be grown in glasshouses to have half a chance of survival because of our unpredictable weather and – God forbid – the odd creepy-crawly. What a load of codswallop! (I really, really like that word, coined by the late, great Cockney actor Sid James, star of *Carry On* films and *Hancock's Half Hour*.)

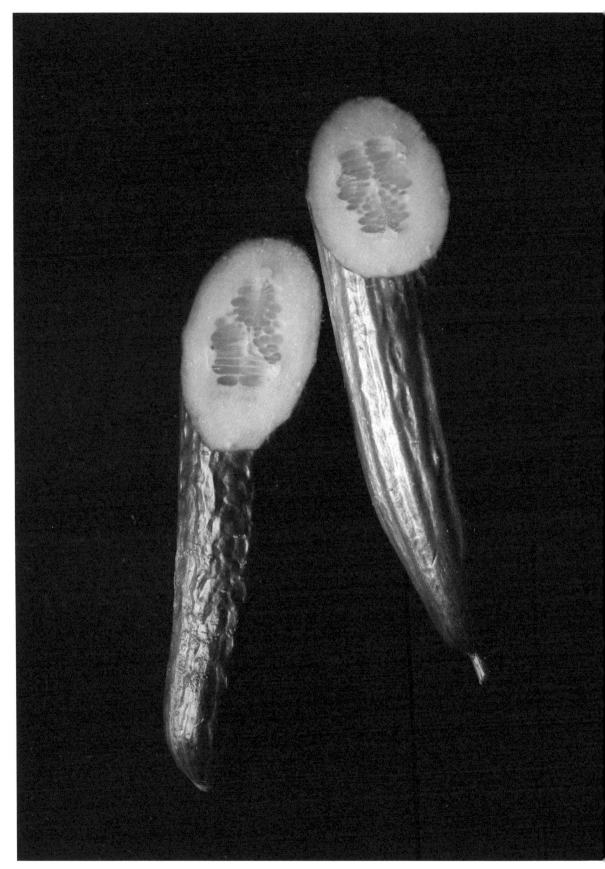

Anticipating the arrival of produce such as Marketmore cucumbers (around mid-June) is very rewarding. In May, though, stick to small, ridged cucumbers from Sicily.

Cucumbers are more than 90 per cent water and most of their delicious flavour is in the skin. Why you would peel a cucumber is beyond me. Glasshouse-grown tomatoes lack almost any flavour – if you don't believe me just do a taste comparison with a glasshouse and an outdoor tomato of the same variety. At Turnips, we test with a selection of produce throughout the year. The differences are especially noticeable with tomatoes, and most strikingly of all with the stunning yellow Beefsteak Pineapple variety: the outdoor, sun-ripened fruit is far superior in flavour to its glasshouse cousin.

But, back to outdoor cucumbers – from Surrey. Early outdoor varieties, such as Burpless Tasty Green, are suitable for growing outdoors when the weather starts to warm up and once the risk of frost has passed – so in about

> "The weather finally seems to be turning, fingers crossed, and with the warmer weather comes more lovely new season produce."

April in the UK's southern counties. These cucumbers have dark green, ridged skin with crisp flesh and are picked around mid-June. Marketmore is another excellent outdoor variety. This one has less-defined ridges and is a good slicing cucumber. "Mid-June?!" I hear you cry. "What does this mean for laying my hands on some Surrey cukes?" Sorry to let you down, but they aren't ready for you yet; we just can't recommend them this week, it's too early. Cucumbers need full sunlight to reach their mouthwatering best, so it's time to be patient. Of course, you can always try the Italian ridged cucumbers from southwest Sicily, instead. The soil in this part of the island is very conducive to vegetable and salad growing and it produces a firmer, thicker-skinned cucumber that is packed full of flavour.

Our stand

Our produce displays at Borough Market are unique. I like to think of them as live art – they draw people in and provide a majestic, colourful backdrop to the bustle of the market. As the seasons change, the displays evolve to reflect the time of year. I have always taken great pains to make our stand beautiful – not only to showcase the natural wonder that is the unbeatable fruit and veg that we sell, but also to steer our customers toward seasonal produce that works well together. So, the Italian winter chicories (see page 34) will sit side by side with Sicilian blood oranges (see page 24), because together they make a winning salad. When you come for summer tomatoes, your eye will be caught by the fragrant bunches of fresh basil sitting right next to them.

Our produce displays, which I first created and are now the work of my son Charlie and his team, led by Gino, snapshot the changing seasons in one giant visual gulp. You can define what time of year it is by the colours you see on our stand, week-in-week-out as new produce arrives. The produce we display inspires the shopping lists at the start of each chapter in the book. This week is no exception. The salad display has moved on from the Italian chicories and now shifts to its spring collection: French radishes, Hampshire watercress, Norfolk asparagus and Sicilian (outdoor-grown) cucumbers.

The Market Report

At Turnips we write regular produce updates for our restaurant clients. We call these our "Market Reports". This is the kind of report they might expect to receive around now: "The weather finally seems to be turning, fingers crossed, and with the warmer weather comes more lovely new-season produce.

"This week we've said goodbye to some winter produce: cime di rapa, pink radicchio, rose Treviso tardivo and even the stripy aubergines (eggplants) are now tailing off. Do not be downhearted, we have...

AMAZING BEANS!!
A fantastic range that includes: Borlotti, Flat, Yellow Bobby, Pelandroni and more from the Milan market.

"French and Italian outdoor heritage tomatoes are on the scene. Coming from Paris and Milan, these tomatoes taste beautiful already and will only get better. Varieties such as: Pineapple, Black Crimée, Green Zebra, Rose and Coeur d'Antan are all available from France. We also have the first Costoluto Liguria and the full colour range of red, yellow and orange Datterinos. Lovely little stripy Zebrino tomatoes have started, but only in small quantities.

"So why not try our 'Turnips Heirloom Mix', which combines the sweet and colourful French outdoor tomatoes with the thicker-skinned more acidic Italian tomatoes – giving you the chance to use the contrasting flavours and textures on your menus.

"Along with the Jerseys (which are now moving to the main crop), we also have the French Noirmoutier and Ile de Ré potatoes. Both these potatoes are grown in seaweed, giving them a beautiful flavour.

"In fruit we've now moved on to the outdoor open-punnet Gariguettes strawberries, which are eating fantastic; French Tulameen raspberries are also now in stock and tasting great. We will be supplying these as standard unless requested otherwise.

"As well as the raspberries, Panach'Fruits blackberries are in stock and will be for the rest of the summer. We are yet to see the Panach'Fruits blueberries, but they should be around soon.

"St George mushrooms have now finally shown up after getting St George's Day out of the way. The first shipment arrived today, and they are currently coming from Bulgaria.

"Mousseron and Fairy Rings also arrived this week. So, we now have some wild mushroom alternatives to the Turkish Morels, which are now fully in swing and available in all different sizes to your preference.

And last but not least... the English outdoor asparagus is in full swing from Jollys' Farm in Norfolk. A lovely accompaniment to go with the wild garlic and wet garlic. We have worked as an agent for Jollys' Farm for many years, allowing us to get unique specifications if required. And finally, we have some of the exclusive French wild asparagus – a little expensive, but well worth it. Enjoy!"

Fresh cucumber salad with horseradish and sesame seeds

This is a lovely spring salad that really shines in the middle of the table. It can be a delicious low-calorie snack or it makes a great side dish for fish or meat main courses. I like to use fresh horseradish, but you can use ready-made horseradish cream if you prefer – you'll need to add a spoonful of sour cream or crème fraîche if you do, to balance the flavours.

Serves 2–4

1 cucumber or 2 small, sliced or diced

1 banana shallot, sliced

2 tbsp olive oil

1 tsp grated fresh horseradish

1 tsp white sesame seeds, toasted

2 tbsp chopped dill

salt and freshly ground black pepper

Tip the cucumber into a mixing bowl. Add the shallot, olive oil, horseradish, sesame seeds and dill and mix well. Season with salt and pepper, then serve immediately, or chill until you're ready to serve.

Superquick pickles

This is the perfect side dish to make while a 30-minute supper is on the go elsewhere in your kitchen. You've got cucumbers in the fridge – let's make quick pickles and enjoy those crunchy cukes!

Serves 4

500g (1lb 2oz) cucumbers (about two to three 12cm/4½in cucumbers), quartered lengthways

3 garlic cloves, crushed

½ bunch of dill, chopped

1 tsp coarse sea salt

This really couldn't be easier. Put the quartered cucumbers in a large sealable freezer bag. Add the garlic, dill and salt. Seal the bag and shake well, so that the salt bruises the cucumbers. Chill for 30 minutes, then enjoy!

22

Yorkshire peas / *Alphonso mangoes* / *French Charentais melon* / *Greek Torpedo watermelon* / *Iranian Cantaloupe melon* / *Raspberries – Panach' Golden, Portuguese Tulameen* / *Strawberries – Gariguette, Mara des Bois* / *French apricots* / *Iranian yellow dates* / *Dill* / *French basil* / *Kentish mint – many varieties* / *Marjoram* / *Norfolk marsh samphire* / *Oregano* / *Rock samphire* / *Sea purslane* / *Sorrel* / *Tomatoes – Early Provence, Italian summer varieties* / *Baby mixed leaves Campania* / *Chalke Valley watercress* / *Italian wild rocket (arugula)* / *Mizuna and Tatsoi leaf* / *Endives – Pis-en-lit (dandelion), Summer fine frisée* / *Feuille de chêne (oak leaf lettuce)* / *Red and green Butterhead lettuce* / *Salanova salad* / *Surrey Little Gems* / *Breakfast radish* / *Italian celery* / *Italian Cucumbers* / *Surrey Downs spring onions* / *Sicilian peppers* / *Beans – Italian broad (fava), Extra fine French* / *Norfolk asparagus* / *Brittany cauliflower* / *Chinese bok choy* / *Young Italian spinach* / *Artichokes – Camus globe, Violet baby artichokes from Apuli* / *Courgettes (zucchini) – French round, Tromba* / *Mushrooms   Chicken of the Woods, Horse* / *Young French leeks* / *Potatoes – Cornish "earlies", Ile de Ré* / *Essex young beetroot* / *Italian fennel* / *Nantes carrots* / *Radishes – Red and white long French, Kent varieties* / *Young turnips*

Yorkshire Pea
A Pea, a Pea, My Kingdom for a Pea

Some say (my wife more than most) that I am very corny. You'll see why in a few weeks' time, in Week 38. Adapting Shakespeare for my vegetable purposes might be considered an example of my corniness, too, but this iconic line from *Richard III* shows how something seemingly insignificant can become more important than a whole "kingdom".

Fresh peas have such as short season that we have almost all but forgotten the fresh version of this most minute of vegetables now that we can buy frozen all year round. But, peas are an important British fresh product. We need to protect them from vanishing entirely – or be lost to the freezer for ever.

> "Sitting down and podding peas in the spring sunshine is a pleasure – a task that even most children enjoy."

When I was young and helping on the family market stall in Pimlico, at this point in the year, peas stood out above all the other vegetables. Fresh peas in pods were grown in Yorkshire and the neighbouring region of Lincolnshire and further afield in Worcestershire, then sold in 7kg (15lb) nets. Trucks and trucks of green beauties would be sent overnight from the northeast to the markets in London. In much the same way that the milkman would turn up with fresh milk every morning, the greengrocer would provide fresh peas every day during the season. It would not be unusual to see 20 or 30 of these heavy-laden pea sacks piled up next to the veg stalls for sale each day.

People ate fresh peas in abundance and, like many children, my siblings and I had the task of podding the peas for tea. It was such a treat to steal the odd pod when mum wasn't looking – those sweet green pearls tasted so delicious. By the time I had my own vegetable stall in the same market, if I sold five bags a week, I would be lucky. Nowadays at Borough Market, we just about get through two. How can this be the case? A fresh raw pea tastes superb, sweet and "green". I'm not sure that even my own son had tasted one until he started working at Turnips. And I am equally unsure that my daughter, who is in her 20s, ever has. Frozen peas have completely dominated the sale of this vegetable, so much so that I very much doubt many people would be able to tell me when the pea is in season.

Unfashionable as it may be, this fresh seed pod has many relatives in the legume family – broad beans, mange tout and sugar snaps among them. Throughout the world many cultures have grown, picked and dried varieties of the humble pea. But it is the British garden pea that has a special place in our history – we've been growing and eating peas since at least Tudor times. They grow exceptionally well outdoors in our northern and eastern regions, and they grace allotments or veg patches throughout the country as they are easy to grow and are often prolific croppers.

As you stealthily snack on the raw pods while cooking dinner, consider that it's time to restore our beautiful, fresh Yorkshire peas to their rightful place with our other world-class products, such as asparagus, watercress, rhubarb, strawberries, sweetcorn and the mighty potato. We have a strong heritage of growing superior fruits and vegetables, a heritage that is slowly declining because of the increase in imports, the rise in popularity of more "international" cuisines, and convenience.

I'll hold my hands up for a confession: I love frozen peas (but they must be petit pois). Throw them in a pan of boiling water and two minutes later you've got one of your five-a-day ready to go with your supper. It doesn't get much easier than that. But whenever you can, stop for just one moment, slow down and take a deep breath. If everything we did was in the name of convenience, how sad would our lives be? How much would we miss? Think: what would we miss by driving everywhere rather than walking? The simple act of sitting down and podding peas in the spring sunshine is a pleasure – a task that even most children enjoy.

Yorkshire peas have a short season of about eight weeks. They are harvested from the middle of May to the end of July, but we can extend the season by making the most of the earlier French crops in much the same way we do for asparagus (see page 101). Fresh British peas will always be sold in the pods – it's an indication of freshness. The bonus is that once you've shelled your peas, you can use the pods to make a delicious stock for soup or risotto.

Turnips is extremely lucky to have served some of London's greatest chefs to have worn whites. However, because of the limited produce throughout the winter months, these chefs are very keen to fast-track spring produce into their kitchens and their dishes. They always insist on the first of the Italian peas and broad beans (*fava*) in early February to go on to their menus in risottos, purées, stews and salads. What's wrong with that?

Peas and broad beans appear at this same time each year.
Our Yorkshire farmers bring them to market within 12 hours
of harvesting – eaten fresh they are wonderfully sweet.

Fresh peas, much like Carpentras strawberries (see page 91), need to be eaten within 48 hours of picking. Italian peas, which are mainly from Vicenza, are beautiful, but transporting them from the farm to the Milan market and then to the UK is a 72-hour affair at best. The peas are already starting to dry and are past their prime when they arrive with us.

By the end of May, when our British peas and broad beans come into season, the chefs have had their fill of these legumes and are already moving on to other produce. I have led a one-man, 20-year campaign to persuade them to remain calm in those early months of the year... to wait for spring to arrive and with it the first of the peas from northern France, which have less distance to travel and will be better flavoured because of it. I have failed in my mission so far, but I'm not a man to give in easily. Although seeing that a very famous brand of pea sells approximately 77.5 million kg (nearly 171 million lb) of garden peas and petit pois every year, I fear that my peas... sorry – *pleas* are falling on deaf ears.

Right now, at this time of the year, we see an explosion of exceptional fresh British produce. As always, Mother Nature knows the best combinations. I can think of nothing nicer than a spring salad of fresh Yorkshire peas, Surrey Little Gems, Chalke Valley watercress, Norfolk asparagus and Kent radishes, with a bowl of Cornish Early potatoes cooked with Kent mint on the side. A supper that is truly flying the flag for British produce from all points of our beautiful country – north, south, east and west.

Whether you prefer the larger garden pea or the smaller petit pois, after you've enjoyed the French season, you can then move to Yorkshire (regarded as the best), Lincolnshire or Worcestershire and for eight weeks buy not quite a 7kg (15lb) sackful, but perhaps at least a paper bagful every other day to enjoy both with and in all sorts of meals.

Yorkshire peas with braised short rib

It's the first week of summer and little green beauties are here. This recipe is a showstopper for peas!

Serves 4

1 tbsp olive oil

4 beef short ribs on the bone

2 Sand carrots, peeled, cut into 1cm (½in) dice

1 large onion, cut into 1cm (½in) dice

3 celery stalks, trimmed and cut into 1cm (½in) dice

½ garlic bulb, cloves separated, peeled and crushed

250ml (9fl oz) red wine

500ml (17fl oz) beef stock

2 rosemary sprigs

3 thyme sprigs

2–3 tsp red wine vinegar, to taste

salt and freshly ground black pepper

For the pea purée

500g (1lb 2oz) fresh Yorkshire peas

4 knobs of butter

Preheat the oven to 160°C/140°C fan/315°F/Gas 2–3.

Heat a heavy-based pan over a high heat. Add the oil and, when hot, season the short ribs with salt and pepper and add them to the pan. Sear for 2–3 minutes each side, until nicely coloured all over. Remove the meat from the pan and set aside. Lower the heat to medium, add the diced vegetables and sweat for about 10 minutes, until softened. Add the garlic and cook for a further 1 minute.

Return the ribs to the pan and add the red wine. Cook for 10 minutes to reduce slightly and then add the beef stock and both herbs. Cover the pan with a lid and transfer it to the oven to braise the ribs for 2–3 hours, until the meat is very tender – check after 2 hours and continue cooking for a little longer if needed.

Meanwhile, make the pea purée. Blanch 350g (12oz) of the peas in salted boiling water for a good 2–3 minutes, until very soft. Drain, reserving the cooking water. Tip the peas into a blender and whizz until smooth, adding a little cooking water if needs be to reach a smooth purée consistency. Add half the butter and season to taste. Strain the purée through a fine sieve into a bowl and cool quickly by sitting the bowl in a sink of iced water to prevent the peas discolouring.

Remove the beef from the oven and transfer the ribs to a plate. Cover and keep warm. Strain the cooking liquid into a smaller pan and reduce over a medium heat, until thickened to a sauce that will coat the back of a spoon. Season to taste and add a little vinegar if needed to balance the flavours.

Blanch the remaining peas in salted water until just tender, then drain them and add them to the sauce with the remaining knobs of butter, stirring to emulsify.

When you're ready to serve, spoon the pea purée equally on to each plate, place a short rib on top and finish with glazed peas in sauce.

King crab with lemon and Yorkshire pea purée

A perfect light dish for a summer's evening, this recipe is not quick to put together, but it is worth it. The king crab sits on a bed of whole and puréed fresh peas garnished with pea shoots and edible flowers.

Serves 4

1 king crab cluster
4 tbsp vegetable oil
1 onion, chopped
1 celery stalk, chopped
1 leek, chopped
1 head of fennel, chopped
150ml (5fl oz) white wine
2 lemongrass stalks
2 lime leaves
250ml (9oz) double (heavy) cream
5 egg yolks
65g (2¼oz) cornflour (cornstarch)
2 platinum-grade gelatine leaves
250g (9oz) whipping cream
2 banana shallots, finely diced
1kg (2lb 4oz) podded fresh peas
1 Sicilian lemon
100g (3½oz) mangetout (snow peas), trimmed
75g (2½oz) pine nuts, toasted
salt and freshly ground black pepper
small handful of pea shoots and edible flowers, to garnish

Start by prepping the crab. Use scissors to carefully cut and separate the crab shells and meat. Use a rolling pin to crush the empty shells into small pieces, which you can use to make the stock, and tip them into a large saucepan. Cut the meaty cluster into 4 equal portions, cover and set them aside in the fridge.

Add 1 tablespoon of the oil to the pan and sweat the shells over a medium heat for 2 minutes. Add the onion, celery, leek and fennel and continue to cook for a further 8 minutes, until the vegetables are soft but not coloured. Add the wine and reduce the liquid by half (about 2–3 minutes). Pour enough water into the pan to cover the shells and vegetables and bring it to a boil. Reduce the heat under the pan and simmer the stock for 45 minutes, then strain it through a fine-mesh sieve into a clean pan.

Add the lemongrass and lime leaves and bring the strained stock to a boil. Reduce by half (about 30 minutes) and then remove from the heat and leave to infuse for 10 minutes.

Discard the lemongrass and lime leaves, add the cream, place the pan back over the heat and bring the liquid back to a boil.

Meanwhile, in a bowl, whisk together the egg yolks and cornflour to a paste. Pour the hot cream and stock mixture on to the paste, whisking continuously until smooth. Strain the mixture back into the pan and cook over a low–medium heat, whisking continuously until thickened. Remove the pan from the heat, pour the sauce into the bowl of a stand mixer fitted with the whisk and leave the sauce to cool slightly.

Meanwhile soak the gelatine leaves in cold water for about 4 minutes, until soft, then remove them from the water, squeezing out the excess and add them to the sauce in the bowl. Whisk on slow–medium speed until the mixture is cold.

Continued overleaf...

In another bowl, whisk the whipping cream until it forms soft and floppy peaks and fold this into the mousse mixture in the stand mixer. Cover and transfer to the fridge to chill.

Tip the shallots into a small saucepan. Add 2 tablespoons of the remaining vegetable oil and cook over a very low heat for about 5 minutes, until soft but not coloured.

Divide the peas into 600g (1lb 5oz) and 400g (14oz). Cook the larger portion in salted boiling water for about 7–8 minutes, until soft. Drain them, then tip them into a food processor and blend until smooth. Spoon the purée into a bowl and chill it in an ice bath to prevent it discolouring. Once cool, season with salt and transfer to the fridge to chill. Blanch the remaining peas in salted water until tender, drain and refresh under cold running water.

Using a serrated knife, peel and segment the lemon and cut the segments into small pieces. Thinly slice the mangetout and place them into iced water to crisp.

Preheat the barbecue or griddle pan for cooking the crab. As the cooking will be very quick, you need to dress the plates first. Mix the blanched peas with the purée, add the lemon pieces, pine nuts, sliced mangetout and shallots and taste, then season accordingly.

Spoon or pipe the mousse on to each plate and top with the pea mixture. Drizzle the crab pieces with the remaining oil, season with salt and cook on the hot barbecue or griddle for no more than 2 minutes, until cooked through.

Place the crab on top of the peas and garnish with pea shoots and edible flowers.

Dried peas

The best time to expand your larder is now. It's possible to dry so many fresh ingredients, setting them aside for future use, and one of my favourite vegetables for drying is peas. Remember one thing, however – when you cook them, allow plenty of time (about 8 hours) for soaking. And don't forget to save the pods – use them to make a light vegetable stock for risotto or soup.

1kg (2lb 4oz) podded fresh peas

Bring a large saucepan of salted water to a boil over a high heat. Add the peas and cook for about 3 minutes, until just tender. Drain and leave the peas to dry on a clean tea towel, or kitchen paper.

Heat the oven to its lowest fan setting. Tip the peas into a baking tray and spread them out in an even layer. Transfer the tray to the oven and dry out the peas for 2–3 hours, until they curl up and become like little stones.

Leave the dried peas to cool and then tip into an airtight container and store them in a cool, dry place for up to 12 months. Soak the dried peas for 8 hours in cold water to rehydrate them before using as normal.

23

Tulameen raspberries / *Alphonso mangoes* / *French Charentais melon* / *Greek Torpedo watermelon* / *Iranian Cantaloupe melon* / *Panach' blackberries* / *Strawberries – Gariguette, Mara des Bois* / *French apricots* / *French basil* / *Iranian yellow dates* / *Dill* / *Kentish mint – many varieties* / *Marjoram* / *Norfolk marsh samphire* / *Oregano* / *Rock samphire* / *Sea purslane* / *Sorrel* / *Tomatoes – Early Provence, Italian summer varieties* / *Baby mixed leaves Campania* / *Chalke Valley watercress* / *Italian wild rocket (arugula)* / *Mizuna and Tatsoi leaf* / *Endives – Pis-en-lit (dandelion), Summer fine frisée* / *Feuille de chêne (oak leaf lettuce)* / *Red and green Butterhead lettuce* / *Salanova salad* / *Surrey Little Gems* / *Breakfast radish* / *Italian celery* / *Italian Cucumbers* / *Surrey Downs spring onions* / *Sicilian peppers* / *Beans – Broad (fava) from Worcester, Extra fine French, Kent Bobby, Runner from Worcester* / *Yorkshire peas* / *Norfolk asparagus* / *Brittany cauliflower* / *Young Italian spinach* / *Chinese bok choy* / *Artichokes – Camus globe, Violet baby artichokes from Apuli* / *Courgettes (zucchini) – French round, Tromba* / *Mushrooms – Chicken of the Woods, Horse* / *Young French leeks* / *Potatoes – Cornish "earlies", Ile de Ré* / *Essex young beetroot* / *Italian fennel* / *Nantes carrots* / *Radishes – Red and white long French, Kent varieties* / *Young turnips*

Tulameen Raspberry
I'm Forever Blowing Raspberries, Raspberries in the Air

Early June for us marks the arrival of French fruits: cherries, strawberries, blueberries, melons, peaches, nectarines – and Tulameen raspberries. Of course, you can get these fruits from all over Europe and beyond, but by using the Turnips System, which is akin to dropping a pebble in the ocean and watching the ripples radiating outward, we look out from London until we find the nearest World Class Standard (we insist upon this for every product) and stop there.

The Tulameen raspberry needs full sunshine and plenty of light to really bring out its stunning flavour. We actually start the season off in mid-May, sourcing these red jewels from Portugal. Weatherwise, Portugal is a few weeks ahead of France, which comes into its own this week. This means that for our restaurant customers, we can lengthen the season for these berries by about two weeks. But, this week, it is to the Vendée region in western France where we're heading for our soft fruit. We've been buying from Panach'Fruits for 20 years. This company focuses on high-quality soft fruits: red, white and black currants, gooseberries, strawberries, blackberries and blueberries – and Tulameen raspberries, which make up three quarters of the company's production. A few years ago the company decided to build six glasshouses covering 15 hectares (37 acres). "*Sacre bleu!*" I hear you cry. The majority of Panach'Fruits' produce, including the raspberries, are grown in the south of

Originally a Canadian cultivar, the Tulameen raspberry is a mid- to late-season variety that grows best in hotter climates. It tastes far sweeter than many other raspberries.

the Vendée, and the blueberries and redcurrants are grown in the west of Maine-et-Loire in glasshouses. Of the area that Panach'Fruits farms, 5 hectares (12 acres) are covered with a glass construction to produce pre-season and post-season fruits. I know what you're thinking... what about my non-glasshouse-grown ethos? What about Turnips' strict policy of only outdoor-grown produce?

When the company first introduced the glasshouses, I was sceptical, but once I tasted their berries, I realized they were right. The raspberries were so good that I couldn't tell the difference compared with those grown outdoors. The glass simply covers the actual soil from the region, and the company uses proper husbandry without pesticides to produce superior fruit. The conditions in that sense, then, are not artificial. For Panach'Fruits it's all about good farming practice to produce excellent flavour, combining new technology with old skills. This is an alternative ethos that I can live with.

However, I draw the line at "extending" the seasons. We do not buy their glasshouse fruit beyond the season it would naturally grow if it were fully outdoors. In other words: protect the plants when necessary, yes; but let us look forward to the seasons just as Nature intended, so we can have the experience of enjoying the anticipation.

Tulameen is a popular raspberry variety around the world – and not only for commercial growers, but also for gardeners. A relatively new variety, it is a cross between Nootka and Glen Prosen and was created in Canada in the 1980s. Tulameen plants are floricans – meaning that they produce fruit on the second year of growth – with a season that begins in late June and continues for about six weeks (two weeks longer than some other varieties). The glossy red berries, which are easy to pick, are late ripening and firm, with a slightly elongated shape and an excellent, sweet, aromatic flavour.

Turnips and Tomas

Turnips Restaurant started life as pop-up in 2020 just as London was coming back to life after the first lockdown of the COVID pandemic. It is essentially a partnership between a family greengrocer and a fine-dining restaurant with fruit and vegetables at its heart. It is set within and under the arches of a bustling market in the heart of the city

"How many other chefs get to see, touch and taste produce as it arrives from the farms or from the markets in Paris and Milan?"

and has at its helm one of the most talented and creative chefs working in London. When we first opened the pop-up, Tomas could talk directly to his customers about his dishes, giving him the confidence to grow the concept.

In most other restaurants, ingredient orders simply arrive from suppliers with some chefs having little understanding of or consideration for the provenance, especially of their fruit and veg. Often chefs place greater importance on the meat or fish they receive. For years there has been very little regard attached to greengrocery produce, but times and minds are changing.

At Turnips, Tomas has the opportunity to cook with produce that most chefs avoid simply because it is too expensive – for them to have such quality produce on their menus would mean buying directly from the growers themselves. Tomas's greengrocer is also his business partner, which gives him unparalleled access to the best produce available in London and a choice that can, and often does, change daily. How many other chefs get to see, touch and taste produce as it arrives from the farms or from the markets in Paris and Milan? Tomas can write and adapt his menus around what is best that day.

With Turnips' no-waste policy, there is a symbiotic relationship between the retail, wholesale and restaurant arms of our business. If stock is left over that no longer meets our exacting standards for premium quality (whether it's a punnet or two of Tulameen raspberries, a box of Tarocco blood oranges or even 8kg/17½lb of ceps, which arrived from the suppliers in error), Tomas and his team will find a use for it, however they see fit. The ceps, for example, could be fermented and made into an intense miso, and the oranges juiced for sale on the market stand and their peels candied and used in desserts.

Tomas is a creative chef with a self-confessed freestyle approach that is influenced by the beautiful displays he sees on his way past the stall to his kitchen every morning – everything from foraged mushrooms, pale Italian aubergines (eggplants) and finger limes to boxes of Sicilian tomatoes. Not many chefs have the ability, or even the opportunity, to think on their feet and embrace the challenge of using produce in fresh ways, and create a constantly changing and evolving menu. His menus – both the small plates and the tasting menu – change frequently, making exciting work for himself and his team.

For Tomas, even the humble onion is no longer just an onion; nor a garlic clove just some added flavouring. He understands that by using Cevenne or Roscoff onions (see page 187) and Lautrec garlic, he is building layers of flavour in his cooking that are unachievable with standard Spanish onions or the bitter-tasting garlic from China.

His Lithuanian heritage has subtle underlying influences in his cooking – whether that is the dumplings or cured fish on the menu or the ever-present preserves, ferments and pickles. The proud father of two, he tells me that he thinks of Turnips Restaurant as his third child – which makes me Le Grand-Père Navet!

Tulameen raspberry, double chocolate

Raspberry and chocolate is one of those classic flavour combinations and this delectable dessert could not showcase this pairing any better. Each component complements the other; the sweet and sharp raspberry sorbet and jelly cut through the beautifully rich brownie and dark chocolate crème.

Serves 6

For the sorbet

400g (14oz) Tulameen raspberries

85g (3oz) caster (superfine) sugar

30g (1oz) glucose powder

For the jelly

3 tbsp raspberry purée (from the raspberries above)

30g (1oz) caster (superfine) sugar

¼ tsp agar agar

For the brownie

280g (10oz) butter, diced, plus extra for greasing

145g (5¼oz) 70% cocoa gianduja chocolate, chopped

4 large eggs

335g (11¾oz) light brown soft sugar

195g (6¾oz) plain (all purpose) flour

30g (1oz) cocoa powder

Continued overleaf...

Start with the sorbet. Purée the raspberries in a food processor until smooth, then pass them through a fine sieve into a saucepan. Set aside 3 tablespoons of purée for the jelly. Then, add the sugar, glucose powder and 65ml (2fl oz) of water to the pan. Set the pan over a low heat to dissolve the sugar and cook until it reaches 65°C/150°F on a sugar thermometer. Strain the compôte into a clean bowl and leave it to cool. Chill the mixture, then churn it in an ice-cream machine according to the manufacturer's instructions. Transfer the sorbet to a freezerproof container, put the lid on and freeze until ready to serve.

Make the jelly. Combine the raspberry purée, sugar and agar agar in a small pan. Bring to a boil while stirring all the time, then cook for 1 minute, until thickened. Pour the mixture on to a tray to cool quickly and set. Once the jelly has set, transfer it to a food processor and blitz it until smooth. Spoon it into a piping bag or squeezy bottle and chill until you're ready to serve.

Make the brownie. Preheat the oven to 200°C/180°C fan/400°F/Gas 6 and grease and line a 22 x 16cm (8½ x 6¼in) baking tin.

Melt the butter and chocolate together in a heatproof bowl set over a pan of simmering water. Stir until smooth, remove from the heat and leave to cool.

In another bowl, whisk the eggs and sugar to a fluffy consistency. Add the cooled chocolate mixture and fold in. Sift the flour and cocoa powder into the bowl and beat until smooth and thoroughly combined. Spoon the brownie batter into the lined tin (it should make a depth of 2cm/¾in) and bake for about 15 minutes, until set. Remove from the oven and leave to cool in the tin.

Continued overleaf...

For the dark chocolate crème

4 egg yolks

70g (2½oz) caster (superfine) sugar

250ml (9fl oz) double (heavy) cream

250ml (9fl oz) full-fat milk

1 platinum-grade gelatine leaf

250g (9oz) 70% cocoa gianduja chocolate, chopped

To serve

20 Tulameen raspberries

6 tbsp dacquoise crumb (see page 182; optional), to serve

melissa or lemon balm cress

Finally, make the crème. In a bowl whisk together the egg yolks and sugar until smooth.

Combine the cream and milk in a small saucepan and place it over a low–medium heat. Leave the mixture to come to just below boiling point (about 4–5 minutes), then slowly pour it into the egg mixture, whisking continuously, until smooth.

Soak the gelatine leaf in cold water for about 4 minutes until soft, and meanwhile return the custard mixture to the pan and heat again to 82°C/180°F, stirring all the time.

Tip the chopped chocolate into a clean bowl. Pour the custard mixture over the chocolate. Remove the gelatine leaf from the water and squeeze out the excess, then add the gelatine to the bowl with the chocolate. Mix until smooth.

Leave the crème until cold, then spoon it into a piping bag fitted with a nozzle if you like.

To serve, cut the brownie into neat 10 x 2cm (4 x ¾in) slices (you should have enough to trim the outside edges from the tin, and then give 6 equal slices) and place 1 slice on each serving plate. Pipe the chocolate crème on top, pipe dots of raspberry jelly among the crème and top with fresh Tulameen raspberries. Place a scoop of sorbet on the side (on a bed of dacquoise crumb, if using) and decorate with melissa or lemon balm cress.

Raspberries in juices

There's no such thing as too many raspberries – but if you do find yourself with an overload, an easy way to preserve them is to can them. You'll have beautiful berries in the middle of winter to serve on top of pancakes or cakes – just add whipped cream.

Makes 2 large jars

3kg (6lb 8oz) raspberries

750g (1lb 10oz) caster (superfine) sugar

Put the raspberries into a large bowl and add the sugar. Stir to combine. Cover the bowl and leave it at room temperature for 24 hours for the sugar to draw the juices from the berries, stirring every 3–4 hours when you can.

The following day, spoon the fruit and the juices into sterilized jars. Seal with the lids and stand the jars in a large saucepan. Pour water into the pan so that it comes halfway up the sides of the jars and place the pan over a high heat. Bring the water to a boil, and boil for 3–5 minutes to pasteurize the contents of the jars.

Remove the jars from the water bath, tightly close the lids and turn the jars upside down to create a vacuum. Leave to cool.

Once cool, turn the jars the right way up and store in a cool, dark place for 6–12 months. Once opened, store in the fridge and use the raspberries within a week.

24

Outdoor French and Italian tomatoes / *Alphonso mangoes* / *French Charentais melon* / *Greek Torpedo watermelon* / *Israeli Galia melon* / *Italian Cantaloupe melons* / *Kent gooseberries* / *Raspberries – French Tulameen, Panach' Golden* / *Strawberries – Gariguette, Mara des Bois* / *French apricots* / *Iranian yellow dates* / *Pêche blanche and pêche jaune* / *Dill* / *French basil* / *Lemon verbena* / *Marjoram* / *Oregano* / *Sorrel* / *Kentish mint – many varieties* / *Norfolk marsh samphire* / *Rock samphire* / *Sea purslane* / *Sussex courgette (zucchini) flowers* / *Fresh almonds* / *Baby mixed leaves Campania* / *Chalke Valley watercress* / *Italian wild rocket (arugula)* / *Mizuna and Tatsoi leaf* / *Endives – Pis-en-lit (dandelion), Summer fine frisée* / *Feuille de chêne (oak leaf lettuce)* / *Red and green*

Butterhead lettuce / *Salanova salad* / *Surrey Little Gems* / *Breakfast radish* / *Italian celery* / *Surrey Downs spring onions* / *Sicilian peppers* / *Beans – Broad (fava) from Worcester, Extra fine French, Kent Bobby, Runner from Worcester* / *Yorkshire peas* / *Norfolk asparagus* / *Brittany cauliflower* / *Young Italian spinach* / *Chinese bok choy* / *Artichokes – Camus globe, Violet baby artichokes from Apuli* / *Courgettes – French round, Tromba* / *Mushrooms – Chicken of the Woods, Horse* / *Young French leeks* / *Potatoes – Cornish "earlies", Ile de Ré* / *Baby veg – Essex beetroot, fennel, and turnips* / *Italian fennel* / *Nantes carrots* / *Radishes – Kent, Red and white long French*

Outdoor French and Italian Tomato
Base Drum, Please – Tom, Tom, Tom, Tom

The tomato industry in Europe is split between glasshouse and outdoor-grown tomatoes. Those on the side of the glasshouse tend to be the more northerly countries, such as Holland and Belgium, and say they can produce stunning tomato varieties for up to ten months of the year. They can farm a much bigger yield by controlling every aspect of the plants' growth – from the amount of water, nutrients and light they receive to the prevalence of the pests that plague a lot of the outdoor crops.

"A tomato is a tomato!" I hear the glasshouse advocates say. They confidently claim that they can produce fruit of outstanding quality and that the tonnes of tomatoes required to feed the masses outweighs the demand for flavour. Those on the side of outdoor farming, however, claim that by leaving the growing to the seasons and Nature, thinking of themselves simply as custodians of the land, and giving the tomatoes only the required quantities of water and (natural) fertilizer, they can nurture a fruit that is sun-ripened in a timely manner and, as a result, has outstanding flavour. So which side should we take? The side of technology or the side of Nature? Turnips chooses Nature's path every time.

France has been growing tomatoes for about 200 years. The first varieties appeared once the Spanish conquistadors returned from the Americas. Nowadays varieties such as Marmande, Coeur de Boeuf, Coeur de Pigeon,

Outdoor French and Italian tomatoes, such as Pineapple,
Coeur de Pigeon, Marmande, Cuore di Bue and Rose, have a
thinner skin and sweeter flavour than earlier varieties.

Pineapple, Green Zebra and Noire de Crimée are some of the most stunning French varieties that flourish in Provence thanks to the warm climate and favourable tomato-growing terroir.

That is the French (via the Spanish). But, when it comes to tomatoes, the Italians are nothing if not passionate. Most regions of Italy have a variety for which they are famous, and dishes to match. Camone and Marinda from Sardinia and Sicily, Costoluto Genovese from Liguria and the full colour range of red, yellow and orange Datterini from the Gargano region to the east of the country on the Adriatic Sea. These sweet, small, date-shaped tomatoes are wonderful roasted whole, or are equally delicious in salads.

But probably the most famous Italian tomato is from Campania in an area around Naples. The San Marzano tomato has a DOP certification ("protected origin"). It is essentially a tomato for cooking and makes perfect pasta sauces. Another DOP tomato is the lesser known Pomodorino Vesuviano, which (you've probably guessed) is grown in the protected area around Mount Vesuvius in the sandy, mineral-rich volcanic soils. Both these tomatoes have provenance and cultivation guarantees with consortiums made up of their producers, who are dedicated to the protection of their varieties.

Traditionally the little Pomodorino Vesuviano tomatoes would be tied in bunches (*piennoli*) and hung from the rafters under a cool porch where their thicker skins mean they will keep until spring. Or, they were cut in half and preserved in jars as *pacchetelle*, a delicacy of the area, which enables the tomatoes to be used in sauces long after the tomato harvest is over.

Finally, Italians give us the Cuore di Bue ("ox heart") tomato, which is Giorgio Locatelli's favourite. This variety grows mainly in Liguria, in the northwest of Italy, and in Calabria, in the south. These large, irregular, ridged, heart-shaped tomatoes are orangey–red with a meaty flesh. With the wonderful summer herbs of oregano and basil to accompany them, they are such a vital part of summer eating – in a simple salad, or in a pasta dish or a wonderful sauce. Life is much more colourful with these tomatoes.

"When it comes to tomatoes, the Italians are nothing if not passionate. Most regions of Italy have a variety for which they are famous, and dishes to match."

There are hundreds, if not thousands of varieties of tomatoes, many with accreditations, but there's only one way to grow them and that is outdoors, in the soil and ripened by the sun. Giorgio Locatelli has such a love for this plant group: "I can't think of life without tomatoes," he says. He calls them "The Steak and Kidney Pie of Italy".

Pesto *Recipe by Jennifer Paterson*

One day at the start of summer, Jennifer Paterson (see page 121) rides her trademark scooter up to my market stall on Tachbrook Street and says: "Anything for me to take home to resurrect?"

"Well, I've got these basil pots," I reply. There are about 20 pots – all looking slightly shabby. "I don't know what you can do with them."

"You'll see – they're perfect. And what about those?" she asks, pointing to the floor at three boxes of "OS" San Marzano tomatoes. (OS is the London market traders parlance for old stock.) I tell Jennifer that they are well past their best and they are heading for the bin.

"Don't you dare!" she exclaims. And with that, she nips home with the basil and returns a short while later and straps three boxes of tomatoes to the back of her scooter with her all-important bungee straps. A few weeks – possibly months – later (she became a daily visitor to the market, so it's hard to remember exactly how much time had passed), she pulls up to the stall again and opens the box on the back of her scooter: "Same deal as always," she says. "Half for you and half for me." She passes me two Kilner jars – one smaller jar full of pesto and another huge one of deep red passata. She smiles, gets back on her scooter and rides off. She later gave me two recipes – one for this pesto, and one for passata (over the page), both of which I still use to this day.

Serves 4

100g (3½oz) basil leaves

2 large garlic cloves, peeled

100g (3½oz) Parmesan, finely grated

30g (1oz) pine nuts

extra-virgin olive oil

Put the basil leaves, garlic, Parmesan and pine nuts in a blender with enough olive oil to make a purée. Blend until smooth.

Passata *Recipe by Jennifer Paterson*

There are no quantities for this sauce, I'm afraid. This is a recipe for when you have a glut of ripe tomatoes, and it doesn't really matter which varieties you use, as long as they are outdoor grown.

Roughly chop the tomatoes, put them into a blender and whizz them until pulped. Strain the pulp through a sieve into a saucepan to remove the seeds and the skins. Add garlic if you like (I love garlic, so I often add an unsociable amount), season, and cook the pulp over a low–medium heat until it has reduced to a consistency that you are happy with. Remove from the heat and leave to cool. Pour the passata into jars up to three quarters full and top up with olive oil. I also love onions, so I usually pop some sautéed onions into the pulp too. This is my dream passata.

Salad of heirloom tomatoes, goat's cheese and basil *Recipe by the Galvin Brothers*

My good friends Jeff and Chris Galvin, although from Essex, have devoted their lives to French cuisine and share their tomato salad using French varieties.

Serves 4

900g (2lb) heirloom tomatoes

200g (7oz) goat's cheese log, such as Ragstone, Dorstone or Aisy Cendré

4 basil sprigs

4 tbsp extra-virgin olive oil

sea salt and freshly ground black pepper

crusty baguette, to serve

Thinly slice the tomatoes – some will just need cutting into quarters – and arrange on your most beautiful plates. Sprinkle lightly with sea salt.

Slice the goat's cheese evenly and arrange it on top of the tomatoes. Grind some black pepper over the top, then drop on the basil sprigs.

Finally, splash some olive oil over each plate to lubricate. This is really delicious served with crusty baguette.

Dried Provençal tomatoes in oil

It's a truly stunning thing to open your fridge and see little jars of different tomatoes in oil all lined up. You can use any variety of Provençal tomatoes in this recipe, but smaller tomatoes will take less time to dry and are easier to pack into jars. They make amazing antipasti, or you can serve them with cheese or in salads.

Makes 2–3 smallish jars

3kg (6lb 8oz) any variety Provençal tomatoes

boiling water, from a kettle

good pinch of caster (superfine) sugar

4–5 large garlic cloves, peeled and thinly sliced

250ml (9fl oz) olive oil

salt and freshly ground black pepper

Cut a cross on the underside of each tomato and tip the tomatoes into a large bowl. Pour over boiling water and leave for 30 seconds to loosen the skins. Drain the tomatoes and refresh them under cold water. Peel off the skins and cut the tomatoes into halves or quarters, depending on size.

Heat the fan oven to its lowest setting.

Place the tomatoes on a wire rack set over a baking tray and sprinkle over the sugar. Season them with salt and pepper. Thinly slice the garlic cloves and place one slice on each tomato piece. Leave the tomatoes to dry in the warm oven for 2–3 hours, until nearly dry but still a little moist.

Pack the tomatoes into jars and cover them with the olive oil. Screw on tight-fitting lids and store the tomatoes in the fridge for up to 3 months. Once opened, eat the tomatoes within 3 weeks.

25

Lettuces – Webb's Wonder, Summer fine frisée / Alphonso mangoes / French Charentais melon / Greek Torpedo watermelon / Israeli Galia melon / Italian Cantaloupe melon / Kent gooseberries / Panach' blackberries / Panach' blueberries / Panach' gooseberries / Raspberries – French Tulameen / Strawberries – Gariguette, Mara des Bois / French apricots / Iranian yellow dates / Pêche blanc and pêche jaune / Dill / French basil / Kentish mint – many varieties / Lemon verbena / Norfolk marsh samphire / Marjoram / Oregano / Rock samphire / Sea purslane / Sorrel / Sussex courgette (zucchini) flowers / Fresh almonds / Tomatoes – Early Provence, Italian summer varieties, Outdoor varieties / Baby mixed leaves Campania / Chalke Valley watercress / Italian wild rocket (arugula) / Mizuna and Tatsoi leaf / Pis-en-lit (dandelion) / Feuille de chêne (oak leaf lettuce) / Italian Cos / Red and green Butterhead lettuce / Salanova salad / Surrey Little Gems / Breakfast radish / Italian celery / Surrey Downs spring onions / Sicilian peppers / Beans – Broad (fava) from Worcester, Extra fine French, Kent Bobby, Runner from Worcester / Yorkshire peas / Norfolk asparagus / Brittany cauliflower / Young Italian spinach / Chinese bok choy / Artichokes – Camus globe, Violet baby artichokes from Apuli / French round courgette / Mushrooms – Chicken of the Woods, Horse / Young French leeks / Potatoes – Cornish "earlies", Ile de Ré / Baby veg – Essex beetroot, fennel, and turnips / Italian Fennel / Nantes carrots / Radishes – Kent, Red and white long French*

Webb's Wonder and Summer Fine Frisée
Salad Days Old and New

Finding the old in the new

On my last trip to *Ortomercato Milano*, the wholesale produce market in Milan, I saw a lettuce that I remembered well from my childhood: Webb's Wonder. I always thought that its name sounded like a philosopher's meaning of life. The big, round lettuce heads have a sweet, crisp heart that I hadn't seen once since my school days (which are now a long time ago). Why did the lettuce heads with the enigmatic name that my dad once sold on his salad stall go out of fashion, and others with them? Webb's Wonders were replaced by "Bud" icebergs from the USA, the sweet and crisp Winter Density made way for the Little Gem, and the Manchester Cos became just plain old Cos. Why?

You've guessed it… the glasshouse revolution! All those lovely old varieties were regional and outdoor grown: Cos from Manchester and Webb's and Density from Woking in Surrey. But, international fruit agents in the USA set up in the UK aiming to import produce from the States, Chile and South Africa. In the winter months, when the Webb's Wonder wasn't growing in Europe, they would ship in a similar lettuce (the iceberg). Customers found that this somewhat bland variety would last longer in the fridge, so before too long we had adopted the same glasshouse farming practices as the Americans. We were able to produce our own lettuces in vast quantities for around nine months of the year, taking away the need for US imports, but also a little bit more of our love for seasonality in our produce. To my knowledge there are now no outdoor-grown lettuces commercially produced in this country any more. The Italians and French did not adopt this practice. In Italy and France, farmers still grow salad varieties that are suited to the climate, such as the spectacular bitter Italian chicories (see page 34).

At Turnips, then, we go to Europe for our "fine" salads and in France to a company called Perle du Nord, which produces, for example, Witloof chicory. Created in 1983, Perle du Nord comprises 120 producers from five agricultural co-operatives in Hauts-de-France, in the north of the country. Forming cooperatives in farming has been a tradition in Europe for many years. Individual producers were finding it difficult to compete for a market share with the big companies. So, they joined forces to defend their interests and provide quality products to their customers.

Perle du Nord salads are grown using traditional but unique farming methods throughout the planting season, which runs from March to early September. They use underground streams for irrigation, and the plants grow and mature naturally in the fields, given a helping hand only with an intermittent misting system and a covering of netting to prevent sun burn and damage from pests, respectively. The fine summer frisée lettuces are covered with terracotta pots for the last five days of growing to "whiten" the hearts – a system called blanching. This creates a stunning, slightly bitter, crunchy lettuce with a depth of flavour that no glasshouse can reproduce. Perle du Nord are also the European endive specialists growing a staggering 47 per cent of the French production of endive – and all outdoors.

The old: an early memory of visiting Covent Garden

Covent Garden had for centuries been London's wholesale fruit-and-vegetable market, in the very heart of the capital just metres from the steps of the Royal Opera House. When I was little, I would go there with my dad to buy for our own market stall. On one occasion, when I must've been no more than nine years old, I vividly remember a large, open-backed lorry parked up on the cobblestones. On the back of that lorry were stacks of wooden

"The big, round lettuce heads have a sweet, crisp heart that I hadn't seen since my school days."

"bushel" boxes. To a small child, it seemed that these boxes reached all the way up to the sky. This was in the farmers' pavilion at Covent Garden where A.E. Burree, a salad grower from Woking, used to pitch up every morning to sell his boxes of salads, radishes and onions off the back of his lorry. I dare say these farmers produced their lettuces in the exact same way as the French farmers do now.

I would love to see a 180-degree turnaround in farming in this country and to see the global modern technologies revert to more traditional methods. All the botanists and scientists, though, believe it will go the other way – to high-tech, futuristic buildings that they will call farms. But they won't be farms as we know them. Who knows what will happen in the next 20 years?

The new: creating Borough Market

In 1989, my wife, Caroline, and I moved from Tachbrook Street in Pimlico to Borough Market in Southwark. We were supplying more restaurants and had outgrown our stalls. We bought our stock from three wholesale markets in London: Covent Garden (now based in Nine Elms on the South Bank), Spitalfields and Borough. We kept the stalls and set up a warehouse in Borough Market on a gut instinct – it just felt perfect. With the move came a new name. As we were now based in Southwark, Fosters of Pimlico no longer seemed appropriate – how we ended up with "Turnips" is a story for another time.

Our business flourished. Then, a cheese retailer and in many ways the foremost champion of British cheeses, Randolph Hodgson (Sir Randolph now) approached us and Monika Linton, a Spanish fine-food importer, to join forces and trial a market day that would open our wholesale doors and let the public see what we provided for the top restaurants in London.

The event proved to be a huge success and we went on to hold similar events four times a year. Henrietta Green was then (and still is) the champion of small producers from all over the British Isles. With her hugely popular Food Lovers' Fair that was held in St Christopher's Place in 1995, she created a platform for fine-food producers and an audience with the public that had not been seen before. Randolph persuaded her to bring her fair to Borough in 1998. Producers and products such as The Ginger Pig, Sillfield Farm wild boar, Furness Fish Morecambe Bay shrimps, Northfield Farm Dexter beef and Mrs King's pork pies were some of the early traders at our monthly, then weekly and eventually daily markets. To this day, all but one are trading at Borough.

The three-day Borough festival was a triumph, the public loved it, the traders from all over the UK loved it and, most importantly, we the incumbents of Borough Market and the market trustees loved it. Our collaboration with Randolph and Monika, and alongside negotiations with the Borough Market Trust, led to a monthly Borough food farmers' market. We invited independent producers. At that time, farmers' markets, driven by Henrietta Green, were becoming increasingly popular and successful up and down the country, and although we weren't technically a farmers' market, we did have many independent farmers attending.

We took the bold step to make the market weekly. We had traders coming from all four corners of the country – we promised them nothing and they paid no rent, at a time when Borough Market was deep in arrears. Thanks to the Vice Chairman George Nicholson and trustee James Todd, we managed to persuade the remaining trustees to go with this high-risk strategy. To begin with things went well, but public support started to wane, traders stopped coming and we lost some stalwarts in the food world. And then Jason from Neal's Yard Dairy came up with the genius idea of putting produce on a barrow and wheeling it out on to London Bridge to promote the market, which was tucked behind Southwark Cathedral, just out of sight. Slowly but surely people came into the market to shop, and interest grew. We formed a committee with the trustees to go out and find the best fishmonger, beef and pig farmers, and the best olive supplier. Within three years, we had established what is now commonly thought of as the best food market in the UK – with over 100 traders of magnificent produce.

*On the flavour spectrum, salad leaves and lettuces go from
bland to bitter, to peppery, to nutty. Webb's Wonder and
Summer Fine Frisée go best together, in joyous harmony.*

Summer salad with preserved Treviso tardivo leaves

While enjoying hot summer days, you really want something refreshing and light to eat. What could be better than some lovely salad leaves and some of those delicious preserved tardivo leaves that we made earlier in the year? The beautiful pickled tardivo will add sharpness to the salad and you'll make the dressing using the pickling liquor, win-win! You could swap the pumpkin seeds for toasted flaked (slivered) almonds, if you prefer, and add anything delicious you have in your fridge, such as mozzarella, olives or pickled walnuts.

Serves 4

1 head of butter leaf salad, leaves separated

1 radicchio, leaves separated

small handful of sorrel leaves

100g (3½oz) green beans, trimmed

1 tbsp Dijon mustard

2 tbsp pickling liquor from the tardivo (see page 38)

6 tbsp olive oil

4 tbsp pickled Treviso tardivo (see page 38), large pieces roughly chopped

2 large tomatoes, diced

2 tbsp pumpkin seeds, toasted

salt and caster (superfine) sugar, to taste

Make sure your washed salad leaves are completely dry – there is nothing worse than soggy salad leaves ruining an amazing dressing.

Bring a saucepan of salted water to a boil and add the green beans. Blanch for 1 minute, then drain and refresh them under cold running water. Pat them dry on kitchen paper and cut them into halves or thirds.

Tear or chop the dry salad leaves into bitesize pieces and tip them into a large mixing bowl.

In another bowl combine the mustard with the pickling liquor and slowly add the olive oil, whisking continuously to emulsify the dressing. Season with salt and sugar to taste.

Add the beans, the pickled tardivo and the tomatoes to the salad leaves, pour over the dressing and add the toasted pumpkin seeds. Mix gently to coat the ingredients in the dressing, then serve.

Pickled mixed radishes

Pickled radishes are something you always should have in your larder – they are delicious added to smoked mackerel sandwiches or to serve with a steak when you need something crunchy and pickled to complement the dish and to cut through the oiliness or smokiness. Get creative and cut the radishes any way that takes your fancy. Any radishes work – breakfast, watermelon or even mooli. A mixture, as in this recipe, makes for an amazing-looking pickle jar.

Makes 1 medium–large jar

1 bunch of breakfast radishes (skin on)

1 red meat radish, peeled

1 watermelon radish, peeled

1 mooli, peeled

200ml (7fl oz) apple cider or white wine vinegar

100g (3½oz) caster (superfine) sugar

pinch of salt

However you want to slice or dice the radishes is up to you – but they must all be the same size. Fill the jar with the prepped radishes.

In a small saucepan, combine the vinegar with the sugar, salt and 300ml (10½fl oz) of water. Place the pan over a high heat and bring the liquid to a boil, then reduce the heat and simmer for 1 minute. Pour the hot pickling liquor over the radishes and seal the jar with the lid. Turn the jar upside down and leave the contents of the jar to cool down.

Once cold, turn the jar the right way up and store it in a cool, dry place for up to 6 months. Once opened, store the pickles in the fridge use them within 1 week.

26

Bing cherries / *Alphonso mangoes* / *French Charentais melon* / *Italian Cantaloupe melon* / *Italian Torpedo watermelon* / *Kent gooseberries* / *Panach' blackberries* / *Panach' blueberries* / *Panach' gooseberries* / *Raspberries – French Tulameen raspberries* / *Strawberries – Gariguette, Mara des Bois* / *French apricots* / *Pêche blanc and pêche jaune* / *Kentish wild strawberries* / *Dill* / *French basil* / *Kentish mint – many varieties* / *Marjoram* / *Norfolk marsh samphire* / *Oregano* / *Sea purslane* / *Sorrel* / *Sussex courgette (zucchini) flowers* / *Fresh almonds* / *Early Tomatoes – Italian summer varieties, Outdoor varieties, Provence* / *Baby mixed leaves Campania* / *Chalke Valley watercress* / *Italian wild rocket (arugula)* / *Mizuna and Tatsoi leaf* / *Endives – Pis-en-lit (dandelion), Summer fine frisée* / *Feuille de chêne* *(oak leaf lettuce)* / *Italian Cos* / *Red and green Butterhead* / *Salanova salad* / *Surrey Little Gems* / *Breakfast radish* / *Italian celery* / *Surrey Downs spring onions* / *Bell peppers* / *Padrón peppers* / *Pimiento Asado del Bierzo* / *Beans – Broad (fava) from Worcester, Extra fine French, Kent Bobby, Runner from Worcester* / *Yorkshire peas* / *Norfolk asparagus* / *Brittany cauliflower* / *Young Italian spinach* / *Chinese bok choy* / *Artichokes – Camus globe, Violet baby artichokes from Apuli* / *French round courgette* / *Mushrooms – Cauliflower, Chicken of the Woods, Horse, Puffball* / *Young French leeks* / *Potatoes – Ile de Ré, Noirmoutier* / *Baby veg – Essex beetroot, carrots, fennel, and turnips* / *Italian fennel* / *Nantes carrots* / *Radishes – Kent, Red and white long French*

Cherry
Bing, Bing, Bing: Jackpot!

The British cherry season is special to me. Wild cherries have been growing in the UK for thousands of years, but it was good old Henry VIII who ordered the first sweet cherry trees to be planted in his orchards in Teynham, Kent, in 1533, after he tasted the fruit in Flanders. His head fruiterer, Richard Harris (remember him from page 18?), planted a "mother" orchard of around 40 hectares (100 acres) from which other superior trees were propagated. We think that this was the start of commercial fruit growing in this country.

Cherry orchards then flourished in Kent for hundreds of years with almost every village and area having commercial orchards growing many varieties. In 1957, a national audit of fruit trees revealed that there were 737,000 cherry trees growing in Britain with over 75 per cent of those in Kent. However, sadly, this is no longer the case.

We have great conditions in this country to grow cherries. But, in recent years, as with many other fabulous products, cheap imports have impacted the home market despite the fact that cherries do not travel well. (Like peas and asparagus, cherries should ideally be eaten soon after picking.) However, it's not all doom and gloom – the UK cherry industry is on the up thanks to the efforts of folk like Raymond Blanc and Henrietta Green, who champion local, regional and British produce and encourage large corporations to follow their lead. In the last few years, there's been an increase in demand for English cherries and new orchards have been planted.

So where do we buy our cherries from at Turnips? The Turnips' cherry season starts in France in May with Folfar and Rainier cherries from the Pyrenees. Then, we travel to the foothills of Mont Ventoux in Provence. We end our wonderful journey back in the UK in Hereford, with Bing cherries, from the end of June. There are many wonderful varieties available, but we concentrate on just a few, focusing on flavour. Once we get to Hereford, our cherry journey reaches its high point, and we stop. We have never seen a decline in English cherries – every year we have been supplied with beautiful fruits from our farm agents in Herefordshire. Depending on the weather, from the last week of June through the whole of July, we revel in the large, deep-red Bing variety that can ably compete with fruit from anywhere else in the world.

Bing cherries were first grown in the late 1880s in Oregon by a horticulturist named Seth Lewelling and his Manchurian Chinese foreman Ah Bing, after whom the cherry is named. Arguably, Bings are the most popular variety in the USA, and they are fast becoming so here. They are large and juicy, with dark purple skin around their deep-red flesh. They are equally delicious eaten fresh or turned into preserves.

> "Cherry orchards then flourished in Kent for hundreds of years with almost every village and area having commercial orchards."

We need to protect and celebrate our world-class British cherries, enjoying them fresh during their short season when they are at their best. I find it's almost impossible to buy a bag of juicy, ripe cherries and not eat at least half of them before I get home. And when the fruit is this good, who can blame any one of us for that? At the same time, I urge you to make the most of this incredible seasonal fruit and preserve as much as you can to enjoy later in the year. You won't regret it.

A fair(way) breakfast

I'm up with the lark this morning and I'm a man on a mission. Last week I spotted a few wild strawberries by the third tee at my local golf club and I'm going to see how many I can pick today. I need to be there at first light as Johnny the green keeper doesn't like me rummaging around in the undergrowth, even though I have permission from the powers-that-be (a bribe of a table at the restaurant goes a long way). It's a ten-minute journey by car. Dawn is just breaking, and it can't be much later than 4.30am – Sapphire, my dog, is somewhat confused as to why she needs to be my accomplice at this hour.

Lovely – the strawberries are still here, and I've filled nearly two punnets on my first recce, but for the next two hours I come up blank. On the eleventh fairway there is an avenue of cherry trees that look promising, but on closer inspection the fruit are bitter and inedible. I decide I'll wait until I get home and tuck into the first delivery of Herefordshire Bings that have just arrived. Then, I find a few chanterelles – enough to put in an omelette, so I'm happy. I dodge Johnny on the 16th fairway and happily Sapphire and I are back home in time for breakfast.

Will it be the omelette, or a nice bowl of bircher muesli topped with fragrant wild strawberries and some of the other beautiful fruits that are around right now? It's a no-brainer: the strawberries are so fragile that they deteriorate while you're looking at them, so they are the first I eat. I'll mix them with some Tulameen raspberries (see page 142), Panach'Fruits blueberries, apricots from Roussillon, a good dollop of Comice Pear Compôte (see page 229) and a final flourish of strawberry mint flowers. There's no need to add honey as the compôte is sweet enough.

I check in with Michael, my trusted forager, who tells me that my fungi are actually "false chanterelles" and I should chuck them out immediately. Remember kids: always double check when picking mushrooms – you may not have a professional forager on speed-dial, but Roger Phillips's book *Mushrooms* is invaluable for identification.

After breakfast, I head to Brogdale to see what fruit they have for me. At Turnips we have a soft spot for our friends at the Brogdale National Fruit Collections in Kent, which includes over 4,000 varieties of fruit trees and bushes grown in more than 61 hectares (150 acres) of farmland – the largest collection of trees and plants of its kind in the world. Although this is not necessarily a specialist grower, Brogdale undertakes important work. With little government funding, Brogdale's maintenance for identifying and preserving heritage fruit relies on donations, visitors, and fruit sales from the vast orchards. The collection even helps to develop new, improved cultivars.

Apples, pears, medlars, plums, damsons, cherries, gooseberries and soft fruits all make their way from Brogdale to our stand at Borough. We cherry pick (see what I did there) from their produce and sell it as "Brogdale to Borough" to our customers. Tulameen raspberries, Mara des Bois strawberries, Earliblue blueberries and, starting in early August, the Loch Ness blackberry.

Brogdale uses traditional farming methods for its produce, all grown outdoors in the correct soil conditions. Heritage fruit has a limited shelf life, so we buy as much as we can get, and anything not sold on the market or to our restaurant customers goes into the Turnips' kitchen to be preserved.

Bing cherries in vodka

This recipe is for adults only! I remember from my childhood that downstairs in the cellar of our house there was a shelf that us kids couldn't reach. On that shelf there were a couple of bottles of dark red liquid, but we didn't know what that liquid was. When I was old enough, my dad allowed me to try it – and he gave me the recipe. This cherry-infused vodka is thick, full of flavour and, of course, has a kick! I have suggested using Bing cherries as they are in season right now, but you can use whatever sweet, dark red cherries you prefer.

Makes about 2.5 litres (85fl oz)

2kg (4lb 8oz) Bing cherries, pitted

800g (1lb 12oz) caster (superfine) sugar

2 litres (70fl oz) vodka (70% alcohol if possible, but the stronger the better)

This recipe couldn't be easier. Tip the cherries into a very large jar or two large jars. Add the sugar, shake to combine, cover and leave on the kitchen counter for 2 days, shaking the jars occasionally.

After 2 days the cherries should have produced a dark red, sugary juice. Pour the vodka into the jars, mix well, cover and store in a cool dark place for at least 6 months before trying.

Once opened, you can enjoy both the boozy cherries and the cherry-infused vodka.

Cherry and dark chocolate tart

In the restaurant we make these tarts in small tins and cut them in half to make two servings (as shown in the photograph), but for easier cooking and serving at home, you make a single tart in an 18cm (7in) fluted tart tin to serve four to six people.

Serves 4–6

For the sorbet

400g (14oz) cherries, pitted

80g (2¾oz) caster (superfine) sugar

25g (1oz) glucose powder

For the sable dough

365g (12¾oz) plain (all-purpose) flour

100g (3½oz) icing (confectioner's) sugar

75g (2½oz) ground almonds

180g (6¼oz) unsalted butter, chilled and cubed

1 extra-large egg

For the chocolate ganache

190g (6¾oz) 57% dark (bittersweet) chocolate, finely chopped

230ml (7¾fl oz) double (heavy) cream

40ml (1¼fl oz) glucose syrup

40g (1¼oz) unsalted butter, cubed, at room temperature

To serve

20 cherries, halved or quartered and pitted

edible flowers and micro lemon balm, to decorate

Make the sorbet. Whizz the pitted cherries in a food processor until as smooth as possible. Pass the purée through a fine-mesh sieve into a saucepan. Add the caster sugar, glucose and 70ml (2¼fl oz) of water. Cook over a low heat to dissolve the sugar, but do not boil.

Strain the purée again into a clean bowl and leave it to cool. Chill it for 2 hours, then churn it in an ice-cream machine, until firm. Scoop the sorbet into a freezerproof container and freeze until you're ready to serve (overnight is best).

Make the dough. Tip the flour, icing sugar and ground almonds into a food processor. Add the butter and whizz on a low speed until the mixture resembles crumble. Add the egg and whizz briefly to combine and bring the mixture together into a dough. Turn the dough out on to a clean work surface and knead it very briefly into a smooth ball. Roll the pastry in between two sheets of baking paper to a disk about 2mm (¹⁄₁₆) thick. Use the pastry disk to line the tart tin, with the excess overhanging. Prick the base with a fork and freeze for 20 minutes.

Meanwhile, preheat the oven to 170°C/150°C fan/325°F/Gas 3. Line the frozen tart case with baking paper and fill it with baking beans. Transfer the lined tart tin to a baking sheet and blind bake the pastry case for 10–12 minutes, until crisp, firm and golden. Using a serrated knife trim any excess pastry from the edge of the tart and whizz the trimmings into a crumble.

To make the ganache, tip the chocolate into a bowl. Bring the cream and glucose to a boil in a small saucepan and pour the liquid over the chopped chocolate. Mix well to melt the chocolate into the hot cream until fully combined. Add the butter and mix again until melted and thoroughly combined. Pour the warm ganache into the baked pastry case, spread it level and chill the tart for 2 hours, until set.

To serve, arrange the cut cherries on the top of the ganache, then slice the tart into servings. Arrange a little pile of pastry crumble alongside each slice and place a scoop of cherry sorbet on top of the crumble. Decorate with edible flowers and micro lemon balm.

27

Padrón peppers / *Alphonso mangoes* / *French Charentais melon* / *Italian Cantaloupe melon* / *Italian Torpedo watermelon* / *Kent gooseberries* / *French Tulameen raspberries* / *Panach' blackberries* / *Panach' blueberries* / *Strawberries – Gariguette, Kent Christine, Mara des Bois* / *Bing cherries* / *French apricots* / *Pêche blanche and pêche jaune* / *Kentish wild strawberries* / *Kentish mint – many varieties* / *Norfolk herbs* / *Norfolk marsh samphire* / *Sea purslane* / *Sussex courgette (zucchini) flowers* / *Fresh almonds* / *Tomatoes – Italian summer varieties, Main crop Provence, Outdoor varieties* / *Baby mixed leaves Campania* / *Chalke Valley watercress* / *Italian wild rocket (arugula)* / *Mizuna and Tatsoi leaf* / *Endives – Pisen-lit (dandelion), Summer fine frisée* / *Feuille de chêne (oak leaf lettuce)* /

Italian Cos / *Red and green Butterhead* / *Salanova salad* / *Surrey Little Gems* / *Breakfast radish* / *Sussex celery* / *Surrey Downs spring onions* / *Bell peppers* / *Pimiento Asado del Bierzo* / *Beans – Broad (fava) from Worcester, Extra fine French, Kent Bobby, Runner from Worcester* / *Yorkshire peas* / *Norfolk asparagus* / *Brittany cauliflower* / *Young Italian spinach* / *Chinese bok choy* / *Artichoke – Camus globe, Violet baby artichokes from Apuli* / *French round courgette* / *Mushrooms – Cauliflower, Chicken of the Woods, Horse, Puffball* / *Young French leeks* / *Potatoes – Ile de Ré, Noirmoutier* / *Baby veg – Essex beetroot, fennel, turnips* / *Italian fennel* / *Nantes carrots* / *Radishes – Kent, Red and white long French*

Padrón Pepper
The Heat is On

As we've seen, King Henry VIII was instrumental in growing some of the fruit and vegetables that we now take for granted (see page 18). Without him, Britain would not be so colourful in produce terms. I know he put a few people to death – I'm not saying he was necessarily a nice guy, I'm just saying that we should be grateful to him for his contribution to our culinary landscape.

Now it's the turn of Christopher Columbus, who voyaged to the New World in 1492 to discover lands, spices and trade routes that would enrich his Spanish masters, King Ferdinand and Queen Isabella. At the time, pepper was one of the most expensive commodities and the race was on to find other routes to the spice-growing regions of the world. On his way westward to East India, Columbus stumbled across the Caribbean and the Americas. While he was there, he was more than likely the first European to encounter chillies. A year later, following his second voyage, he returned to Spain with chilli seeds, and within the next 50 or so years, chillies had spread across the world.

Evidence of chilli use – for health and in cooking – has been found in Central and South America dating as far back as around 6,000BCE. Once in Europe, chillies grew first in monastery gardens in Portugal and Spain, planted for medicinal purposes, but they soon became a cheap substitute for the highly expensive black pepper.

With summer comes heat, in more ways than one! Source outdoor-variety chillies from very hot countries – such as Spain for your Padrón peppers, which give good flavour, too.

Today, chilli is one of the most important culinary flavourings in the world. From the Far East to India, across Africa, Europe and, of course, the Americas, it has been on a pretty impressive journey to appear in regional cooking in every corner of the globe. Peppers are members of the nightshade family, which also includes tomato, aubergine (eggplant) and potato, so it's not surprising that these three ingredients have a particular affinity for one another and are used in many tapas dishes.

There are hundreds of varieties of chilli, but at Turnips we concentrate on a just few that give us year-round supply from all over the world. The heat of any individual chilli is assessed according to the internationally recognized Scoville Heat Scale, which runs from a score of 0 (not at all spicy-hot) to 2.2 million (don't even try). More on that on the opposite page, but in the meantime, I want to make the point that heat and flavour are not the same thing. Flavour varies depending on where and how the chillies are grown. Jalapeños, one of the most popular chillies, are firm, smooth, torpedo-shaped, deep green and relatively mild Scoville-wise (2500–8000 Scoville Heat Units/SHU), with a fresh and grassy flavour. The best come from Mexico. The lantern-shaped Scotch bonnet from the West Indies appears in colours from green and yellow to orange and red, and has a hot, fruity and sweet flavour. Although Scotch bonnets are not the hottest chillies you'll find, they are punchy enough for the most serious heat junkies (100,000–350,000 SHU). Thai bird's eye chillies (from Thailand, obviously) are small, finger-shaped and red or green. These give good heat (50,000–100,000 SHU) – proving that size isn't everything.

However, rather than any blow-your-socks-off chillies, the chilli I really want to focus on is the Spanish Padrón pepper. First grown by 17th-century Franciscan monks in their monastery gardens, this chilli began its life in Europe in the town of Padrón in Galicia, northwestern Spain, using seeds that had been brought over from Mexico. Dark green and similar in size to a fresh jalapeño (about 5cm/2in long), but with an irregular and ridged shape, Padrón peppers are harvested when underripe and have thin and slightly

> "There are hundreds of varieties of chilli, but at Turnips we concentrate on just a few that give us year-round supply from all over the world."

soft flesh, with a waxy skin that is less thick than other chillies. Sautéed whole over a high heat in a little olive oil until the skins blister, Padrón peppers are often served hot as a tapas dish, scattered with sea salt. You eat the lot – including the seeds – except the stalk, which acts as a useful handle to pick up each pepper with your fingers. What really defines this *pimentón*, though, compared with any other, is that the heat is not consistent from pepper to pepper. There's an element of playing chilli Russian (or Spanish) roulette: you can go from a delicious, fresh burst of flavour (about 500 SHU) to a moderate heat explosion in your mouth (about 2,000 SHU) that takes you that little bit by surprise. There's a one-in-ten chance of hitting the hot-pod-jackpot. Keep in mind the Galician saying "*Os pementos de Padrón, uns pican e outros non*" – "Padrón peppers, some are hot, some are not".

The province of A Coruña, where Padrón lies, is well known for its lush, green landscape and maritime climate with milder temperatures than most of Spain. The high rainfall, fertile soil and fairly constant temperature provides the ideal growing conditions for these peppers, which have a season from May to September. The peppers get hotter in flavour as the season progresses. Padrón grown in a specific area of A Coruña district in Galicia have a PDO (Protected Designation of Origin) from the Spanish government and are given the name Pemento de Herbón.

The Scoville Heat Scale

How do you test how hot a chilli pepper is? Don't fear – you don't have to eat each one in a side-by-side taste test. But when cooking with chillies, it's important know what level of heat you can expect from each variety.

In 1912, a pharmacologist named Wilbur Scoville invented a method, now known as the Scoville Heat Scale, whereby it is possible to measure the pungency and heat from peppers and chillies based on their capsaicin content. Capsaicin is the chemical compound that causes the burning sensation when we eat or touch chillies.

To derive the relative heat of the chilli or pepper, an alcohol extract of capsaicin oil from dried chillies was diluted in sugar water and the dilution increased until the sensation of heat disappeared when tested by a panel of tasters. The score on the scale, the Scoville Heat Unit (SHU), represents the level of dilution required for the sensation of heat to disappear completely. For example, if a pepper rates at 5,000 SHUs, then the extract would need to be diluted 5,000 times before the heat is barely detectable.

It's not an exact science and Scoville found that there were still some varied heat levels in the same varieties. He put this down to different farming practices and growing conditions, crop by crop.

And the process of developing chillies and measuring their heat is not over. Farmers are still hybridizing chillies and each new hybrid variety needs to be officially named and given a Scoville rating. There's even an ongoing competition to create the world's hottest chilli.

Fermented Scotch bonnet sauce

I'm in love with the acidic and spicy flavour of sriracha sauce and I use it on almost anything. If you can get hold of Scotch bonnets, you can make something very similar yourself. It's delicious added to mayo, which will temper the heat, or you can use it straight if you prefer things super-spicy. Make sure you wear rubber gloves when you prep these little peppers – they are really, really hot and will sting your skin!

Makes 1 small jar

500g (1lb 2oz) Scotch bonnet chillies, deseeded and finely chopped

2 large red peppers, deseeded and sliced

1 garlic bulb, cloves separated, peeled and chopped

4 tomatoes, diced

2 Cevenne onions, thinly sliced

about 2 tsp Maldon salt or fermenting salt

500ml (17fl oz) filtered water

Tip the Scotch bonnets, peppers, garlic, tomatoes and onions into a bowl. Weigh the vegetables (if you have digital scales, zero the weight of the bowl first to give just the vegetable weight), make a note of the weight, and tip them into a large, sterilized jar.

Calculate 1 per cent of the weight of the vegetables, add this weight of salt to the filtered water and stir to dissolve.

Pour the brine over the vegetables to just cover. Press down with a fermenting weight and leave the veg at room temperature to ferment for 2 weeks, opening then re-sealing the jar every day or so to burp the contents.

After a fortnight, all the vegetables will be very soft and smell hot and sour. Strain them through a sieve over a bowl. Blend the vegetables in a food processor until smooth, adding a little of the strained brine if you need it. Pour the sauce into a clean jar and store it in the fridge for up to 6 months. Use the sauce within 1 month once opened.

Padrón peppers stuffed with pork

When it comes to spicy snacks, this one will be like Russian roulette – with one in ten Padrón peppers being very spicy, it's a gamble! These peppers make an amazing canapé to start your meal or a beautiful beer snack.

Serves 4

1 tbsp olive oil

1 banana shallot, finely sliced

3 garlic cloves, crushed

300g (10½oz) pork mince (ground pork)

½ tsp smoked paprika

4 spring onions (scallions), trimmed and finely sliced

20 Padrón peppers, stalks removed and seeds shaken out

150g (5½oz) cheddar, grated

salt and freshly ground black pepper

Preheat the oven to 180°C/160°C fan/350°F/Gas 4.

Heat the oil in a small frying pan over a medium heat. Add the shallot and garlic and sweat for 5 minutes, until softened. Tip the vegetables into a bowl and leave them to cool slightly. Add the pork, paprika, and half of the spring onions and season well with salt and pepper. Mix to combine.

Spoon the pork mixture into the peppers. Place the peppers on a baking tray and bake them for 10–15 minutes, until the pork is cooked through and golden brown.

Cover the peppers with the grated cheese and return them to the oven for a minute or so until melted and bubbling. Transfer to a serving plate and scatter with the remaining spring onions to serve.

Scottish Girolle mushrooms / King Kesar mangoes / French Charentais melon / Italian Cantaloupe melon / Italian Torpedo watermelon / French Tulameen raspberries / Panach' blackberries / Panach' blueberries / Strawberries – Gariguette, Kent Christine, Mara des Bois / Bing cherries / French apricots / Pêche blanc and pêche jaune / Kentish wild strawberries / Wild bilberries / Kent gooseberries / Kentish mint – many varieties / Norfolk herbs / Norfolk marsh samphire / Sea purslane / Sussex courgette (zucchini) flowers / Fresh almonds / Tomatoes – Italian summer varieties, Main crop Provence, Outdoor varieties / Baby mixed leaves Campania / Chalke Valley watercress / Italian wild rocket (arugula) / Mizuna and Tatsoi leaf / Endives – Pis-en-lit (dandelion), Summer fine frisée / Feuille de chêne (oak leaf lettuce) / Italian Cos / Red and green Butterhead / Surrey Little Gems / Breakfast radish / Surrey cucumbers / Sussex celery / Surrey Downs spring onions / Bell peppers / Padrón peppers / Pimiento Asado del Bierzo / Beans – Extra fine French, Kent Bobby, Runner beans from Worcester / Kent broccoli / Boston cauliflower / Rainbow chard / Natural vine spinach / Young Italian spinach / Chinese bok choy / Somerset Savoy cabbage / Artichokes – Camus globe, Violet baby artichokes from Apuli / Tiger aubergine (eggplant) / Courgettes – Brittany round, French round / Mushrooms – Cauliflower, Chicken of the Woods, Horse, Puffball / Somerset leeks / Potatoes – Ile de Ré, Noirmoutier / Baby veg – Essex beetroot, fennel, turnips / Italian fennel / Kent radish / Somerset bunched carrots

Scottish Girolle
Girolle in One

Off the west coast of Scotland, we find a special, orange curiosity (no, not Donald Trump on his Turnberry golf course) – the Girolle (or Chanterelle) mushroom. From early July until October (weather depending), you will find these stunning fungi buried in their mossy duvets among the Alpine trees of birch, beech, Scots pine and oak. Like Morels and St George mushrooms (see pages 49 and 97, respectively), Girolles are wild – they have a very specific season and require very specific growing conditions. It is impossible to cultivate them. Each mushroom we sell at Turnips has been picked by a licensed forager.

This golden beauty is a much sought-after mushroom – huge quantities are sold in the London markets and to fine-dining establishments all over the country. At the beginning of the season, when Girolles are scarce, they command a high price. But, as the season gets under way and they become more abundant, cost falls significantly. The trick to guaranteeing your supply is to find your own "sender" agent up in Scotland, who will courier the mushrooms southward to London. On numerous occasions rows have erupted in the markets because the vendor might have sold a reserved mushroom order to another buyer who offered more cash (gazumping is not limited to the property market!). This is an underhand practice that was scorned upon in the early days when a handshake was enough to seal the deal.

The Turnips' supply of Girolles has been well provided for by Scotch Johnny for years now. Known as Jock to his friends (and you need to be one if you stand a chance of getting your hands on his specimens – if you know what I mean!), he has an agreement to have sole pickings of mushrooms on one landowner's 810-hectare (2,000-acre) piece of heaven up in Scotland. It's a highly competitive market and there's a lot of "mushroom poaching" that goes on, so it pays to keep schtum on the finer details of who, what, where.

During the summer months, Scotland's conifer and deciduous woodlands provide the best growing conditions, coming alive with these delicious fungi. The mushrooms grow in circles among the moss and heathers, with the bracken providing camouflage, and they return year after year to the same places. Over the season from early July until October, foraging trips with mushroom hunters never fail to amaze me: these guys have their secret areas and know the exact spots where they will find what they're looking for. Further south in the UK, the landscape is less wooded and the chance of finding Girolles in any quantity is unlikely.

Girolles have an almost apricot aroma with a firm texture and fruity, peppery flavour. They smell woodsy, of the forest from where they grow. Cook them gently and simply to preserve their delicate texture and flavour, pairing them with soft herbs such as parsley, tarragon, chervil and chives. Add them to creamy sauces or sauté them in garlic and butter and fold them into an omelette to elevate a humble supper to great heights. Don't be tempted to soak them in water – simply use a soft brush to remove any dirt and then trim the stems with care. Each and every Girolle has been carefully cut from the forest floor by hand – treat it with love and respect.

Aesthetics mean that the French tend to prefer the smallest Girolles and they'll often cook them whole. Not me, though. I think Scottish Girolles are best when you use large mushrooms and simply tear them with your fingers to reveal the stunning white flesh and release their fruity aroma.

> "Girolles have an almost apricot aroma with a firm texture and fruity, peppery taste, they smell woodsy and of the forest from where they grow."

At Turnips, we are wild about mushrooms and have garnered a roaring lunchtime trade with our now legendary wild mushroom risotto (see page 176), cooked fresh on the stand each day, all year round. We use some cultivated mushrooms and whatever wild mushroom is in season at any given time: Morels in late winter, St George in spring, Girolles in summer and ceps, porcini and Penny Buns in autumn.

Turnips' wild mushroom risotto

The longest-serving vegetable stand in Borough Market, Turnips also produces one of the market's most popular cooked-food highlights – its wild mushroom risotto. Made using pearled spelt – an ancient grain that takes on all the flavour of the wild 'shrooms, rather than risotto rice – it is super-quick and super-tasty.

Serves 4

For the stock

1 small onion, roughly chopped

1 small leek, roughly chopped

100g (3 ½ oz) button or chestnut mushrooms, roughly chopped

1 garlic clove, roughly chopped

30g (1oz) mixed dried wild mushrooms

handful of parsley stalks

small bunch of thyme sprigs

2–3 rosemary sprigs

For the risotto

3 tbsp olive oil

4 large shallots, finely chopped

2 garlic cloves, 1 finely chopped, 1 crushed

300g (10 ½ oz) organic pearled spelt

200ml (7fl oz) white wine

100g (3 ½ oz) butter

350g (12oz) mixed wild mushrooms, torn into bitesize pieces

150g (5 ½ oz) chestnut or button mushrooms, halved or quartered

100g (3 ½ oz) Parmesan, grated

small bunch of flat-leaf parsley, chopped

small bunch of chives, chopped

salt and freshly ground black pepper

Start by making the stock. Place the onion, leek, fresh mushrooms and garlic into a large saucepan and cover with about 3 litres (105fl oz) of water. Add the dried mushrooms and all the herbs and place the pan over a high heat. Bring the water to a boil, then reduce the heat and simmer gently for at least 45 minutes – but up to 2 hours would be better to eke out all that flavour. Strain the stock into a clean pan and keep warm.

To make the risotto, heat 1 tablespoon of the olive oil in a saucepan and add the shallots and chopped garlic. Fry over a low heat for 5 minutes, until soft but not coloured. Season with salt and pepper.

Stir in the pearled spelt, coating the grains in the shallots, and add the white wine. Continue to cook for a few minutes, until the wine has almost evaporated, then add one third of the warm stock. Cook over a medium heat, stirring all the time, until the grains have absorbed most of the stock. Add a second third and continue cooking, stirring frequently, until that has been absorbed, too. Add the final third, then lower the heat and simmer for about 15 minutes, stirring most of the time, until the risotto is the consistency of loose porridge and the spelt grains are tender and coated in a rich, creamy sauce.

Meanwhile, cook the mushrooms. Heat the remaining olive oil in a large frying pan with half the butter over a medium heat. Once melted and hot, add all the mushrooms and the crushed garlic. Season with salt and pepper and cook for about 7–8 minutes, until the mushrooms are tender and lightly browned.

Add the remaining butter and two thirds of the Parmesan to the risotto, and check the seasoning, adding more salt and pepper to taste as necessary.

Divide the risotto between 4 shallow serving plates, spoon equal amounts of the sautéed mushrooms on top, and scatter with the remaining Parmesan and chopped herbs. Serve immediately.

Pickled Girolles

OMG – I'm absolutely in love with pickles! But when it comes to Girolles, it's love on a higher level. Whether you are buying Girolles from the market or foraging for them yourself, I think they will make a meal about as good as it gets. You need only a few store-cupboard ingredients for these pickles – and by now if you've already been pickling and preserving throughout the year, you'll be familiar with them. If you can make a larger batch than the amount stated in this recipe – you won't regret it later. Pickled Girolles make a lovely side dish or addition to a salad – which is perfect, really, as, if you have worked your way through the book so far, you already have the shallots and carrots!

Makes 1 medium–large jar

500g (1lb 2oz) Girolles

2 Sand carrots, peeled and coarsely grated

2 banana shallots, sliced

3 garlic cloves, sliced

1 bay leaf

200ml (7fl oz) white wine vinegar

100ml (3½fl oz) white wine

5 black peppercorns

2 tbsp salt

4 tsp caster (superfine) sugar

Carefully clean your mushrooms with a soft brush to remove any dirt. Place them directly into the sterilized storage jar together with the carrots, shallots, garlic and bay leaf.

Pour the vinegar into a small saucepan over a medium heat. Bring it to a boil and leave it to bubble away and reduce by half (about 4–5 minutes). Add the wine and 100ml (3½fl oz) of water and return the liquid to a boil. Add the peppercorns, salt and sugar and stir to dissolve. Pour the liquid over the mushrooms.

Seal the jar tightly with the lid and turn it upside down to create a vacuum. Leave the contents of the jar to cool, then turn the jar the right way up and store the mushrooms in a dry, cool place for up to 6 months. Once opened, store in the fridge and use within 2 weeks.

Dorset blueberries / King Kesar mangoes / French Charentais melon / Italian Cantaloupe melon / Italian Torpedo watermelon / Kent gooseberries / French Tulameen raspberries / Loganberries / Panach' blackberries / Bing cherries / Pêche blanche and pêche jaune / Wild bilberries / Curry leaves / Kentish mint – many varieties / Norfolk herbs / Norfolk marsh samphire / Methi leaves / Sea purslane / Edible flowers from Surrey / Fresh almonds / Tomatoes – Italian summer varieties, Main crop Provence / Baby mixed leaves Campania / Italian wild rocket (arugula) / Mizuna and Tatsoi leaf / Surrey salad leaves / Endives – Pis-en-lit (dandelion), Summer fine frisée / Feuille de chêne (oak leaf lettuce) / Italian Cos / Red and green Butterhead / Surrey Little Gems / Breakfast radish / Sussex celery / Surrey cucumbers / Surrey Downs spring onions / Padrón peppers / Pimiento Asado del Bierzo / Kent broccoli / Boston cauliflower / Rainbow chard / Natural vine spinach / Young Italian spinach / Chinese bok choy / Somerset Savoy cabbage / Camus globe artichoke / Tiger aubergine (eggplant) / Courgettes (zucchini) – Brittany round, Sussex / Mushrooms – Cauliflower, Chicken of the Woods, Puffball, Scottish Girolle, Summer cep / Somerset leeks / Potatoes - Belle de Fontenay, Charlotte, Maris Bard "earlies", Noirmoutier / Essex young beetroot / Italian fennel / Kent radish / Somerset bunched carrots

Dorset Blueberry
Out of the Blue

When Americans talk about European blueberries, they mean wild varieties. Throughout the UK we have different names for wild blueberries: in the North we call them bilberries; in the West Country, whortleberries; in Wales, wimberries; and in Scotland, blaeberries. You might be lucky to find them in small farmers' markets across Europe, but no one grows them commercially. Most exciting for this week, though, is the arrival of the first Dorset blueberries. And, whether it's these or the early season French Panach'Fruits blueberries (*myrtilles*), we owe our blueberry love to North America.

In the early 1950s, David Trehane, a Dorset-based market gardener and horticulturist, took up the offer of free blueberry plants from a parson on Lulu Island in British Columbia, Canada. Those first 80 plants thrived in the sandy, acidic soils of Dorset. Much encouraged by this success, David went on to plant a further 0.4 hectares (1 acre) of around 1,000 bushes. His endeavours became the first commercial blueberry plantation in this country.

> "Those first 80 plants thrived in the sandy, acidic soils of Dorset."

In 2018, the Trehane Blueberry Farm became a Pick Your Own (PYO), rather than growing for wholesale and for supermarkets. For years, the family had battled against cheaper imported berries with uniform shape, standard size, less flavour and a longer shelf life. They decided that instead of lowering their standards to produce more commercial varieties, they would change

Is it any wonder that a fruit that looks so amazing is a superfood? Dorset blueberries' intense flavour is derived from bushes planted in the 1950s by the Trehane family.

direction. Trehane now grows eight varieties of blueberry, including some of the originals that David brought over from Canada. The berries vary in size, firmness and sweetness. Each bush is pruned by hand and the farm has now been certified as organic. For eight weeks of the year, the family opens the farm gates for visitors to enjoy picking and eating their beautiful fruit. The success of this venture has meant that, for Turnips, over the last couple of years it has become increasingly difficult to get wonderful Trehane berries. But, we are still thankful to be able to buy as much as we can.

Blueberries are the one soft fruit that bucks the trend when it comes to shelf life. Supermarket imported berries will lurk happily in the back of the fridge for up to two weeks. Rather than filling your blueberry boots all year round, limit your hit to an eight- to ten-week window, starting with French Panach'Fruits in the middle of June and moving on to the Dorset Blues from mid-July to the end of August. For those of you with green fingers who want to turn them blue, blueberry bushes grow best when cross-pollinated, so always plant a variety to ensure the best crop.

Move over, Alphonso

It's the third week in July, summer is in full swing, the heat is ramping up and there's a steady stream of fantastic fruits coming into the warehouse. Among them, though, as the Alphonso season comes to an end (we enjoyed them fresh in May; see page 111) is our incredible Alphonso mango pulp direct from Mumbai. Adnaan, our man in accounts, has a cousin in India who sources it for us. Each year at the end of the Alphonso season, the Indian farmers make preserves, purées, canned mango slices – and the pulp. We, in turn, make our smoothies, juices and ice creams from it. By moving further north through India, we can extend our season for supplying fragrant fresh mangoes, too – the Kesar mango has just started to arrive from Gujarat in western India.

A while ago I was fortunate enough to visit Mr Singh, our mango supplier, in the Western International Market near Heathrow. I clearly remember the first time Mr Singh invited me down to the market. At the time, Pacific Rim or "fusion" cuisine was very much in vogue and I was buying many products from him for my restaurant customers. For this style of cooking, the chefs needed such exotics as green mango and paw paws, bird's eye chillies, baby shallots, pea aubergines, and lots of mangoes.

When I arrived at Mr Singh's warehouse, he summoned me over and we went out to the back where his trucks unloaded the produce. Sitting there on the forecourt were three large metal containers, each about the size of half a shipping container. He unlocked one of them, opening the doors to release a heat that was something else. After the heat, though, came a wave of sweet, fruity perfume. He explained that the farmers pick the mangoes from the trees while they are still slightly underripe. While the sun's heat is still on them, the mangoes are sealed in the metal containers that are air-freighted to the UK the next morning. Meanwhile, the warmth in the containers continues to ripen the fruit to perfection, which results in this burst of heat and sweet mango aroma when the doors are opened. It was an experience that I'll never forget.

Panach'Fruits blueberries, jasmine, white chocolate

One day, Charlie brought some amazing blueberries and when we tasted them, we knew they deserved something special and so we came up with this stunning dessert. The recipe is a little difficult and more cheffy than others in this book, but the end results are more than worth the effort. Prepare all of the elements the day before you plan to serve. You will need eight individual mousse moulds – ours have hollows for the final layer of jelly, but regular oval silicone moulds are easier to get hold of.

Serves 8

For the almond dacquoise

150g (5½oz) icing (confectioner's) sugar

150g (5½oz) ground almonds

200g (7oz) egg white

60g (2oz) caster (superfine) sugar

For the meringues

50g (1¾oz) caster (superfine) sugar

50g (1¾oz) egg white

50g (1¾oz) icing (confectioner's) sugar

¼ tsp blueberry powder

For the white chocolate and jasmine mousse

1 platinum-grade gelatine leaf

165g (5¾oz) white chocolate, finely chopped

60ml (2fl oz) full-fat milk

200ml (7fl oz) double (heavy) cream

1 tsp jasmine tea

For the sorbet

600g (14oz) Panach'Fruits blueberries

85g (3oz) caster (superfine) sugar

25g (1oz) glucose powder

Continued overleaf...

Preheat the oven to 190°C/170°C fan/375°F/Gas 5 and line a large baking tray with baking paper.

Make the dacquoise. Sift the icing sugar and ground almonds together into a bowl. Whisk the egg white and caster sugar together until they will hold soft peaks. Gradually add the sifted icing sugar and ground almonds to the meringue, folding in using a silicone spatula. Spread the dacquoise on to the lined tray and bake for 10 minutes, until firm. Reduce the oven to 120°C/100°C fan/235°F/Gas ½−1.

Leave the dacquoise to cool, then cut out 8 pieces the same shape as the mousse mould and use one piece to line the base of each mould. Crumble the trimmings, tip them on to a baking tray and dry them out in the cool oven for about 20 minutes. Leave to cool and then whizz the crumbs in a food processor until they look like breadcrumbs.

For the meringues, reduce the oven to 100°C/80°C fan/200°F/Gas ½ and line a small baking tray with baking paper.

Whisk the caster sugar and egg white until they hold stiff peaks. Sift the icing sugar and blueberry powder into the bowl and fold in until thoroughly combined.

Spoon the meringue into a small piping bag, snip the end into a 2–3mm (1/16–⅛in) nozzle and pipe very small meringue droplets on the lined baking tray. Bake for 30–40 minutes, until crisp and firm.

Make the mousse. Soak the gelatine leaf in a bowl of cold water for 5 minutes. Tip the white chocolate into another bowl.

Combine the milk, 30ml (1fl oz) of the double cream and the jasmine tea in a small saucepan and bring to a boil. Drain the gelatine and squeeze out any excess water, add it to the hot milk mixture and stir until melted. Strain the mixture into the bowl over the white chocolate and leave to melt for 2 minutes without stirring.

Continued overleaf...

For the ganache

2 platinum-grade gelatine leaves

170g (6oz) white chocolate, finely chopped

100ml (3½fl oz) full-fat milk

1 tsp glucose syrup

210ml (7½fl oz) double (heavy) cream

For the jelly

160g (5¾oz) blueberry purée (from the sorbet)

50g (1¾) caster (superfine) sugar

¼ tsp agar agar

To serve

handful of blueberries, halved

edible flowers

Meanwhile, whip the remaining cream to soft peaks. Fold the cream into the white chocolate mixture and spoon the mousse into the individual moulds on top of the dacquoise base in an even layer. Freeze the mousses until they are solid.

To make the sorbet, whizz the blueberries in a food processor until they are as smooth as possible. Pass the purée through a fine-mesh sieve into a saucepan, then separate out 160g (5¾oz) and set it aside for the jelly. Add the caster sugar, glucose powder and 70ml (2¼fl oz) of water to the pan. Cook the mixture over a low heat to dissolve the sugar, but do not let the syrup boil.

Strain the syrup into a clean bowl and leave it to cool. Then, chill it for 2 hours. Once it's chilled, churn the sorbet mixture in an ice-cream machine according to the manufacturer's instructions, until set. Scoop the sorbet into a freezer-proof container and freeze it until you're ready to serve.

To make the ganache, soak the gelatine leaves in a bowl of cold water for 5 minutes. Tip the white chocolate into another bowl. Pour the milk and glucose into a small saucepan and place it over a low–medium heat. Drain, squeeze out and add the gelatine. Bring the mixture to a boil, then pour it over the chopped chocolate. Mix well to melt the chocolate into the hot milk. Slowly add the cream, mixing until smooth. Spoon the mixture into a piping bag and chill it for 24 hours before using.

To make the jelly, pour the blueberry purée into a small pan, add the sugar and agar agar and place the pan over a medium heat. Stirring continuously, bring the mixture to a boil, then cook for 1 minute and pour it on to a tray to quickly cool and set. Once the jelly has set, blend it in a food processor until smooth, then strain it through a fine-mesh sieve into a bowl. Spoon the jelly into a piping bag or little squeezy bottle and chill.

Remove the mousse moulds from the freezer 30 minutes before you intend to serve and carefully unmould each one on to a serving plate, gently arranging each so that the mousse is uppermost.

Pipe or spoon a little jelly on top of each mousse to create a final layer over the mousse (in the restaurant, we fill a hollow in our moulds, as in the photograph), then arrange some crumbled dacquoise around one side. Pipe jelly and ganache dots on top of the crumble and arrange halved blueberries, meringues and edible flowers among them. Spoon a little pile of crumble alongside the mousse, then top it with a scoop of sorbet to serve.

Pickled blueberries

Pickled blueberries pair particularly well with gamey, wild red meats, such as venison or boar. You could adapt this easy recipe to use sea buckthorn berries, if you prefer.

Makes 1 small–medium jar

500g (1lb 2oz) blueberries
240ml (8fl oz) rice wine vinegar
3 tbsp caster (superfine) sugar
pinch of salt
1 star anise
2 allspice berries
1 thyme sprig

Pick over the blueberries and remove any that are overripe and damaged, then wash them in a sieve under cold, running water and pack them into a sterilized jar.

In a small saucepan, combine the vinegar, sugar, salt, star anise, allspice and thyme and place the pan over a medium heat. Bring the liquid to a boil, then reduce the heat and simmer for 30 seconds. Pour the hot liquid over the berries to cover.

Seal the jar with the lid and stand it in a clean saucepan. Pour enough water into the pan to come two thirds of the way up the side of the jar. Bring the water to a boil over a medium heat and simmer for 5 minutes to pasteurize the contents of the jar.

Remove the jar from the pan and leave it to cool. Store the pickled blueberries in a cool, dry place for up to 1 year. Once opened, store in the fridge and consume within 1 week.

Roscoff onions come from Brittany to the UK, originally brought here by "Johnnies", French onion-sellers who, in the 1950s, literally "pedalled" their wares from their bicycles.

30

Roscoff onions / *King Kesar mangoes* / *French Charentais melon* / *Italian Cantaloupe melon* / *Italian Torpedo watermelon* / *Dorset blueberries* / *French Tulameen raspberries* / *Kent gooseberries* / *Loganberries* / *Panach' blackberries* / *Bing cherries* / *Peaches – Italian Flat, Pêche blanche, pêche jaune, Pêche de Vigne* / *Plums – French Mirabelle, Italian Drago Sanguine* / *Nectavigne* / *Wild bilberries* / *Curry leaves* / *Kentish mint – many varieties* / *Norfolk herbs* / *Norfolk marsh samphire* / *Methi leaves* / *Sea purslane* / *Edible flowers from Surrey* / *Tomatoes – Italian summer, Main crop Provence* / *Baby mixed leaves Campania* / *Mizuna and Tatsoi leaf* / *Surrey salad leaves* / *Endives – Pis-en-lit (dandelion), Summer fine frisée* / *Feuille de chêne (oak leaf lettuce)* / *Italian Cos* / *Red and green Butterhead* / *Surrey Little Gems* / *Breakfast radish* / *Surrey cucumbers* / *Sussex celery* / *Surrey Downs spring onions* / *Padrón peppers* / *Pimiento Asado del Bierzo* / *Italian Friggitelli peppers* / *Kent broccoli* / *Boston cauliflower* / *Rainbow chard* / *Natural vine spinach* / *Young Italian spinach* / *Chinese bok choy* / *Somerset Savoy cabbage* / *Artichokes – Brittany baby, Camus globe, Jerusalem* / *Tiger aubergine (eggplant)* / *Courgettes (zucchini) – Brittany round, Sussex, Trombetta* / *Mushrooms – Cauliflower, Chicken of the Woods, Puffball, Scottish Girolle, Summer cep* / *Cevenne onions* / *Somerset leeks* / *Potatoes – Belle de Fontenay, Charlotte, Maris Bard "earlies", Noirmoutier* / *Squash – Italian Turban, Potimarron* / *Celeriac* / *Essex young beetroot* / *Italian fennel* / *Somerset bunched carrots* / *Kent radish* / *Kohlrabi*

Roscoff Onion
Oh Johnnie Boy! The Brits, the Brits are Calling!

We grow onions in Kent, Essex and Surrey, "home counties" that surround London. From Kent, we source a brown onion that is ideal to use in stocks and basic cooking. But if you're looking for an onion for optimum flavour, you'll need something else. I want you to think of onions as a cornerstone of your cooking, not something to chuck in with barely more than a passing glance. Cooking is all about layering flavour, which starts from the ground (or onion) up. Why spend money on special ingredients if you don't lay solid flavour foundations first?

> "But, what makes a great onion? It needs to be sweet and have a great depth of flavour and – importantly – it needs to caramelize perfectly."

But, what makes a great onion? It needs to be sweet and have a great depth of flavour and – importantly – it needs to caramelize perfectly. The term caramelized when talking about cooking onions is a misnomer. The process is a Maillard reaction, in which sugars and amino acids in the protein content of the onion break down in the presence of heat to produce that amazing umami flavour and golden colour.

To find these superior onions, we travel to the town of Roscoff in Brittany, France. Twinned with Great Torrington in Devon, this picturesque little town with its striking architecture became a major ferry crossing in the 1970s. It's from here that the "Onion Johnnies" would make their way to the UK, dressed in berets and blue-and-white-striped tops, to sell their strings of onions from their push bikes.

In which case, then, the stereotypical image of a Frenchman on a bike with strings of onions around his neck is not without credence. In around 1815, Henri Ollivier filled a cargo boat with his onions to try his luck selling them in England. He tapped into a brand-new market, and from then until just after World War II, onion sellers travelled to Britain, literally pedalling their wares up and down the country. These sellers were often called Yann, a common Breton name for Jean in French or John in English, and so were given the nickname Onion Johnnies. At their peak in the 1920s, there were around 1,400 Onion Johnnies plying their trade in Britain, selling onions door to door throughout the summer and autumn. At the end of the season, they would return to France, only to come back to the same patch again the next year.

The onions are still sold plaited into a braid with the largest onion, the *penn kapitenn*, or captain of the ship, at the bottom. Not only do the braids look beautiful, but they provide the perfect way to hang and store the onions.

Grown in the fertile soils of Brittany (in an area called the "Golden Belt" for its prolific production of early fruit and veg) since the 17th century, Roscoffs have a mellow, sweet flavour. Their pink skins lend them the occasional name of rosé onions. The oceanic climate and light rainfall mean that Roscoffs need little intervention to develop their flavour and were awarded the French AOC in 2009 and the PDO (see page 15) by the European Union in 2010. The Roscoff onion festival occurs in the town in August every year.

With the arrival of the Roscoff, the onion journey is complete. We saw the imported Chilean large white onion when our European onions were not available from March to June, then the first shoots of the Three-cornered leek from Kent in late February. We have the Catalans' beautiful Calcot onions from Spain from February to early May, and then we move to Italy for the stunning Cipollini onion from May to September. And, finally, we have the Roscoff, which arrives around now and you can store right up until next February. Who said onions were dull? Certainly not Johnnie.

Land of plenty

We see an abundance of world-class fruit and veg when international seasons converge. There's an eclectic mashup of produce currently available, including courgette (zucchini) flowers from Liguria, Muscat grapes from Provence, Italian flat peaches, and baby fennel from Essex. Just a glance at this week's shopping list will give you an idea of the wealth of beautiful produce available.

We took our first delivery of English apples this week, from Hertfordshire – the brilliantly crisp and refreshingly sweet Discovery apple, which starts the apple season in the UK. You can't store these apples and, like so many "earlies", you have to eat them quickly once they've been picked.

Fried Roscoff onions

If you have some friends coming over and have a fridge full of ice-cold beers, this is a very quick snack solution to serve alongside the drinks. It's simply a matter of mixing flour and spices, adding onions and frying. The fried onions are also the perfect accompaniment to steak or a garnish to a braised Roscoff (see page 190).

Serves 4

2–3 Roscoff onions, peeled and sliced into rings

200ml (7fl oz) buttermilk

sunflower oil, for deep-frying

140g (5oz) plain (all-purpose) flour

1 tsp hot smoked paprika, plus optional extra to serve

1 tsp garlic powder

salt and freshly ground black pepper

garlic mayonnaise, to serve

Tip the onions into a bowl. Add the buttermilk and mix to thoroughly coat. Leave the onions to soak in the buttermilk at room temperature for 30 minutes.

Meanwhile, pour the oil into a deep-sided saucepan (or use a deep-fat fryer, if you have one) and heat it to 170°C/325°F on a cooking thermometer.

Tip the onions into a sieve and shake off the excess buttermilk. Return the onions to the bowl, then add the flour, paprika and garlic powder. Season well with salt and pepper, and mix to coat.

A few at a time, deep-fry the onions in the hot oil for about 2 minutes, turning carefully, until golden brown and crispy all over. Lift the onions out of the oil using a slotted spoon and set them aside to drain on kitchen paper while you cook the next batch. Season with salt and more paprika if you like, and serve with garlic mayonnaise for dipping.

Braised Roscoff onion with Brillat-Savarin cheese sauce

When it comes to onions, Roscoff is the king of alliums... mild, sweet and not too oniony; brilliant flavour when cooked, but also edible raw. This starter is an easy but beautiful showstopper. I suggest you use Brillat-Savarin cheese for the sauce, but you could instead use brie at a pinch. And please do add a scattering of your favourite pickles to the finished dish – wild garlic capers (see page 68) would be especially good.

Serves 4

2 large Roscoff onions, halved with the skins on

200ml (7fl oz) vegetable or chicken stock

4 thyme sprigs

2 rosemary sprigs

2 garlic cloves, finely chopped

salt and freshly ground black pepper

For the cheese sauce

2 tbsp vegetable or light olive oil

1 banana shallot, sliced

3 garlic cloves, chopped

50ml (1¾fl oz) white wine

50ml (1¾fl oz) double (heavy) cream

150g (5½oz) Brillat-Savarin cheese, diced

1 tsp lemon juice

1 tbsp wild garlic capers (see page 68; optional but recommended)

4 slices of sourdough or brioche, toasted, to serve (optional)

To garnish (optional)

fried Roscoff onions (see page 189)

½ quantity of herb mayonnaise (see page 222)

microchickweed

Preheat the oven to 160°C/140°C fan/315°F/Gas 2–3.

Place the onion halves in a small, heavy roasting tin. Pour over the stock and tuck half the herbs and all the garlic around the onions. Season with salt and pepper, cover with foil, and pop the tray in the oven. Braise for 25–30 minutes, until the onions are soft but not breaking apart. Lift the onions from the stock, strain the stock into a bowl, then cool and chill the onions and the stock until ready to use.

Prepare the cheese sauce. Heat 1 tablespoon of the oil in a small saucepan over a medium heat. Add the shallot and garlic and sweat over a low heat for about 5 minutes, until softened. Add the remaining rosemary and thyme and the white wine. Bring to a boil and reduce by half (about 1 minute). Then, add 100ml (3½fl oz) of the reserved stock and cook for 10 minutes, until reduced by half again. By now your kitchen will be full of amazing aromas. (You can freeze any unused stock for another time, if necessary.)

Add the cream, bring the liquid to a boil, then remove from the heat and pick out the herbs. Use a stick blender to blend the sauce until smooth. Add the cheese and blitz again until smooth and then pass the sauce through a fine-mesh sieve. Season with salt and pepper and add the lemon juice to sharpen and balance the flavour.

When you're ready to serve, peel the skins from the braised onions. Heat the remaining oil in a frying pan over a medium heat. Add the onion halves, cut side down, and fry for about 2 minutes, until golden brown on the cut side. (If you happen to have the barbecue lit for something else, you can cook the onions over coals for a delicious, smoky flavour.)

To serve, place 1 onion half in each bowl, add the capers, if using, and pour the sauce around the onion, then garnish with fried Roscoff onions, herb mayo, and microchickweed, if you wish. Enjoy with toasted sourdough or warm brioche to make the dish more substantial.

31

Mirabelle and Pershore plums / King Kesar mangoes / French Charentais melon / Italian Cantaloupe melon / Italian Torpedo watermelon / Italian green figs / Currants from Kent – black, red, white / Dorset blueberries / French Marquette strawberries / French Tulameen raspberries / Kent gooseberries / Panach' blackberries / Bing cherries / Peaches – Doughnut, Italian Flat peach, Pêche de Vigne / Nectavigne / Curry leaves / Kentish mint – many varieties / Methi leaves / Norfolk herbs / Norfolk marsh samphire / Purple basil / Sea purslane / Edible flowers from Surrey / Pumpkin flowers / Hazelnuts / Tomatoes – Italian summer, Main crop Provence / Surrey salad leaves / Endives – Pis-en-lit (dandelion), Summer fine frisée / Feuille de chêne (oak leaf lettuce) / Italian Cos / Red and green Butterhead / Surrey Little Gems / Breakfast radish / Cucumbers – Italian round Caroselli, Surrey / Sussex celery / Italian Friggitelli peppers / Jalapeño peppers / Pimiento Asado del Bierzo / Coco de Paimpol beans / Kent broccoli / Boston cauliflower / Rainbow chard / Natural vine spinach / Young Italian spinach / Artichokes – Brittany baby, Camus globe / Tiger aubergine (eggplant) / Courgettes (zucchini) – Brittany round, Sussex, Trombetta / Mushrooms – Cauliflower, Chicken of the Woods, Puffball, Scottish Girolle, Summer cep / Onions – Cevenne, Roscoff / Somerset leeks / Potatoes – Belle de Fontenay, Charlotte, Maris Bard "earlies", Noirmoutier / Squash – Italian Turban, Potimarron / Celeriac / Essex young beetroot / Italian fennel / Kent radish / Kohlrabi / Somerset bunched carrots

Mirabelle Plum
A Plum Job

Even though at Turnips we import Italian and Spanish plums from early summer (Italy produces a deep-red-fleshed plum called Sangue di Drago – "Dragon's Blood" – and the Spanish grow a decent dark-skinned plum with red or yellow flesh), it is not until we start to see world-class standard plums arrive from France in early August that we really highlight them. France produces some of the best plum varieties within specified growing regions and with accreditations aplenty. The President group of plums are large, oval, dark blueish–black-skinned fruits with juicy yellow flesh. One of the most highly prized in this group is Prunc d'Ente, a variety grown in a protected area around the Lot-et-Garonne. Here, plums are mostly dried to create the stunning Agen prunes, which were awarded a PGI status (see page 24) in 2002. The greenish yellow Reine Claude de Bavay plums, or greengages, are much celebrated in France when they come into season. These smallish round fruit, with speckled skin, are super-sweet with a fragrant, slightly floral and honey flavour.

The town of Moissac in the L'Occitanie region of southern France is commonly thought to be best growing region for plums. In July and August, the market vendors proudly display their Label Rouge certificate alongside their produce, confirming that their plums are from the defined area and are harvested by hand when perfectly ripe. And then we come to the Mirabelle.

Unique and easily recognizable, Mirabelle de Metz plums are round and petite, with a golden yellow, sometimes blushing skin, often covered in a white bloom. The flesh is pale yellow, honey sweet, and juicy. Mirabelles are wonderful baked into sweet tarts and pastries and are often turned into jams and liqueurs, but they are so delicious to eat fresh, just like sweets.

It is thought that Mirabelle plums have been cultivated in France since the 1500s, grown in a protected area in Lorraine around the towns of Nancy and Metz, which also produces the Nancy plum. The area produces 70 to 80 per cent of the world's Mirabelles and, for two weeks in August, Metz itself holds a Mirabelle Festival with tastings, feasts, regional produce, dancing and singing, and which culminates in the crowning of the Mirabelle queen.

Of course, this is not to undermine the beauty of our own UK varieties. Most famously we have the Marjorie Seedling, Victoria and President plums, perfect for picking ripe from your garden and best eaten before the wasps and birds get to them. The Victoria plum makes a very fine tart or crumble.

I recently learned that the UK has its own plum festival in Pershore, Worcestershire, in the Vale of Evesham, well known for its fresh produce. It's a beautiful abbey town on the banks of the River Avon and has been associated with plum growing since the early 19th century. In my 30 years of working with fruit and veg, I had no idea the festival existed. But, then, apart from the Rhubarb Festival in Wakefield, the Alresford Watercress Festival in Hampshire and the British Asparagus Festival in Evesham, I don't know of any other UK celebrations of fruit and vegetables. Held throughout August, culminating on the Bank Holiday weekend, Pershore's plum festival attracts around 30,000 visitors each year, who experience eccentric English village life at its best – not least people dressed up in rotund purple onesies, shouting poems about Little Jack Horner!

> "It is thought that Mirabelle plums have been cultivated in France since the 1500s."

Growers in the area have created many wonderful specimens, all of them egg-shape with thin skin and juicy flesh. Here is the full list of Pershore early, mid- and late-season fruits. Mirabelle, eat your heart out!

Mid-July: Herman, Cherry Plum
Late July: Opal, Rivers' Early Prolific, Sanctus, Hubertus
Early August: Oullins Gage, Czar, Blue Tit, Blaisdon Red
Mid-August: Pershore Yellow Egg, Purple Pershore, Victoria, Swan Avalon, Belle de Louvain, Excalibur, Heron, Ontario
Late August: Cambridge Gage, Cox's Emperor, Keeves, Warwickshire Drooper, Grove's Late Victoria
Early September: Kirke's Blue, Giant Prune, Seneca, Laxton's Cropper, Edwards, Pond's Seedling, Monarch
Mid-September: Haganta, Valor, President, Common Damson
Late September: Guinevere, Marjorie's Seedling

Roasted plums in rum with Chantilly cream

I'm a massive fan of plums – especially when it comes to Reine Claude – for me those are hitting the plum jackpot! This recipe takes a maximum of 30 minutes' hands-on time to pull together into a boozy, fruity dessert. If you have some delicious homemade granola in your cupboards, scatter a little on top for a bit of extra texture and nutty crunch.

Serves 4

12 Reine Claude plums, halved and destoned

100ml (3½fl oz) spiced rum

50g (1¾oz) dark brown soft sugar

1 tbsp grated fresh ginger

2 star anise

1 cinnamon stick

finely grated zest and juice of 1 lime

a little granola, to serve (optional)

For the Chantilly cream

250ml (9fl oz) double (heavy) cream

60g (2oz) icing (confectioner's) sugar

1 vanilla pod, seeds scraped out

Preheat the oven to 180°C/160°C fan/350°F/Gas 4.

Tip the plums into a large bowl. Add the spiced rum, sugar, ginger, star anise and cinnamon and toss the plums to coat in the spices. Add the lime zest and juice and mix to combine.

Scoop everything into a roasting tin and bake for about 25 minutes, until the plums are softened but still holding their shape – the precise timing will depend on how ripe the plums are.

Meanwhile, whip the cream with the icing sugar and vanilla seeds until it holds soft, floppy peaks. Cover and chill until you're ready to serve.

Cool the roasted plums to room temperature, then serve them with spoonfuls of the Chantilly cream and perhaps some granola scattered over the top.

Mirabelle chutney

You can guarantee that Mirabelle plums will be sweet. They are little yellow beauties that will distract you as you're picking them, tempting you to eat them like sweets! Mirabelles are also delicious in cakes, jams and chutneys, like in this recipe.

Makes 1 medium jar

2 tbsp vegetable oil

4 banana shallots, thinly sliced

1 thumb-size piece fresh ginger, peeled and finely chopped

2 garlic cloves, finely chopped

1 large thyme sprig (optional)

1kg (2lb 4oz) Mirabelle plums, halved and destoned

100g (3½oz) caster (superfine) sugar

60g (2¼oz) yellow mustard seeds

2 star anise

1 cinnamon stick

3 cloves

100ml (3½fl oz) apple cider vinegar

1 tsp salt

Heat the oil in a large saucepan over a low heat. Tip the shallots, ginger and garlic into the pan and add the thyme, if using. Sweat for about 5 minutes, until the shallots are soft but not coloured.

Add the plums, sugar, mustard seeds and spices and cook, stirring often, for about 15 minutes, until the plums have softened.

Add the vinegar and salt and cook for a further 45 minutes, until the mixture starts to thicken, become jammy and will coat the back of a spoon. Taste the chutney and add a little more sugar to sweeten or vinegar to sharpen, as needed.

Remove the pan from the heat and pick out the star anise, cinnamon stick and cloves. Spoon the chutney into sterilized jars while it's still hot. Seal the jar with a lid, then turn it upside down to create a vacuum and leave the chutney to cool. Once cold, store the chutney in the fridge for up to 6 months. Use within 2 months once opened.

32

Pêche de Vigne / *King Kesar mangoes* / *Sucking mangoes* / *French Charentais melon* / *Italian Cantaloupe melon* / *Italian Torpedo watermelon* / *Plantain* / *Bramley apples* / *Italian green figs* / *Currants from Kent – black, red, white* / *Dorset blueberries* / *French Marquette strawberries* / *French Tulameen raspberries* / *Kent gooseberries* / *Kentish blackberries* / *Panach' blackberries* / *Bing cherries* / *Peaches – Doughnut, Italian Flat* / *Plums – French Mirabelle, Pershore* / *Nectavigne* / *Curry leaves* / *Kentish mint – many varieties* / *Methi leaves* / *Norfolk herbs* / *Norfolk marsh samphire* / *Pea aubergines (eggplants)* / *Purple basil* / *Thai basil* / *Edible flowers from Surrey* / *Pumpkin flowers* / *Hazelnuts* / *Tomatoes – Italian summer varieties, Main crop Provence* / *Surrey salad leaves* / *Endives – Pis-en-lit (dandelion), Summer fine frisée* / *Feuille de chêne (oak leaf lettuce)* / *Red and green Butterhead* / *Surrey Little Gems* / *UK Cos* / *Breakfast radish* / *Cucumbers – Italian round Caroselli, Surrey* / *Italian Friggitelli peppers* / *Jalapeño peppers* / *Pimiento Asado del Bierzo* / *Beans – Coco de Paimpol, Snake* / *Kent broccoli* / *Boston cauliflower* / *Rainbow chard* / *Camus globe artichokes* / *Tiger aubergine* / *Courgettes (zucchini) – Brittany round, Sussex, Trombetta* / *Mushrooms – Bay Bolete, Chestnut, Cauliflower, Chicken of the Woods, Hen of the Woods, Judas Ear, Scottish Girolle, Slippery Jack* / *Onions – Cevenne, Roscoff* / *Somerset leeks* / *Potatoes – Belle de Fontenay, Charlotte, Javelin, Maris Bard "earlies", Noirmoutier, Ratte* / *Squash – Italian Turban, Potimarron* / *Casava* / *Celeriac* / *Italian fennel* / *Kent radishes* / *Kohlrabi* / *Somerset bunched carrots* / *Somerset heirloom beetroot* / *Yams*

Pêche de Vigne
Life's a Peach

Most people are aware only of the yellow-fleshed peach varieties, but it's the white- and red-fleshed ones that have a higher demand from the top restaurants. I believe the French peach varieties are the best and our Paris agents source ours at Rungis, the largest wholesale produce market in the world. From June to September, we import 75 different varieties of peach from France, incorporating white, yellow and red-fleshed fruits. My particular favourites are the large, juicy, white-fleshed Monsolle (which has a very short shelf life) and the yellow-fleshed Diamond Princess (a mid-season variety with a wonderful sweetness). But it is the beautiful red-fleshed peaches that not only taste stunning but have a great story.

The main peach-growing regions in France are Rhône-Alpes, Roussillon, Gard and Crau. We go to the region around Lyon to find the "vineyard peach", or Pêche de Vigne, which has many different varieties, a short season and ripens at same time as the grapes on the vines.

In the vineyards around Lyon, growers would plant a peach tree at the end of each row of vines, in much the same way as Bordeaux *vignerons* (winemakers) would plant a rose. Owing to the plants' susceptibility to mildew, the tree would warn the *vigneron* that mildew was coming before it hit the vines, giving them a chance to take pre-emptive and remedial action. Now, though, the peaches are grown for their own merits.

Not all Pêche de Vigne varieties have red flesh, but commercial ones generally do. The flesh can be a stunning crimson, raspberry red or even deep pink with a darker stained or marbled appearance. The skin of the peaches is covered in a light fuzz that gives little indication of the beauty that lies within. The flavour of these exquisite stone fruits is of cherries, berries, plums and (of course!) peaches; they are sweet, but not overwhelmingly so.

Nico Ladenis and his peach Melba

I supplied Nico Ladenis at his triple Michelin-starred restaurant Chez Nico for around 15 years. Each year, in the height of summer, Nico would call me: "Find me the most beautiful peaches around. They must be sweet, they must be semi-firm, and they must be French." So off I'd go to find perfect peaches at the market for Nico – he also added the proviso that they had to be very cheap. French peaches are many things, but they are never cheap.

Everything has its price – and not all vegetables are created equal, whether it's a box of cucumbers or a sack of carrots. This is something that chefs and the public are just beginning to understand, and I hope that you've learned from reading this book: a peach is never just a peach. How expensive that peach (or cucumber or carrot...) is depends on where and how it's grown. Mass-produced peaches, mostly for the home market with a longer shelf life and seemingly less flavour, from countries such as Turkey, Spain, Greece and Italy, are generally cheaper. French farmers, though, with their tireless pursuit of perfection, grow beautiful peaches – but at a price. This does drop once the season reaches its peak – however, they will still

> "Find me the most beautiful peaches around. They must be sweet, they must be semi-firm, and they must be French."

be more costly than peaches from elsewhere. Once I'd found the right peaches for Nico, the long negotiation with the salesman started. It's a skill keeping everyone happy!

One hundred boxes of peaches with 22 in a box is a lot of peaches all heading to one 80-seater restaurant. Nico would get his brigade of around 10 chefs to peel all 2,200 fruit after the lunch service, when they would normally be on their break. Under this system, it might take them three days altogether and it was a race against time with the risk of over-ripening. Understandably, Nico's chefs were never exactly overjoyed at the prospect of the impending peaching session, so I would sweeten the job for them and arrange for a delivery of a crate of beers along with the fruit. Once the peaches were peeled and stoned, the chefs would cook the peach flesh and preserve it in syrup in sterilized jars. Then, instead of having to pay top dollar for jarred fruit from the fine-food vendors, Nico had the joy of using his own peaches in syrup for a fraction of the price. He kept the peaches until winter, when he put his classic peach Melba dessert on the menu.

A tricolour of peaches make up over 70 French varieties that range in flavour from heady-sweet (yellow), to floral (white), to sharp wine influences in the (red) Pêche de Vigne.

A truly authentic peach Melba is made using fresh peaches and served on a bed of vanilla ice cream accompanied by a fresh raspberry sauce. Auguste Escoffier, the French restaurateur and cookery writer, developed the original recipe in 1892 at the Savoy Hotel in London and in honour of Nellie Melba, an Australian Opera singer. Escoffier's French roots inspired the dish's French name Pêche Melba, which is still widely seen on French menus – here and over the English Channel.

My aromatic walkway

I've noticed mint growing all over the garden at the front of my house. A few years ago our East Sussex herb man supplied me with some mature plants that I grew to create an "aromatic walkway" to my front door. I planted rosemary into a low hedge on either side of the path, sage and thyme in front of the rosemary, bay either side of the door, two large pots of basil in front of the bay – and six varieties of mint to really give an aromatic welcome to our visitors.

It is stunning even if I say so myself. Who knew there were so many varieties of mint? (Our herb man grows 19.) But boy, do I regret not putting that mint into pots! If you've ever planted mint in your garden – you'll know what I mean... that stuff can really grow.

The beauty of herbs comes to the fore at this time of year. They bring a freshness to all dishes and, at Turnips, we connect different herbs with specific fruits and vegetables. Rosemary, thyme and sage we associate with wild mushrooms, and curly and flat-leaf parsley with cultivated mushrooms. For the tomatoes, we combine basil, marjoram and oregano; and fennel with dill and its own herb top. But mint is a truly versatile herb – think of its association with both fruit *and* vegetables.

We display our new potatoes, and especially the first of the Jerseys, with bunches of Moroccan mint, but it also works well with strawberries or peaches, one of my favourite combinations.

Pêche de Vigne tarte Tatin

It's a glorious summer evening, you have friends coming round and you want to impress them with something beautiful, quick and simple. Try this easy-going recipe for tarte Tatin, which takes very little time to prepare and bake, especially if you use store-bought pastry.

Serves 4

75g (2½oz) granulated sugar

40g (1½oz) unsalted butter

1 tbsp double (heavy) cream

4 Pêches de Vigne, halved, destoned and thinly sliced (peeled, if you wish)

plain (all-purpose) flour, for rolling out

320g (11¼oz) shortcrust pastry

whipped cream or vanilla ice cream, to serve

Preheat the oven to 190°C/170°C fan/325°F/Gas 3.

Combine the sugar and butter in a small frying pan or saucepan and set the pan over a low heat. Stir the butter and sugar continuously with a spatula, until the mixture starts to caramelize and turns a lovely amber colour. Add the cream, stir to combine and pour the mixture into the bottom of a solid-based 18cm (7in), circular baking tin.

Arrange the peaches neatly over the creamy caramel, in an even layer. Dust the work surface with the flour and roll out the pastry to create a disk slightly larger than the tin. Place the pastry on top of the peaches and tuck the sides in around the edges.

Bake for about 25–30 minutes, until the pastry is golden brown. Remove the tart from the oven and leave it to cool for a couple of minutes, then place a plate on top of the tin and quickly flip it over, inverting the tart on to the plate. Remove the tin and serve with whipped cream or vanilla ice cream.

Spiced canned peaches

Canned peaches are one of my fondest childhood food memories. I always used to think how sweet, sugary and tasty they were. And now I make my own. They are perfect to use in trifles or to have with yogurt and nuts for breakfast.

Makes 2 large jars

1 tsp citric acid or lemon juice

10 peaches, preferably Pêche de Vigne, halved or quartered and destoned

4 bay leaves

½ lemon, sliced

150g (5½oz) caster (superfine) sugar

2 star anise

4 cloves

1 large cinnamon stick

6 juniper berries

Bring a saucepan of water to a boil. Fill a bowl with iced water, add the citric acid or lemon juice and stir to combine.

Blanch the peach halves in the boiling water for about 20 seconds and then remove them from the pan and plunge them into the cold water. Carefully peel the skins from the peaches and pack them into sterilized jars with the bay leaves and lemon slices.

In a saucepan combine the sugar, spices, juniper berries and 400ml (14fl oz) of water. Bring the liquid to a boil, then reduce the heat to low and simmer for 2–3 minutes to extract the flavour from the spices. Pour the hot syrup over the peaches to cover – you may not need it all, depending on the size of your jars. Seal the jars with the lids and stand the jars in a deep saucepan. Pour enough boiling water into the pan to come halfway up the sides of the jars. Place over a high heat and simmer for 10 minutes to pasteurize the contents of the jar.

Remove the jars from the pan and turn them upside down to create a vacuum. Leave to cool. Once cold, turn the jars the right way up and store the peaches in a dry, cool place for up to 1 year. Once opened, store in the fridge and consume within 3 days.

1 tsp citric acid or lemon juice

10 white peaches, halved and destoned

75g (2½oz) caster (superfine) sugar

100ml (3½fl oz) Amaretto Disaronno

Alternative 1: canned peaches with amaretto
This recipe follows a similar method to the one above, but add the Amaretto to the syrup before pouring into the jars – the result is a beautiful almondy boozy flavour!

1 tsp citric acid or lemon juice

10 white peaches halved and destoned

100g (3½oz) caster (superfine) sugar

2 star anise

10 pink peppercorns

1 cinnamon stick

1 vanilla pod, halved

Alternative 2: peppery spiced canned peaches
Follow a similar method, using peppercorns, star anise, cinnamon and a vanilla pod in the sugar syrup, which is a little less sweet in this version of the recipe.

33

Kentish cobnuts / *King Kesar mangoes* / *Sucking mangoes* / *Italian Torpedo watermelon* / *French Charentais melon* / *Plantain* / *Bramley apple* / *Italian green figs* / *Currants from Kent – black, red, white* / *Dorset blueberries* / *French Marquette strawberries* / *French Tulameen raspberries* / *Kentish blackberries* / *Panach' blackberries* / *Bing cherries* / *Peaches – Doughnut, Pêche de Vigne* / *Plums – French Mirabelle, Pershore* / *Nectavigne* / *Curry leaves* / *Kentish mint – many varieties* / *Methi leaves* / *Norfolk herbs* / *Norfolk marsh samphire* / *Pea aubergines (eggplants)* / *Purple basil* / *Thai basil* / *Pumpkin flowers* / *Tomatoes – Ailsa Craig and Red Alert from Essex, Italian summer varieties, Main crop Provence* / *Surrey salad leaves* / *Endives – Pis-en-lit (dandelion), Summer fine frisée* / *Feuille de chêne (oak leaf lettuce)* / *Red and green Butterhead* / *Surrey Little Gems* / *UK Cos* / *Breakfast radish* / *Cucumbers – Italian round Caroselli, Surrey* / *Italian Friggitelli peppers* / *Jalapeño peppers* / *Pimiento Asado del Bierzo* / *Beans – Coco de Paimpol, Snake* / *Kent broccoli* / *Boston cauliflower* / *Rainbow chard* / *Camus globe artichokes* / *Tiger aubergine* / *Courgettes (zucchini) – Brittany round, Sussex, Trombetta* / *Mushrooms – Bay Bolete, Cauliflower, Chestnut, Chicken of the Woods, Hen of the Woods, Judas Ear, Scottish Girolle, Slippery Jack* / *Onions – Cevenne, Roscoff* / *Somerset leeks* / *Potatoes – Belle de Fontenay, Charlotte, Cyprus Nicola (for mashing), Javelin, Italian Spunta (for chipping), Maris Bard "earlies", Noirmoutier, Ratte* / *Squash – Italian Turban, Potimarron* / *Casava* / *Celeriac* / *Italian fennel* / *Kent radishes* / *Kohlrabi* / *Somerset bunched carrots* / *Somerset heirloom beetroot* / *Yams*

Kentish Cobnut
The Nutcracker in More Ways than One

Late summer brings Kentish cobnuts, but are cobnuts just hazelnuts in fancy frocks? In the hazelnut world, there is the cobnut, filbert and hazelnut. As we commonly know them, hazelnuts are also known as filberts, particularly in the USA. And cobnuts are sometimes also called filberts. However, in truth, cobnuts are the cultivated form of hazelnuts. They are longer and more torpedo-shaped than hazelnuts and always sold as fresh rather than dried.

Wild hazelnuts grow in woods and hedgerows up and down the country. You can easily identify them by the pale green, yellowy catkins or lambs' tails that are the male flowers and appear in late winter and early spring and before the trees are in leaf. For cobnuts, though, we go to Kent, a county close to my heart because it is my home. Lying to the southeast of London, Kent is known as the Garden of England and is famous for myriad fresh produce – but hops and cobnuts are those that for me have the greatest association. This is not least because of the beautiful oast houses that lie dotted through its countryisde and which in times past were used for drying hops for beer-making. Kentish cobnuts are a truly British product, with a short season and specific growing region – in a nutshell, the message that I am trying to promote overall.

One hundred years ago, there were around 2,800 hectares (7,000 acres) of cobnut orchards in Kent, where they are known as plats. Now there are only around 101 hectares (250 acres) remaining. However, as our interest in and awareness of local and seasonal produce increases, so does the popularity of these fresh nuts. Thanks to some forward-thinking farmers and landowners, who are replanting and restoring old orchards, the area dedicated to cobnuts is set to increase once again. The cobnut even has its own society: the Kentish Cobnut Association, formed in 1990, promotes the industry and represents the 150 or so growers, offering courses in growing and pruning. The Association also hosts an annual Nutters' Supper, which sounds intriguing.

There is barely any difference in the methods of farming and harvesting of cobnuts since Victorian times. They grow with very little intervention and require few (if any) pesticides. Grown on trees, some of which have been producing for decades, the nuts are hand-harvested by "nutters", first around the feast day of St Philibert on August 20. Picking continues through to September, in a race against the squirrels, who are also rather partial to them.

The nuts are encased in a distinctive green, frilled casing, and at the start of season the shells are still green, too. Initially crisp and juicy with a milky, sweet flavour, the nuts can sweeten further as they age. They have a similar texture to fresh coconut and the delicate flavour is sweeter and fresher than their dried hazelnut cousins, which are available all year round. Store them fresh in the fridge (just like any fresh product), because at room temperature they will dry out and the husk will become crisp and fall off. Eat them simply with a seasoning of salt, or in recipes when you want a milkier, fresher nut – they are particularly delicious in salads. Try them roasted, when they become more nutty and slightly caramel in flavour. In this way they are wonderful in granola, bakes or paired with chocolate. By mid-season the husks and shells surrounding the nuts start to turn golden brown and dry.

"Initially crisp and juicy with a milky sweet flavour, the nuts can sweeten further as they age."

As a child you might well have played conkers with horse chestnuts tied to a length of string. Let me introduce you to the game nutcracker, in which you tie on a cobnut or hazelnut instead and use it to hit your opponent's head (or to give it it's Cockney name, nut). I can see why this might have fallen out of favour in school playgrounds!

We are so used to seeing packets of dried nuts on sale all year round that you'd be forgiven for thinking that nuts have no season at all – but they are a fresh product with seasons like any other. The nut season starts in early summer with almonds from Italy; then we move to England and in particular to Kent for cobnuts, before crossing the Channel to France for wet walnuts from early September and we end with sweet chestnuts – more of which in a few weeks' time, in mid-October. What a glorious thought that nutters go nutting from Puglia to Kent to Grenoble.

Hazelnut and chocolate spread

Who doesn't love a snack of toast laden with hazelnut and chocolate spread? I'm guessing, not many! This mouthwatering recipe uses less sugar and has the bonus of being homemade. You'll need a powerful food processor to get the texture right.

Makes 1 small jar

150g (5½oz) blanched hazelnuts, plus optional extra chopped to serve

1–2 tsp hazelnut oil

1 tbsp caster (superfine) sugar

2 tbsp cocoa powder

1 tsp vanilla extract

170g (6oz) 70% dark (bittersweet) chocolate, chopped

80g (2¾oz) milk chocolate, chopped

Preheat the oven to 180°C/160°C fan/350°F/Gas 4.

Tip the hazelnuts into a roasting tin and roast them for about 8 minutes, until golden. Keep an eye on them and check them after 5 minutes, as you don't want them to burn.

Tip the nuts into a food processor and blitz until smooth, scraping down the sides of the bowl from time to time. Add 1 teaspoon of hazelnut oil, or a little more if needed, to make the mixture easier to blend. Once the nuts are smooth, add the sugar, cocoa and vanilla and blend for another minute.

Meanwhile, melt both chocolates in the microwave or in a heatproof bowl set over a pan of simmering water. Add this to the hazelnut mixture and blitz again until smooth and shiny. Pour the spread into a clean jar, leave it to cool and then seal it with a lid. Store the spread in the fridge for up to 3 months, or 3 weeks once opened, and enjoy on toast for breakfast (sprinkled with a few extra chopped hazelnuts if you like), or even stirred into your coffee!

Apple and kohlrabi slaw with Kentish cobnuts

Kohlrabi is one of my favourite vegetables. It is crisp with a mild, peppery flavour, and is versatile and delicious, cooked or raw. Now that cobnuts are in season, we can combine the two into a super-sexy, non-traditional slaw that's amazing with beef and Sand carrot stew, or alongside fried chicken or burgers.

Serves 4

2 large apples (such as Granny Smith or Golden Delicious – nothing too sweet)

2 kohlrabi, peeled

100g (3½oz) cobnuts, shelled and sliced or chopped

1 garlic clove, peeled and crushed

2 tbsp mayonnaise

1 tbsp chopped flat-leaf parsley

finely grated zest and juice of 1 lime

salt and freshly ground black pepper

Peel the apples if you like – it's not necessary, though, and the skin will add extra colour, flavour and texture. Coarsely grate the kohlrabi and apples into a large mixing bowl.

Add the cobnuts, garlic, mayonnaise, parsley, and lime zest and juice, and season with salt and pepper. Mix to combine, then serve.

34

Cavaillon melon / *King Kesar mangoes* / *Sucking mangoes* / *French Charentais melon* / *Italian Torpedo watermelon* / *Plantain* / *Apples – Bramley, Discovery, Scrumptious, Worcester Pearmain* / *Pears – Bartlett, Clapp's Favourite* / *Currants – black, red, white* / *Kentish blackberries* / *Bing cherries* / *Damsons* / *Peaches – Doughnut, Pêche de Vigne* / *Plums – French Mirabelle, Pershore* / *Nectavigne* / *Kentish mint – many varieties* / *Norfolk herbs* / *Norfolk marsh samphire* / *Pea aubergines (eggplants)* / *Purple basil* / *Thai basil* / *Pumpkin flowers* / *Kentish cobnuts* / *Tomatoes – Ailsa Craig and Red Alert from Essex, Main crop Provence* / *Surrey salad leaves* / *Summer fine frisée* / *Feuille de chêne (oak leaf lettuce)* / *Red and green Butterhead* / *Surrey Little Gems* / *UK Cos* / *Breakfast radish* / *Italian Friggitelli peppers* / *Jalapeño peppers* / *Pimiento Asado del Bierzo* / *Beans – Coco de Paimpol, Snake* / *Essex sweetcorn* / *Kent broccoli* / *Boston cauliflower* / *Chard – Rainbow, Swiss* / *Cabbages – Kent red and white, Somerset kale* / *Tiger aubergine* / *Courgettes (zucchini) – Brittany round, Sussex* / *Mushrooms – Bay Bolete, Chestnut, Hen of the Woods, Judas Ear, Penny Bun, Scottish Girolle, Slippery Jack* / *Onions Cevenne, Roscoff* / *Somerset leeks* / *Potatoes – Belle de Fontenay, Charlotte, Cyprus Nicola (for mashing), Italian Spunta (for chipping), Javelin "earlies", Maris Bard "earlies", Ratte* / *Squash – Italian Turban, Potimarron, Spaghetti* / *Casava* / *Celeriac* / *Kent radishes* / *Kohlrabi* / *Somerset bunched carrots* / *Somerset heirloom beetroot* / *Yams*

Cavaillon Melon
MEL-O-Ncholy – You Must Be Kidding!

Let me take you on a tour through southern Europe, for melons. In Greece, we find the Torpila watermelon. Torpedo-shaped, it has a dark and pale green striped exterior with deep red, juicy flesh. In Turkey, the Karpuzu, which has been grown for hundreds of years in Karaköprü and surrounding regions, is an elongated watermelon that looks like a giant courgette (zucchini). In Italy, the orange-fleshed Cantaloupe reigns supreme. And, finally, we land in France.

A few years ago my wife and I took a cruise through the Mediterranean from Greece to France on what became a voyage of discovery for the best-tasting melon. From Athens, where we had views of the Acropolis from our hotel room, we boarded a ship bound for Turkey to visit the site of the lost city of Ephesus. Then on to Italy, and Luca, and the Leaning Tower of Pisa. We sailed to Monaco and finally docked in Marseille, in the south of France. Each time the ship reached a new port, we disembarked to see the sights and taste the delights. The heat was incredible, and we'd make a bee-line for stalls selling sliced local melon – quite a contrast to the dull, flavourless melons we were served for breakfast on board the ship. Watermelons in Greece, a honeydew-type melon in Turkey, Cantaloupe slices in Italy... I soon came to realize that melon summed up the Mediterranean in red, green, orange and yellow.

The final days of our trip were ashore in Marseille, where the hotel breakfast was a beautiful buffet feast, including local hams and yogurts, and cheeses from a creamery down the road. There were soft fruits, including fraise de bois, and, of course, local melon. The orange-fleshed melon had a floral aroma, exquisite flavour and sweetness unlike any other we'd had before. It was the best of all the marvellous fruit we'd tasted on the trip – I'd go so far as to say it was the best melon I'd ever eaten. I knew it was a classic Charentais, a name unique to this type of melon in France and known elsewhere as Cantaloupe, but I didn't know which specific variety. The chef was summoned: he explained to me that it was a Cavaillon Charentais, from Provence.

Cavaillon is a small town to produce what's commonly accepted as the best melon in the world. The inhabitants are rightly proud of this achievement and there's a 9-tonne melon sculpture to greet you as you approach. The melons are well protected by a brotherhood – the Confrérie des Chevaliers de l'Ordre du Melon Cavaillon, who wear black hats and long, dark green velvet robes with orange sashes. In July, during the annual Féria du Melon, pyramids of melons go on display, and and there are tastings, music, parades and feasts. There is a finale of 100 white Camargue horses running through the streets.

I love the guesswork for how this melon ended up in France. One story credits 14th-century monks for bringing melon seeds from Cantalupo near Rome, where melons were grown in the papal gardens of the Pope's residence in Avignon. At the time, melons were considered a delicacy and more than one Pope was said to have died from over consumption of the fruit. Another story credits Charles VIII of France, some 200 years earlier, for introducing melons to the area after plundering Italy. Whichever is true, melons have been growing in this region for a very long time.

The Cavaillon has had famous fans, too. The 19th-century writer Alexandre Dumas (*The Three Musketeers*, *The Count of Monte Cristo*) donated volumes of his books to the library in Cavaillon and in return was paid 12 melons a year until his death.

Round and small enough to sit comfortably in your hand (serving two people... or one Pope), Cavaillon Chanterais have pale green skin that is either smooth or embroidered (*brodé*) with a fine netting and has between nine and eleven bluish-green stripes from the base to the stalk. The flesh is

> "Cavaillon is a small town to produce what's commonly accepted as the best melon in the world."

juicy and apricot-coloured, with an intense floral aroma of honeysuckle, jasmine, honey and ripe apricots. To tell if a melon is ripe, pick it up – it should feel heavy in the hand for its size and it should smell heady, sweet and, well, "melony".

Thanks to the rapid train network through France, we can transport these melons from Provence to Paris, and then ship them to Britain for us to enjoy throughout the season, which starts in mid-June and ends in September.

France, Italy, Spain, Greece and Turkey compete to produce the finest orange-fleshed melon. Our vote goes to a small town in Provence, France, called Cavaillon. Try it and see!

Compressed Charentais melon

This was one of our first pre-desserts that we served in the restaurant when we opened. The compressed melon looks like a normal melon wedge, but when you bite into it, the flavour is so different and unexpected it blows your mind! It's perfect to serve at a party on a hot, sunny day – perhaps with a little tequila poured over to booze it up! For this recipe, you will need a vacuum machine and crushed ice on which to serve the melon.

Serves 4–6

1 Charentais melon, halved and deseeded

100g (3½oz) caster (superfine) sugar

½ red chilli, deseeded

1 tbsp finely chopped galangal

2 lemongrass stalks, bruised

finely grated zest and juice of 1 lime

Cut each melon half into 4 wedges (to give 8 in total) and place them in a vacuum pouch.

Tip the sugar into a saucepan, add 100ml (3½fl oz) of water and bring the water to a boil. Add the chilli, galangal, lemongrass, and lime zest and juice. Remove the pan from the heat and leave the syrup to cool and the flavours to infuse.

Strain the syrup into the vacuum pouch, seal and pass the pouch through the vacuum machine.

Chill for 2–3 hours to allow the flavours to penetrate the melon wedges, then remove from the pouch and serve the wedges on top of crushed ice.

Charentais melon sorbet with galangal and chilli

If you have already made the compressed melon (opposite) and loved it (why wouldn't you?) here is another recipe that uses similar flavours to make a sorbet. Not only is this sorbet delicious as a dessert or as a palate cleanser, but it is also good to serve as a cocktail – simply, place a scoop of sorbet into a glass and then pour Champagne over the top.

Serves 4–6 as a dessert

100g (3½oz) caster (superfine) sugar

5cm (2in) piece of galangal, peeled and thinly sliced

900g–1kg (2lb–2lb 4oz) Charentais melon, peeled, deseeded, and flesh chopped into small dice

¼ Scotch bonnet chilli, deseeded and finely chopped

juice of ½ lime

2 tbsp glucose syrup

In a small saucepan combine the sugar, galangal and 150ml (5fl oz) of water. Place the pan over a medium–low heat and slowly bring the mixture to the boil to dissolve the sugar. Simmer for 1 minute, then remove the pan from the heat and leave it until the mixture is cold and the galangal flavour has infused the syrup.

Tip the melon and chilli into a food processor with the lime juice and glucose syrup. Strain the sugar syrup into the food processor to remove the galangal and blend until the mixture reduces to a smooth purée. Strain the purée into a clean bowl, cover and chill it overnight.

The following day, churn the mixture in an ice-cream machine following the manufacturer's instructions, until firm. Transfer the sorbet to a freezer container and freeze it for about 2 hours, until firm, before serving.

35

French figs / *Finger limes* / *Cavaillon melon* / *French Charentais melon* / *Italian Torpedo watermelon* / *Plantain* / *Apples – Bramley, Discovery, Scrumptious, Worcester Pearmain* / *Pears – Bartlett, Clapp's Favourite* / *Quince* / *Currants – black, red, white* / *Kentish blackberries* / *Muscat grapes* / *Damsons* / *Plums – French Mirabelle, Pershore* / *Reine Claude Greengages* / *Kentish mint – many varieties* / *Norfolk herbs* / *Norfolk marsh samphire* / *Pea aubergines (eggplants)* / *Purple basil* / *Thai basil* / *Pumpkin flowers* / *Kentish cobnuts* / *Tomatoes – Ailsa Craig and Red Alert from Essex, Italian Vesuvio, Main crop Provence, San Marzano* / *Chalke Valley watercress* / *Surrey salad leaves* / *Summer fine frisée* / *Feuille de chêne (oak leaf lettuce)* / *Red and green Butterhead* / *Surrey Little Gems* / *UK Cos* / *Breakfast radish* / *Italian Friggitelli peppers* / *Jalapeño peppers* / *Pimiento Asado del Bierzo* / *Beans – Coco de Paimpol, Snake* / *Essex sweetcorn* / *Kent broccoli* / *Cauliflowers – Cape, Boston, Romanesque* / *Chard – Rainbow, Swiss* / *Cabbages – Kent red and white, Somerset kale* / *Tiger aubergine* / *Courgettes (zucchini) – Brittany round, Sussex* / *Lautrec pink garlic* / *Mushrooms – Bay Bolete, Chestnut, Judas Ear, Hen of the woods, Penny Bun, Scottish Girolle* / *Onions – Cevenne, Roscoff* / *Somerset leeks* / *Potatoes – Belle de Fontenay, Charlotte, Cyprus Nicola (for mashing), Italian Spunta (for chipping), Javelin "earlies", Maris Bard "earlies", Ratte* / *Squash – Delica, Italian Turban, Potimarron, Spaghetti* / *Casava* / *Celeriac* / *Kent radishes* / *Somerset bunched carrots* / *Somerset heirloom beetroot* / *Turnips – French, Kohlrabi* / *Yams*

French Figs
What's the Fig Idea?

Try as we might, in the UK we simply can't recreate the flavour of fruits that thrive in hotter climates. The fig is definitely one of those fruits, flourishing as it does in the warm, dry, frost-free environment of southern Europe. There are around 700 named varieties (very few of them commercially grown), the majority of which come from around the Mediterranean. Figs are commonly thought of as an autumn fruit, but I believe the best come from France in late summer. When you see autumn recipes in magazines and newspapers using figs and blackberries, you'll be cooking with fruit from Turkey and Morocco because by then the beautiful fruits from closer to home will be long gone.

In early July, for our restaurant clients we import Italian figs from Milan via Tim, our Covent Garden agent. These figs have an amazing flavour, similar to British botanist James Wong's suggested Brunswick variety, with "rose-scented fragrance and a sugar content so high it literally drips from the eye (the hole at the base of the fruit)". However, they arrive so ripe that they have a ridiculously short shelf life and the chefs need to use them immediately. We prefer instead to wait for the French Languedoc-Roussillon figs to start in late August.

The Figue de Solliès is the most widespread of all the varieties and accounts for 75 per cent of the market. This fig is firm and teardrop-shape with deep purple skin, darker veining, and juicy, dark red flesh. It has crisp, crunchy seeds. The flavour is sweet like honeydew melon or red fruits and has a perfect balance between sweetness and acidity. Other similar, large, juicy purple or violet figs of the Bourjassotte variety, which grow in the mineral-rich, warm soil of the area, include the Rouge de Bordeaux, Sultane and the Marseillaise. Normally, when a particular variety or type of fruit is the most commonly grown, they tend to be uninspiring – but not these figs.

Solliès-Pont, a small town in the Provence-Alpes-Côte-d'Azure region of France is renowned for the quality of its figs, which have held an AOC (see page 15) since 2006. As usual, among other things, the figs must be grown and packaged in a specific area and be of a minimum size, colour and sweetness. Figs are a delicate fruit and are hand-picked, graded and packed every two days from late August into October. The customary festival to celebrate the succulent fig takes place at the end of August in Solliès-Pont village.

Seasons that merge

"Behold, the days are coming," declares the Lord, "when the ploughman shall overtake the reaper and the treader of grapes him who sows the seed; the mountains shall drip sweet wine, and all the hills shall flow with it. I will restore the fortunes of my people Israel, and they shall rebuild the ruined cities and inhabit them; they shall plant vineyards and drink their wine, and they shall make gardens and eat their fruit." Amos 9: 13–14

We are in Week 35 and two thirds of the way through the summer–autumn season, which starts in Week 26 and finishes in Week 39. Figs are the perfect example of a fruit that is thought of as belonging to one season, but really begins in another: can we really call the fig an autumn fruit when the best specimens come from more southernly European countries in the height of summer in July and August? It is all about setting boundaries. Most people probably consider tropical fruits as summer fruits, but if we want to enjoy true world-class tropical fruits, they are in season in the UK in winter–spring. Likewise, strawberries are spring–summer and figs are summer–autumn – when the seasons are regarded as merged timelines, harvests make much more sense. Early, mid and late varieties overlap rather than

> "Early, mid and late varieties overlap rather than separating tidily into each season. In the same way colours in the natural world blur into each other as the seasons change."

separating tidily into each season. In the same way, colours in the natural world blur into each other as the seasons change: the hot summer colours turn to muted warmer tones as we approach autumn – and that's the wonder of the natural world. The changing colours and flavours are what makes each season worth waiting for.

Fig chutney with apples

When figs arrive, you need to move quickly as their season is quite short – the flavour when they are at their super-ripe best is like sweet heaven. You can make desserts or salads with beautiful-looking fresh figs, but when you go to the market ask for less-than-perfect fruits – the ones that some people wouldn't buy – as these will make amazing chutney, which you can enjoy later in the year. This recipe makes only one jar, but you can double or triple it easily enough.

Makes 1 medium jar

1 tbsp vegetable oil

1 large Cevenne onion, finely chopped

2 garlic cloves, finely chopped

3 Granny Smith apples, peeled, cored and diced

10 figs, diced

1 cinnamon stick

4 star anise

50g (1¾oz) yellow mustard seeds

120g (4¼oz) dark brown soft sugar

150ml (5fl oz) balsamic vinegar

salt and freshly ground black pepper

Heat the oil in a saucepan over a low heat. Tip in the onion and garlic and sweat for about 10 minutes, until soft and translucent.

Add the apples to the pan, cover them with a disk of baking paper (a cartouche) and cook them slowly for about 10 minutes, until softened. I love my chutney with texture and little apple bits, so I now remove 2 tablespoons of the mixture and set them aside.

Add the figs to the pan and cook for another 10 minutes over a low heat, until softened. Add the cinnamon stick, star anise, mustard seeds, sugar and vinegar, mix to combine and leave to simmer for about 30–45 minutes, stirring occasionally to make sure that the chutney doesn't stick to the bottom of the pan, until thickened to a jammy consistency.

Return the reserved apples to the pan, season with salt and pepper and mix to combine. Spoon the chutney into a sterilized jar, seal with a lid and leave to cool.

Store the chutney in a cool, dark place for up to 6 months. Once opened, store in the fridge and use within 1 month.

Roasted figs with kaimaki ice cream and ouzo

Ripe figs are like gold dust, but when you do find them, try making this Greek-inspired recipe for a gooey ice cream that everyone will love. Salep is a powder made from orchid bulbs and is used in Middle Eastern countries for teas and in baking. Mastic is resin from the mastic tree – the taste is bitter at first, but mellows to a refreshing flavour reminiscent of pine and cedar.

Serves 4

For the figs

10 ripe figs, halved

300g (10½oz) caster (superfine) sugar

2g ascorbic acid (or citric acid or juice of ½ lemon)

1 star anise

4 tbsp ouzo

For the kaimaki ice cream

120g (4¼oz) caster (superfine) sugar

4g mastic crystals

500ml (17fl oz) full-fat milk

125ml (4fl oz) double (heavy) cream

6g salep

Tip the figs into a large bowl. Add the sugar, acid or lemon juice, star anise and ouzo and mix well to combine. Cover and leave at room temperature overnight for the sugar to draw the juice from the figs.

Meanwhile, start the ice cream base, which needs 24 hours before churning and freezing. Whizz 20g (¾oz) of the sugar with the mastic in a food processor to combine to a fine powder.

Pour the milk and cream into a saucepan, place over a medium–low heat and bring the liquid to just below boiling. Add the remaining sugar, the mastic and sugar mixture and the salep and whisk to combine. Lower the heat to the lowest setting and heat for 30 minutes to infuse the milk and cream. Leave the milk and cream mixture to cool and then cover and chill it overnight.

The following day churn the ice cream in an ice-cream machine according to the manufacturer's instructions until firm. Spoon the ice cream into a freezerproof container and freeze until you're ready to serve (at least 4 hours, if possible).

Heat the oven to 180°C/160°C fan/350°F/Gas 4 and line a medium roasting tin with baking paper. Tip the figs and all the juice into the tin and roast for about 15 minutes, until very soft.

Serve the roasted figs in bowls with scoops of the ice cream on top.

36

Penny Bun mushrooms / Finger limes / Cavaillon melon / French Charentais melon / Plantain / Apples – Bramley, Hereford Cox Orange Pippin, Kent Russet / Pears – French Vassout Comice pear, Kent Conference, Kent Victoria / Quince / Currants – black, red, white / Kentish blackberries / Muscat grapes / Damsons / Reine Claude greengages / Plums – French Mirabelle, Pershore / Kentish mint – many varieties / Italian Monk's Beard / Norfolk herbs / Norfolk marsh samphire / Pea aubergines (eggplants) /Purple basil / Thai basil / Kentish cobnuts / Tomatoes – Ailsa Craig and Red Alert from Essex, Italian Vesuvio, Main crop Provence, San Marzano / Chalke Valley watercress / Surrey salad leaves / Summer fine frisée / Feuille de chêne (oak leaf lettuce) / Red and green Butterhead / Surrey Little Gems / UK Cos / Breakfast radish / Italian Friggitelli peppers / Jalapeño peppers / Pimiento Asado del Bierzo / Snake beans / Essex sweetcorn / Kent broccoli / Cauliflower – Boston, Cape, Romanesque / Cime di rapa / Chard – Rainbow, Swiss / Cabbages – Cavolo Nero, Kent red and white, Normandy Savoy, Somerset kale / Tiger aubergine / Courgettes (zucchini) – Brittany round, Sussex / Garlic – Lautrec pink, French smoked, Turnips' black / Mushrooms – Bay Bolete, Chestnut, Hen of the Woods, Penny Bun, Scottish Girolle / Onions – Cevenne, Roscoff / Somerset leeks / Potatoes – Belle de Fontenay, Charlotte, Italian Spunta (for chipping), Lancashire Agria, Northumberland Yukon Gold, Ratte / Squash – Delica, Italian Turban, Potimarron, Spaghetti / Casava / Celeriac / Somerset bunched carrots / Somerset heirloom beetroot / Turnips – French, Kohlrabi / Yams

Penny Bun Mushroom
Penny Buns are in My Ears and in My Eyes

At Turnips we source our wild mushrooms from all over Europe, starting in Turkey in February with Morels. We travel across the continent to end our journey in the UK in September with Penny Buns. Here, we rely on a network of foragers – it might be Michael from Essex, but it could be Anne from Cornwall – because Nature offers no guarantees.

Michael offered to take me out with him to look for Penny Buns. He told me to wear wellington boots. "Michael," I said, "I'm a greengrocer, I spend my life outdoors. You don't need to tell *me* what to wear!" I ignored him and wore my usual Doc Martens that I bought off a bloke selling them from his van in New Covent Garden Market.

My son Charlie and I met Michael in Essex at 4am – serious foragers set off while it's still dark to pick mushrooms at daybreak. Penny Buns should not be picked when wet, as they can deteriorate quickly. Ideally, you want a crisp autumn morning dappled with sunshine after a light rainfall. Michael parked under a Ministry of Defence sign: "Don't worry, I've got permission."

"What the hell is this?" I asked. "It's a military training ground where they recreate the Afghan terrain and let off bombs." This information added a certain frisson. The MoD land was covered with craters ankle deep with rainwater. It quickly became clear that my knock-off DMs were as waterproof

If you don't want maggots as a side course, ask your vendor to minutely slice the stem of the Penny Bun. If there are no tiny holes, you have a perfect mushroom to enjoy.

as bath sponges. Michael led us into the woods and told us to look for patches of heather and fallen leaves. The caps of Penny Buns are the same colour as autumn leaves, but wipe away the leaves and you'll find the most perfect mushrooms. The skill is knowing when to pick them. In the right conditions, Penny Buns can emerge, grow up to a kilo (2lb 4oz), and start to putrefy within a week. Once the mushrooms get big, they can get stronger in flavour and attract flies. And that means maggots…

Head down, scouring the forest floor, I tripped over a fallen tree and nearly knocked over some old boy who was also out foraging. Midway through my apology, I realized that this old boy was none other than legendary restaurateur Antonio Carluccio. Having foraged since he was a child in Italy, Antonio was passionate about mushrooms. We agreed that Penny Buns in the UK tend to look fresher because the damp makes the caps tacky, whereas French ceps or Italian porcini look drier, even wilted, but that isn't necessarily a sign of poor quality.

> "I'm a greengrocer, I spend my life outdoors. You don't need to tell *me* what to wear!"

Penny Buns are a good-size mushroom with caps 8–25cm (3–10in) across. When cooked, they are firm and meaty with a buttery, umami-rich, nutty flavour. They dry well. Young *Boletus edulis* (the botanical name) are delicious raw in salads – they're crisp and velvety with a woody, almost smoky flavour. It's best to cook the more mature mushrooms. To check for age, look at the pores on the underside of the caps – a fresh Penny Bun will be pale grey, then it will turn yellow, then olive green when it's getting past it. They have an incredible, intense depth of flavour, almost Parmesan-like, so a little goes a long way. The drier the climate, the stronger the flavour (and greater the chance of maggots).

Antonio found that Brits would rarely pick Penny Buns, regarding them as "something suspicious". In Italy, by contrast, most people would happily chow down on porcini – maggots and all. This day, the great chef opened his rucksack and pulled out a little gas burner, a home-baked sourdough loaf and a box of eggs. He scraped away the spongy underside of the mushrooms, explaining that otherwise they'd be soggy. He glugged some olive oil into a frying pan, added a knob of butter and some garlic and set the pan over the burner. In those woods on that perfect autumn morning, with the sun just beginning to dry my feet, a wonderful sense of calm came over me.

Antonio sliced the Penny Buns straight into the pan, they sizzled and browned in the garlicky oil and a deep, earthy smell filled the air. He scattered over chopped parsley and a generous smattering of flaky salt and black pepper – Antonio's rucksack could rival Mary Poppins' carpet bag for contents. He cracked the eggs into the pan, whisked them into an omelette and toasted great hunks of the sourdough over the open fire. The mushroom omelette was divided into four and served on top of the hot, crunchy toast. There were Charlie and I, sitting on a fallen log in the middle of a wood on MoD land and sharing breakfast with a Greek forager from Essex and an Italian culinary legend. Life doesn't get much better than that.

Potatoes and ceps   *Recipe by Antonio Carluccio*

Here is a recipe from Antonio's own book *Complete Mushroom Book: The Quiet Hunt*.

Serves 4

200g (7oz) fresh ceps
600g (1lb 5oz) waxy firm potatoes
85g (3oz) butter
90ml (3fl oz) olive oil
12 sage leaves
salt and pepper, to taste

Clean, trim and finely slice the ceps and peel the potatoes. Boil the potatoes in salted water until soft. Drain and leave them to cool, then slice thickly.

Fry the cep slices in half the butter and half the oil until brown, then set aside. Fry the potatoes and two thirds of the sage leaves in the rest of the butter and oil.

Mix the ceps and potatoes together in a large dish and season to taste. Scatter the remaining sage leaves over. Serve either as a starter or a side dish with meat or fish.

Jarred Penny Buns

This is a simple preserving technique to make the most of the short season for these mushrooms, keeping them in your larder for later in the year. Once you've opened the jar, you can simply boil or pan-fry the drained Penny Buns.

Makes 2 x 1 litre (35fl oz) jars

250g (9oz) Penny Bun mushrooms, chopped into bitesize pieces
1 tbsp caster (superfine) sugar
1 tbsp fine sea salt
2 tbsp apple cider vinegar
2 bay/cherry/blackcurrant leaves

Put the Penny Buns in a pan and cover them with cold water. Place the pan over a high heat and bring the water to a boil. Drain and repeat. The water should run clear.

In another saucepan, heat 1 litre (35fl oz) of water with the sugar, salt, apple cider vinegar and leaves. Stir the water over a medium heat until the sugar and salt have dissolved. Add the cleaned mushrooms and gently simmer for 15–20 minutes, depending on size, until tender.

Divide the mushrooms between 2 sterilized jars and pour over the cooking liquor, ensuring the mushrooms are fully submerged. Immediately seal with the lids, turn the jars upside down to create a vacuum and leave them until the contents of the jars are cool.

Once the pickles are cool, turn the jars the right way up and store in a cool, dark place or in the fridge for up to 6 months. Once opened, store in the fridge and use within 3 weeks.

Penny Bun dumplings with herb mayonnaise and wasabi

This starter is a real celebration of the Penny Bun mushroom. Packed with herbs to bring freshness, with a warming heat from wasabi for added brightness, this is a finely balanced dish with layers of texture. Although there are quite a few stages to follow, don't be put off – none is particularly difficult. Remember to start at least a day before serving, so your cauliflower mushrooms have enough time to pickle.

Serves 4

For the pickled cauliflower mushrooms

100ml (3½fl oz) rice vinegar

50g (1¾oz) caster (superfine) sugar

pinch of salt

100g (3½oz) cauliflower mushrooms, cut into floret clusters

For the herb mayonnaise

75g (2½oz) flat-leaf parsley, leaves picked

50g (1¾oz) chives, roughly chopped

200ml (7fl oz) vegetable oil

2 egg yolks

1 tbsp Dijon mustard

generous pinch of sea salt flakes

For the mushroom purée

50g (1¾oz) butter

1kg (2lb 4oz) button mushrooms, trimmed and roughly chopped

100–200ml (3½–7fl oz) mushroom stock

Continued overleaf...

Combine the vinegar, sugar, 150ml (5fl oz) of water and the salt in a non-reactive pan, stirring until the sugar has dissolved. Bring the liquid to a boil, then leave to cool until lukewarm. Place the cleaned mushrooms in a sterilized jar, pour over the pickling liquid, seal the jar with the lid and leave at room temperature for 24–72 hours.

To make the herb mayonnaise, put the parsley leaves in a food processor with the chives. Add the oil and blitz quickly until smooth. Pour the herb oil through a sieve lined with muslin (cheesecloth) and leave it to slowly drip through into a small bowl. Pour the oil into a small plastic container and freeze it for about 2 hours, until solid.

Spoon the oil from the frozen herb water to separate them. Discard the water and leave the oil to warm to room temperature. In a small bowl whisk the egg yolks and mustard with the salt until pale. Very slowly and gradually whisk in the herb oil to make mayonnaise. Cover and chill until ready to serve.

Make the purée. Melt the butter in a large frying pan over a medium heat. Add the mushrooms, season well and fry until they are browned and have released all their water. Tip the mushrooms into a food processor, add 100ml (3½fl oz) of the stock and blitz together until smooth, adding more stock, if necessary – the mixture should be the consistency of sour cream. Set aside.

Continued overleaf...

For the dumplings

450g (1lb) potato flour

300g (10½oz) plain (all-purpose) flour, plus extra for rolling out

good pinch of salt

340ml (11½fl oz) boiling water

4 tsp sesame oil

For the dumpling filling

2 tbsp olive oil

200g (7oz) Penny Bun mushrooms, cut into 5mm (¼in) slices

4 tsp finely chopped chives

For the wasabi sauce

1 tbsp olive oil

2 banana shallots, finely sliced

2 garlic cloves, crushed

150ml (5fl oz) white wine

500ml (17fl oz) full-fat milk

2–3 tsp wasabi paste

100g (3½oz) spinach

2g soy lecithin

To serve

100g (3½oz) Penny Bun mushrooms, sliced

knob of butter

1 tbsp olive oil

handful of parsley cress (optional)

salt and freshly ground black pepper

To make the dumplings, mix the flours together in a bowl with the salt. Pour over the boiling water and the sesame oil and mix to roughly combine. Tip the dough on to your work surface and knead until smooth and elastic. Return the dough to the bowl, cover and leave to rest for 30 minutes.

Meanwhile, make the filling. Heat the olive oil in a frying pan over a high heat. Add the mushrooms and fry them for about 4–5 minutes, or until soft. Leave to cool, then finely chop them, mix them with the chives and season them with salt. Spoon the filling into a piping bag and set it aside while you make the wasabi sauce.

Heat the oil in a frying pan over a low heat. Add the shallots and garlic and cook for about 5 minutes, until translucent. Add the white wine, bring to a boil and let the liquid bubble away until reduced by half (about 5 minutes). Add the milk and bring the liquid to a boil again – it might look like it's split, but it will emulsify later. Put the mixture in a blender, season with salt and wasabi paste to taste. Add the spinach in stages, blitzing each time, until the sauce is a vibrant green. Pass it through a fine-mesh sieve and chill it until you're ready to serve.

Lightly flour your work surface and roll out the rested dumpling dough to a thickness of 2–3mm (¹⁄₁₆–⅛in). Use two round cutters of 5cm and 6cm (2in and 2½in), to stamp out 24 circles of dough – 12 in each size. Pipe roughly 1 teaspoon of dumpling filling into the centre of each of the smaller disks. Brush the edges with water and cover each with a larger disk. Press the edges around the filling to seal and to expel any air bubbles. You should make 12 dumplings in total.

Pan-fry the remaining Penny Buns to serve in the butter and oil for about 4–5 minutes, until tender and golden brown and season with salt and pepper to taste. Meanwhile, cook the dumplings in a steamer for about 7 minutes, until cooked through.

Warm the mushroom purée in a small pan. Spoon 3 dots of purée on to each plate and place a dumpling on top of each dot. Next, arrange the pan-fried Penny Buns in the middle of the plates, along with 2 drained pickled mushrooms. Pipe over dots of herb mayonnaise and a little more purée.

Blitz the wasabi sauce until foaming, add the soy lecithin and blitz again so that the sauce retains the bubbles. Spoon wasabi foam on top of the mushrooms in the centre of the plate and arrange the parsley cress on top before serving.

37

Vassout Comice pears / *Finger limes* / *Cavaillon melon* / *Apples – Bramley, Hereford Cox Orange Pippin, Kent Russet* / *Kent Conference pears* / *Quince* / *Kentish blackberries* / *Muscat grapes* / *Damsons* / *Plums – French Mirabelle, Kent Victoria, Pershore* / *Reine Claude greengages* / *Kentish mint – many varieties* / *Italian Monk's Beard* / *Norfolk herbs* / *Norfolk marsh samphire* / *Purple basil* / *Thai basil* / *Kentish cobnuts* / *Tomatoes – Ailsa Craig and Red Alert from Essex, Italian Vesuvio, Main crop Provence, San Marzano* / *Chalke Valley watercress* / *Italian rocket (arugula)* / *Surrey salad leaves* / *Endives – Escarole, Winter frisée* / *Late chioggia radicchio* / *Feuille de chêne (oak leaf lettuce)* / *UK Cos* / *Breakfast radish* / *Pimiento Asado del Bierzo* / *Essex sweetcorn* / *Kent broccoli* / *Cauliflower – Boston, Cape, Romanesque* / *Chard – Rainbow, Swiss* / *Cime di rapa* / *Cabbages – Cavolo Nero, Kent red and white, Normandy Savoy, Somerset kale* / *Garlic – Lautrec pink, French smoked, Turnips' black* / *Mushrooms – Bay Bolete, Beefsteak Fungus, Chanterelle, Chestnut, Common Puffball, Hen of the Woods, Horse, Penny Bun, Scottish Girolle, Trumpet* / *Onions – Cevenne, Roscoff* / *Somerset leeks* / *Potatoes – Belle de Fontenay, Charlotte, Lancashire Agria, Northumberland Yukon Gold, Ratte* / *Squash – Delica, Italian Turban, Potimarron, Spaghetti* / *Celeriac* / *Somerset bunched carrots* / *Somerset heirloom beetroot* / *Turnips – French, Kohlrabi*

Vassout Comice pear
A Partridge in a Pear Tree

The Vassout family's 39 hectares (86 acres) of orchards are about 48km (30 miles) north of Paris. Having grown orchard fruits for three generations and almost 100 years, this is the oldest family of orchardists in the Ile de France. They produce exceptional apples and pears. Someone once told me that the land the Vassouts farm has been given a royal decree stating that it will always be used for fruit farming – I can't substantiate that, but it's a lovely story!

The trees in the Vassout orchards are meticulously hand-pruned twice a year, once in winter and then in late summer, when they remove excess foliage and the smallest, marked fruits so that each apple and pear is fully exposed to the sunlight to ripen evenly and blemish-free. The process is labour intensive and creates a much-reduced yield (with a high cost), but the results are truly world-class fruit. This is farming with passion.

To release their flavour, pears need to ripen, but even then so many pears are flavourless. Vassout's, though, is a story of perfection – there's no need to add sugar and spice to their pears. The family grows Guyot, Williams Blanches, Williams Rouge, Beurré Hardy, Conference, Passe Crassane and Comice. Some are intended specifically for cooking; each is distinct. Williams, Passe Crassane and Beurre Hardy keep their form when cooked; Comice does not. Lusciously textured, juicy, and earthy in flavour, this thin-skinned pear oozes with juice like nectar. The season for these exemplary pears is quite short: they harvest from early September and will store up to mid-January.

Generally, Conference and Comice pears are considered to have the best flavour, and both are grown in southern Britain and northern France, which share similar terroir and climate. I believe that Comice are the best, and if it weren't for the Vassout family, we would stay in Kent to source ours. But, the skill and husbandry of Vassout puts their fruit in the premier league. Once hand-picked, each fruit is graded, then the tips of the stems are dipped in red wax and each fruit is wrapped in paper. The process is above and beyond.

In the UK, the government-run Department for Environment, Food and Rural Affairs (DEFRA) is responsible for grading our fresh produce. They "class" fruit using the Specific Marketing Standard, which includes quality and labelling rules for each stage of production and marketing. What it does not judge, though, is flavour. So, you can buy a wonky, out-of-shape, blemished Class 2 Comice pear and its flavour could be far superior to a Class 1 picture-perfect Williams. Looks aren't everything: use your taste buds not your eyes.

In my world, food is all about enjoyment. I believe that if we can adopt a simplistic love of seasonal food, we can go a long way in the quest to slow down the imminent climate crisis. Whether you are foraging for blackberries, growing basil in window boxes or popping to Turnips (or your local greengrocer) for some delicious blood oranges or Norfolk asparagus, sourcing local, seasonal produce and cooking your meals from scratch is not only healthier, but also reduces how much we rely on global food chains.

Oana's story – a tale of perfection

"The Pear, the whole Pear and nothing but the Pear, so help me boss." By now I hope you'll have seen how the recipes in this book cover all levels of difficulty, from some very simple preserving methods to highly technical culinary wizardry from the chefs at Turnips. At Turnips we are very fortunate in having a team of talented individuals working in our restaurant kitchen, including our pastry chef Oana – "The Pudding Lady". Oana has fully embraced the Turnips mantra of "All taste, no waste" and creates stunning desserts using the ever-changing seasonal produce

> "The fruits are hand-picked and graded, the tips of the stems are dipped in red wax and each fruit is wrapped in paper."

available to her. She cooks with unbelievable skill and finesse and her attention to detail is exquisite. At this time of year, she has a complicated and intricate Vassout pear dessert on our menu (it is probably not a dish you could try to recreate at home) that uses the pears in their entirety, even making a crisp from the skin. It comprises a caramel chocolate mousse, ganache, sesame and almond crumble, almond dacquoise, pear compôte, pear gel and, finally, a delicate pear sorbet – it's a taste explosion that everyone should experience at least once.

Pear cake with white chocolate and vanilla Namelaka

Stunning Vassout pears are full of flavour and very crisp and are perfect for baking. This simple cake is served with chocolate and vanilla Namelaka, which is a cross between a mousse and ganache, and the combo will stop everyone talking when dessert is served – and for all the right reasons!

Serves 4–6

For the white chocolate and vanilla Namelaka

2 platinum-grade gelatine leaves

185g (6½oz) good-quality white chocolate, finely chopped

100ml (3½fl oz) full-fat milk

½ vanilla pod

200ml (7fl oz) whipping cream

For the cake

3–4 ripe Vassout Comice pears, plus extra to serve

250g (9oz) unsalted butter, at room temperature, plus extra for greasing

250g (9oz/1½ cups) caster (superfine) sugar

4 eggs, lightly beaten

finely grated zest of 1 lemon

¼ tsp vanilla extract

250g (9oz/1¾ cups + 2 tbsp) plain (all-purpose) flour

1 tsp baking powder

pinch of salt

Prepare the Namelaka the day before you plan to serve, as it needs to chill overnight. Soak the gelatine leaves in a bowl of cold water for 5 minutes to soften. Tip the white chocolate into another bowl.

Pour the milk into a small saucepan and add the halved vanilla pod. Place over a medium heat and bring the milk to just below boiling, then remove the pan from the heat. Drain the rehydrated gelatine from the bowl and squeeze out any excess water. Add it to the hot milk and whisk until the gelatine has melted and is thoroughly combined. Remove the vanilla pod, then pour the hot milk over the chocolate and mix well with a silicone spatula until smooth. Add the cream, and using a stick blender mix to a perfectly smooth emulsion. Leave to cool, then cover and chill overnight.

Make the cake. Preheat the oven to 180°C/160°C fan/350°F/Gas 4 and grease and line the base of a 23cm (9in) cake tin. Peel, quarter and core the pears and cut them into 5mm (¼in)-thick slices.

Using a stand mixer, cream the butter and sugar until light and fluffy. Gradually add the eggs, mixing well between each addition. Add the lemon zest and vanilla and mix again. Sift the flour, baking powder and salt into the bowl and mix again to a smooth batter.

Spoon half the mixture into the cake tin and spread level. Arrange the pear slices on top and then cover with the remaining cake mixture and spread level again. Bake for about 60 minutes, until well risen and golden brown and a skewer inserted into the middle comes out clean. Leave the cake to cool.

Spoon the Namelaka into a piping bag fitted with a 1cm (½in) plain or fluted nozzle. Cut the cake into slices, decorate with the Namelaka and serve with extra slices of fresh pear.

Comice pear compôte

At Turnips, we had an amazing pear dessert on the menu and decided to make it into something to sell on the retail stand. This compôte has been a huge hit with our customers and I would suggest doubling or even tripling this recipe – it will take a little longer to prepare and cook but you will have double the amount of joy sitting in your fridge. The compôte is delicious with muesli, other cereals or pancakes, or as a topping for cakes.

Makes 1 small jar

75g (2½oz) jam sugar

1 vanilla pod, seeds scraped out, pod reserved

2 Vassout Comice pears, peeled, cored and chopped into 5mm (¼in) cubes

In a saucepan, combine the sugar with 200ml (7fl oz) of water, and the vanilla seeds and empty pod. Bring the liquid to a boil over a high heat to dissolve the sugar.

Add the pear and cook over a low heat for about 10 minutes, until the pear is very soft, but still holding its shape.

Remove the vanilla pod and spoon the compôte into a sterilized jar. Seal with the lid, turn the jar upside down to create a vacuum and leave to cool. Store either in the fridge or in a cool dry, place for up to 3 months. Once opened, store in the fridge and use within a week.

38

Essex sweetcorn / Finger limes / Cavaillon melon / Prickly pear / Sharon fruit / Apples – Bramley, Hereford Cox Orange Pippin, Kent Russet / Kent medlars / Pears – French Vassout Comice, Kent Conference / Quince / Kentish Blackberry / Muscat grapes / Damsons / Plums – Kent Victoria plums / Reine Claude greengages / Italian Monk's Beard / Norfolk marsh samphire / Chestnuts / Kentish cobnuts / Tomatoes – Ailsa Craig and Red Alert from Essex, Italian Vesuvio, Main crop Provence, San Marzano / Chalke Valley watercress / Italian rocket (arugula) / Endives – Escarole, Winter frisée / Late chioggia radicchio / Feuille de chêne (oak leaf lettuce) / Pimiento Asado del Bierzo / Essex sweetcorn / Cauliflowers – Boston, Cape, Romanesque / Chard – Rainbow, Swiss / Cime di rapa / Cabbages – Cavolo Nero, Kent Brussels tops, Kent Hispi, Kent red and white, Normandy Savoy, Somerset kale / Garlic – French smoked, Lautrec pink, Turnips' black / Mushrooms – Bay Bolete, Beefsteak Fungus, Chanterelle, Chestnut, Common Puffball, Hen of the Woods, Horse Penny Bun, Scottish Girolle, Trumpet / Onions – Cevenne, Roscoff / Somerset leeks / Potatoes – Belle de Fontenay, Charlotte, Lancashire Agria, Northumberland Yukon Gold, Ratte / Squash – Delica, Italian Turban, Potimarron, Spaghetti / Celeriac / Italian chervil root / Parsley root / Red meat radish / Somerset heirloom beetroot / Turnips – French, Kohlrabi

Sweetcorn
The Cob Father

If I were to ask 100 people when they think sweetcorn is in season, I'm fairly sure that 99 of them wouldn't have a clue. In the UK, in January, you can buy vacuum-packed corn-on-the-cob from Peru. After that, it's possible to source it from Egypt, and then from Portugal and other mid-European countries. It's not until we hit France that the corn is freed from the packs, fresh and of better quality.

Even though you can get sweetcorn from all over the world all year round, it doesn't mean that you should: corn is always better from closer to home. But it's not just as simple as proximity (when is it ever?). It is not until September that the best UK sweetcorn is available and then you can enjoy exceptional varieties that are grown in Essex, the Isle of Wight and Cornwall. In fact, in the sandy coastal soil, where the best potatoes and asparagus grow, you'll also find the best sweetcorn.

The corn season in Cornwall and on the Isle of White begins a little earlier than now, usually sometime in mid-August, with a variety called Illini Xtra Sweet. For this reason, when we source our sweetcorn, we travel West to East along the south coast of the UK and once we reach Essex, we stop buying from elsewhere and focus on the nearest (and best) harvest to us. The Essex corn has larger ears and the kernels are sweeter and far juicier than corn from most other regions.

Corn, like peas and asparagus, doesn't travel well. It needs to be cooked and eaten soon after harvesting for us to fully enjoy its crisp texture and juicy, sweet flavour. As a result, growers need to know exactly when to harvest the ears of corn: they should be at the "milk" stage – when a pierced kernel will produce a milky liquid – which indicates they are at peak sweetness. Time is critical: a corn cob's rapidly declining goodness hugely effects the sweet flavour.

This is a great vegetable to plant in your garden or allotment because it's easy to grow and needs so little prep before you can enjoy it. If you're buying sweetcorn, though, always buy the cobs while they are still encased in their husks, which should be green and fresh-looking to indicate the corn is likely at its best. The husk also acts as a brilliant wrapper if you're cooking on a barbecue – it helps to keep the kernels crisp and juicy over the fierce heat of the coals.

For over 30 years we have been buying North Maldon sweetcorn from an agent in Spitalfields fruit-and-vegetable wholesale market in Leyton, to the east of London. North Maldon is in Essex, on the Blackwater Estuary, in an area where over the centuries land was reclaimed from the marshes for farming. The fertile, alluvial soil helps to produce heavy yields of crops and perfect growing conditions for "The Sweet Stuff". North Maldon Growers Ltd is a co-operative farming business of four local Essex families, who have been wholesale producers of UK-grown hand-picked fresh vegetables since 1964. As well as sweetcorn, they grow pumpkins, courgettes (zucchini) and brassicas. Their deliciously sweet and juicy, hand-picked whole corn-on-the-cob is branded as Goldhanger Corn after the village near where it is grown. The season starts in late August (but we tend to wait until early September when the sweeter varieties appear) and goes on to about the end of October.

For a long while we never really had a connection with the farmers who grew our sweetcorn; we just knew this was the best-tasting corn nearest to us at Borough Market. (In flavour it equals the first of the Isle of White sweetcorn and surpasses any foreign imports.) Given this anonymity, then, imagine my surprise when, a few years ago, I met Ron, the head supplier of North Maldon Sweetcorn, at a prestigious golf club in Surrey. The meeting was purely by serendipitous chance. My friend John had invited me to play at the famous Wentworth course, and suggested he would introduce me to a friend of his, another member, while I was there – because we'd have a lot in common. Enter Ron. On that day I lost a golf match, but secured a brilliant deal for the most succulent sweetcorn in the whole of Essex.

"Even though you can get sweetcorn from all over the world all year round, it doesn't mean that you should: corn is always better from closer to home."

Popped corn

Most people think sweetcorn season is all year round – but it's not! At the height of the season, in September, you can use corns fresh in many ways (salsas, creamy corn or cooked whole on the cob and served with butter). If you're a fan of a challenge, you can also try this. Handcrafted from start to finish, making your own popcorn does take a bit of time but it's not labour intensive.

Makes 1 bowl

2 corn-on-the-cobs
50g (1¾oz) butter, melted
sea salt flakes, to season

Peel the husk and any strings from the cobs and discard. Meanwhile, bring a large saucepan of salted water to a boil. Add the de-husked cobs and blanch them for 2 minutes, until the kernels are just tender.

Drain the cobs and plunge them into a bowl of iced water to stop them cooking any further. Leave them to cool and then drain them again and pat them dry with kitchen paper.

Stand the cobs upright on a board and, slicing downward, strip the kernels using a sharp knife. Place the kernels in a dehydrator and leave them to dry according to the manufacturer's instructions, for about 1 day.

When the corn is completely dry, tip it into a paper bag and then put this bag into another bag with the openings facing each other so that the kernels cannot escape. Microwave the corn in the paper bag, on full power for 2 minutes, until popped.

Tip the popped corn into a large bowl, mix with the melted butter to coat and season with sea salt flakes.

Sweetcorn salsa

When the weather gets a little bit moodier, you really want something fresh and colourful on your dinner plate. You can make this beautiful salsa to go with your ribeye or whole roasted fish, or try wrapping the salsa in blanched Napa cabbage leaves for an amazing canapé.

Serves 4

2 corn-on-the-cobs

1 Granny Smith apple, peeled, cored and finely diced

1 banana shallot, finely chopped

1 red chilli, deseeded and finely chopped

finely grated zest and juice of 1 lime

2 tbsp olive oil

1 tbsp chopped coriander (cilantro) leaves

1 tbsp chopped flat-leaf parsley leaves

runny honey, to sweeten, if necessary

salt and freshly ground black pepper

Stand the corn upright on a chopping board and, using a sharp knife, cut down the length of the cob to strip away the kernels without cutting into the core.

In a bowl combine the corn kernels with the apple, shallot and chilli. Add the lime zest and juice, olive oil and chopped herbs, mix to combine and season with salt and pepper to taste. The flavours should be tangy and sharp from the chilli and lime, but add a little honey if you feel it needs sweetening.

Cover the corn and chill it for 2–3 hours for the flavours to mingle, then remove it from the fridge and leave it for about 20 minutes, to serve it at room temperature.

39

Delica squash / *Finger limes* / *Cavaillon melon* / *Prickly pear* / *Sharon fruit* / *Apples – Bramley, Hereford Cox Orange Pippin, Kent Russet* / *Kent medlars* / *Pears – French Vassout Comice, Kent Conference* / *Quince* / *Kentish Blackberry* / *Muscat grapes* / *Damsons* / *Plums – Kent Victoria* / *Reine Claude greengages* / *Italian Monk's Beard* / *Norfolk marsh samphire* / *Chestnuts* / *Kentish cobnuts* / *Tomatoes – Ailsa Craig and Red Alert from Essex, Italian Vesuvio, Main crop Provence, San Marzano* / *Chalke Valley watercress* / *Italian rocket (arugula)* / *Endives – Escarole, Winter frisée* / *Late chioggia radicchio* / *Feuille de chêne (oak leaf lettuce)* / *Pimiento Asado del Bierzo* / *Essex sweetcorn* / *Cauliflower – Boston, Cape, Romanesque* / *Chard – Rainbow, Swiss* / *Cime di rapa* / *Cabbages – Cavolo Nero, Kent Brussels tops, Kent Hispi, Kent red and white, Normandy Savoy, Somerset kale* / *Garlic – French smoked, Lautrec pink, Turnips' black* / *Mushrooms – Bay Bolete, Beefsteak Fungus, Chanterelle, Chestnut, Common Puffball, Hen of the Woods, Horse, Penny Bun, Scottish Girolle, Trumpet* / *Onions – Cevenne, Roscoff* / *Somerset leeks* / *Potatoes – Belle de Fontenay, Charlotte, Lincolnshire Agria, Northumberland Yukon Gold, Ratte* / *Squash – Italian Turban, Potimarron, Spaghetti* / *Celeriac* / *Italian chervil root* / *Parsley root* / *Red meat radish* / *Somerset heirloom beetroot* / *Turnips – French, Kohlrabi*

Delica Squash
A Squash and a Squeeze

So here we are in the week before the autumn–winter season starts. It's a time of transition for fresh produce: stone fruits are giving way to the seeded and orchard fruits – there are no more peaches, nectarines and mangoes; plums are on the wane. Now it's all about the figs, grapes, apples, pears and quinces. In the vegetable world, the leafy varieties are being replaced by root veg.

With perfect timing, as the summer squashes pare back, the hardier pumpkins and squashes of autumn come. One of the first to arrive is the Delica pumpkin (a type of Kabocha squash), from Lombardy in northern Italy. This is squat and round, with bumpy, thick, dark grey–green, mottled skin. Cut it open and the smooth flesh is bright orange and has a sweet, nutty flavour that pairs well with woody herbs, such as rosemary, sage and thyme (which are also hitting their stride) and with cheese. The Delica holds its shape well when it's cooked and is delicious roasted or steamed and added to risotto; puréed and used as a filling for pasta; and even candied and paired with chocolate.

In northern Italy the pumpkins are *naturalmente stagionata*, or naturally seasoned. They are harvested when mature and stored for between one and two months in a heated, dry atmosphere, which reduces the water content in the pumpkin, firms the flesh and allows the natural sugars to develop, which in turn improves the flavour immensely. By "curing" the pumpkins in this way, producers can store them in a dark, dry room for months. The tip of the stem is covered in a red wax seal, which denotes quality and provenance and prevents them drying out. As a result of this process, the Italians often served the pumpkins during Lent as a meat substitute.

Life beyond the supermarket

In the spirit of full disclosure, I admit I absolutely love supermarkets. Like everyone, I lead a busy life and value convenience. However, I feel passionately that supermarkets need to stand side-by-side with niche stores, markets and farmers' markets. We are not competitors – we offer something completely different, but complementary. You will not, for example, see the Delica squash in many UK supermarkets. The same goes for other world-class European and international products. Instead, you will mostly find heavily subsidized, mass-produced imports that leave our own farmers and growers struggling.

When supermarkets first started selling fresh produce, many farmers couldn't wait to get in on the action. They no longer had to worry about selling small orders to a multitude of wholesalers – they could shift their whole stock in one fell swoop. However, the system put them at the mercy of the store giants. Now, price wars, less diversity of fresh produce and poorer quality have left the farming industry in crisis. We have lost thousands of farms in the last decade alone. Those farmers who do not want to go down the route of growing inferior produce on a grand scale need our help, and their high-end, seasonal fruit and vegetables should be available to everyone. If we can increase their turnover by buying more, natural business forces would bring down their prices making better food more affordable for everyone.

> "I feel passionately that supermarkets need to stand side by side with niche stores, markets and farmers' markets. We are not competitors – we offer something completely different, but complementary."

If you're a regular supermarket shopper, take note of what you're putting in your basket: the same bag of apples, plastic-wrapped broccoli, maybe a bag of carrots. If you shop online, you even get reminders to add last week's purchases into this week's virtual cart. Soft fruits are largely restricted to four varieties (strawberries, raspberries, blueberries and blackberries), regardless of whether you are shopping during the UK season or not, when you could be enjoying so many more. If you want to eat strawberries with your breakfast yogurt all year round, you will need to source them from all across the globe, but by doing so you'll be missing out on other seasonal berries, like mulberries and tayberries. Extending the natural season of one product can be to the detriment of another and some once-popular fruits and vegetables have now been all but forgotten.

I want to offer an alternative way of thinking about and shopping for fresh produce and to encourage you to embrace seasonal shifts in your cooking. Pumpkins and squashes are here in all their autumn glory.

Squash salad with pickled walnuts and blue cheese

My family absolutely loves "meaty" vegetarian salads. Pumpkin and squash are perfect for the job and mean that this salad is great as either a starter or a main meal. You can use whichever blue cheese you like, but my favourite is Cashel Blue.

Serves 4

1 butternut squash, peeled, deseeded and cut into 1cm (½in) cubes

2 thyme sprigs, leaves picked

2 rosemary sprigs

4 garlic cloves, chopped

3 tbsp olive oil

1 baby gem lettuce, chopped into bitesize pieces

1 red onion, sliced

2 pickled walnuts, drained and roughly chopped or sliced

100g (3½oz) blue cheese (such as Cashel Blue)

100g (3½oz) rocket (arugula) leaves

nasturtium leaves (optional)

2–3 tbsp sherry vinegar

salt and freshly ground black pepper

Preheat the oven to 180°C/160°C fan/350°F/Gas 4 and line a baking tray with baking paper.

Place the squash on the lined baking tray. Add the thyme, rosemary and garlic and season well with salt and pepper. Drizzle with the olive oil and mix to coat the squash. Cover the tray loosely with foil and roast for 20–25 minutes, until the butternut squash is soft and tender but not mushy. Remove the rosemary sprig, tip the squash into a bowl and leave it to cool to room temperature.

Add the lettuce, onion and walnuts to the bowl with the squash, crumble in the blue cheese, season with salt and pepper and mix gently to combine.

Finally, add the rocket leaves, nasturtium leaves (if using), and the sherry vinegar to taste. Mix to combine and serve immediately.

Gratin of pumpkin *Recipe by Jennifer Paterson*

This recipe is as much about the person as it is about the pumpkin. Jennifer Paterson's life was far from simple. She was a wild child with a turbulent youth that saw her excommunicated from her family, but she found solace in the church. This led her to a simple way of living, including in her cooking. "Incredible flavours need no supporting acts, just some friends" – my wife, Caroline, and I struck up a dear friendship with Jennifer. We saw her most weeks, rain or shine, at our stall in Pimlico. "What shall we eat this week?" she might ask. Well, Jennifer, this week it is pumpkin.

Serves 4–6

900g (2lb) piece of pumpkin, peeled, depipped and defibred

seasoned plain (all-purpose) flour

oil

450g (1lb) onions, sliced

225g (8oz) tomatoes, peeled, fresh or canned

salt, pepper, sugar

breadcrumbs and butter

Slice the pumpkin into 1cm (½in) by 7.5cm (3in) pieces. Shake them in flour. Fry them in oil until golden, batch by batch, drain on kitchen towels.

In another pan, cook the onions gently in oil until soft but not browned. Add the tomatoes and stew until you get a moist sauce. Season with salt, pepper, and a little sugar.

In a gratin dish, layer the slices of pumpkin and the onion mixture, adding a little extra seasoning. Finish with a layer of pumpkin and scatter it evenly with breadcrumbs. Melt 30g (1oz) or so of butter and drizzle it over the crumbs.

Bake in the oven at 180°C/160°C fan/350°F/Gas 4, until bubbling round the sides, about 45 minutes. Finish by browning the top under the grill (broiler). To make a change you could also add gruyère cheese to the crumbs. Serve immediately.

Muscat grapes / *Finger limes* / *Cavaillon melon* / *Prickly pear* / *Sharon fruit* / *Apples – Bramley, Kent Russet, Hereford Cox Orange Pippin* / *Kent medlars* / *Pears – French Vassout Comice, Kent Conference* / *Quince* / *Damsons* / *Egyptian yellow Bahri dates* / *Jordanian Medjool dates* / *Plums – Kent Victoria* / *Reine Claude greengages* / *Dried fruit – Corsican apricots, Prunes d'Agen* / *Italian Monk's Beard* / *Norfolk marsh samphire* / *Kentish cobnuts* / *Marron glacé* / *Sweet chestnuts* / *Wet walnuts* / *Tomatoes – Italian Vesuvio, Main crop Provence, San Marzano* / *Chalke Valley watercress* / *Italian rocket (arugula)* / *Endives – Escarole, Winter frisée* / *late Chioggia radicchio* / *Feuille de chêne (oak leaf lettuce)* / *Sweet peppers* / *Essex sweetcorn* / *Cauliflower – Boston, Cape, Romanesque* / *Cime di rapa* / *Chard – Rainbow, Swiss* / *Cabbage – Cavolo Nero, Kent Brussels tops, Kent Hispi, Kent red and white, Normandy Savoy, Somerset kale* / *Jerusalem artichokes* / *Garlic – French smoked, Lautrec pink, Turnips' black* / *Mushrooms – Bay Bolete, Chestnut, Hen of the Woods* / *Onions – Cevenne, Roscoff* / *Somerset leeks* / *Potatoes – Belle de Fontenay, Charlotte, Lincolnshire Agria, Northumberland Yukon Gold, Ratte* / *Squash – Delica, Italian Turban, Potimarron, Spaghetti* / *Celeriac* / *Horseradish* / *Italian chervil root* / *Parsley root* / *Parsnips* / *Red meat radish* / *Somerset heirloom beetroot* / *Turnips – French, Kohlrabi*

Muscat Grape
In Vino Veritas

This week we enter the autumn–winter season. It's the time of year when our thoughts are focussed around the bounty of the harvest, and at the same time we look forward to next year and planting the seeds now for our early spring produce, such as garlic. We celebrate the end of one growing season while we anticipate the future – it's an incredible moment in the year. Some vegetables are into their second flush, new season "earlies" have turned into main crop "storers" – for example, we started with Jersey potatoes, then moved on to Ile de Ré and now enjoy Lincolnshire Agria and Maris Piper. In fruits, the early season seed varieties, such as raspberries, strawberries and gooseberries, which over the summer gave way to stone fruits, now begin to make a return. Apples, pears, figs and late-season melons are accompanied by European grapes. Who knew that the true grape season was actually at the end of summer?

Table grapes
When most people think about grapes, they immediately think of wine... or maybe that's just me! In fact, grapes fall into two categories: those that are grown for winemaking (understandably highly prized, but not so relevant to this book) and those that are classified as table or eating grapes. Wine grapes, such as Cabernet Sauvignon, Tempranillo Blanco and Riesling, are generally smaller, thicker-skinned, seeded and even when fully ripe have a higher acidity than table grapes, making them somewhat unpleasant to eat. It's the European table grapes that I want to highlight this week. From Italy, we see the stunning

Uva Fragola or "strawberry grape", which is round and deep red to purple, with a sweet, berry flavour. Then there's the lesser-known French variety Chasselas. A beautiful, seeded green–yellow grape with accents of blush as it ripens, a Chasselas is small in size but big on flavour. The Muscat du Ventoux grape from Vaucluse is, however, my pick of the bunch.

The Vaucluse is an inland area nestled between three mountain ranges: Mont Ventoux to the north, Monts du Vaucluse to the east and the Massif du Lubéron to the south. It's the same region of Provence that gave us Carpentras strawberries in April (see page 91) and Cavaillon melons in August (see page 209) – an orchard, olive grove and market garden all rolled into one.

Muscat du Ventoux grapes have been growing in the region for over 100 years, are hand-harvested and run from the end of August for around 12 weeks, ending in October. They are large, dark purple, almost blue–black in colour and hang sumptuously from the vines in loose, conical bunches. They have a sweet muscat scent and a flavour that is a perfect balance of both syrupy and acidic with hints of rose, violet and berries. They are wonderful to serve at the end of a meal on a cheeseboard or as an idle fruit-bowl snack, or churned into sorbet.

> "These sumptuous table grapes are dark purple, almost blue–black in colour and hang from the vines in loose, conical bunches."

Wet walnuts

Heading slightly further north and west to the Périgord and east to Grenoble, we find fresh walnuts. Périgord varieties such as Marbot, Grandjean, Corne and Franquette, all of varying sweetness, are available for a short window until mid-October. Granted AOC status (see page 15), they are sold as Noix du Périgord – the region's limestone soils, altitude and temperate climate making the perfect combination. Most of the walnuts are organic and grown with little or no intervention and some trees produce for over 50 years. If you ever visit, follow the Route de la Noix, which meanders through the valleys and hills of the Dordogne, and take in the walnut groves, restaurants and artisan producers of walnut products, such as the region's famous walnut oil. The season extends until mid-November, with the PDO (see page 15) Noix de Grenoble, which grow in the mountainous Isere, Drôme and Savoie regions. This mild-tasting and creamy nut was the first fruit to receive an AOC.

Walnut oil from either of these nuts, with its low smoking-point and its superb nutty flavour, is sold all over the world. A versatile oil, it's delicious in myriad dishes as a seasoning or drizzled over salads.

Once the fresh walnuts are over, producers dry and sell the remaining main crop throughout France and export them all over Europe. Ideally, they need eating within a few months to enjoy the delicious and unique nuttiness.

Muscat grape sorbet

I'm not a big fan of desserts, but there is something about grapes. They are little sweet-and-sour bubbles covered with a thin, tart skin. You can do so much with them besides just sticking them on a cheeseboard.

This recipe uses Muscat grapes to make a delicious, easy sorbet that will save you when you're watching telly and craving something sweet. You could add spices such as cinnamon to the sorbet mixture, but the grapes are so delicious that I don't think it really needs any extra flavour. However, a little sweet dessert wine added to the cooking pot might not go amiss.

Serves 4

1kg (2lb 4oz) black Muscat grapes, plus extra chopped to decorate

120g (4¼oz) caster (superfine) sugar

finely grated zest and juice of 1 lemon

2 thyme sprigs

Pick the grapes from the stems and place them into a food processor with the sugar and lemon zest and juice. Blitz for 20 seconds, until finely chopped, and pour the mixture into a saucepan. Add the thyme and bring the mixture to a boil. Reduce the heat and simmer for 15–20 minutes, until thickened enough to coat the back of a spoon.

Pass the grape mixture through a fine-mesh sieve to remove the solids. Pour the liquid into a container, leave it to cool and then cover it and chill it overnight.

Churn the sorbet mixture in an ice-cream machine according to the manufacturer's instructions until firm, then serve in scoops decorated with a few extra chopped, fresh grapes. The sorbet will keep in a freezerproof container in the freezer for up to 1 month.

Pickled grapes with creamy mussels

When it comes to shellfish, for me it's all about mussels. Ever since I first tasted them when I was about 19 years old, I just can't get enough of them. Simply steamed with white wine or beer, mussels are beautiful – but they are even more delicious if you add these pickled grapes. You can keep any leftover pickled grapes in the fridge for up to three months – serve them alongside a cheeseboard.

Serves 4

1 bunch of green or red grapes

40g (1½oz) caster (superfine) sugar

80ml (2½fl oz) apple cider vinegar

pinch of salt

1.5kg (3lb 5oz) fresh mussels

150ml (5fl oz) white wine

2 tbsp olive oil

2 banana shallots, sliced

1 small fennel bulb, thinly sliced (save the fennel fronds for the sauce)

3 garlic cloves, chopped

5 thyme sprigs

100ml (3½fl oz) double (heavy) cream

large knob of butter

10 dill sprigs, leaves picked

a few flat-leaf parsley leaves, to garnish (optional)

toasted sourdough, to serve

Start this recipe the night before you plan on serving the mussels, so that the vinegar has a chance to pickle the grapes into sweet-and-sour flavour bombs.

Pick the grapes from the stems and tip them into a bowl.

In a saucepan, combine the sugar and vinegar and 120ml (4fl oz) of water. Bring the liquid to a boil, add the salt and pour the mixture over the grapes. Leave them to cool and then cover and chill them overnight.

Scrub the mussels, pull out the beards and discard any mussels that are open. Tip the mussels into a large bowl and pour over the white wine – I usually make them drunk before they hit the hot pan!

Take a large saucepan that will easily hold all the mussels. Add the oil, shallots, fennel, garlic and thyme and sweat everything over a low heat for about 5 minutes, until the vegetables are softened and transparent.

Increase the heat to full power and quickly, before the vegetables have a chance to burn, add the mussels and wine. Cover with a lid and steam the mussels for a couple of minutes, until they start to open.

Remove the lid, add the cream and cook until the liquid thickens slightly. Roughly chop about 15 of the pickled grapes, add them to the pan and mix well. Spoon the mussels and grapes into warm bowls and quickly return the pan to the heat. Add the butter and mix to melt into and emulsify the sauce. Add the dill and fennel fronds, and pour the sauce over the mussels. Serve immediately scattered with parsley (if using) and with the toasted sourdough and a glass of well-chilled white wine.

Corsican chestnuts / Bergamot / Finger limes / Green clementines / Lemons – Cedro, Menton / Cavaillon melon / Prickly pear / Apples – Bramley, Hereford Cox Orange Pippin, Kent Russet / Kent medlars / Pears – French Vassout Comice, Kent Conference / Quince / Muscat grapes / Egyptian yellow Bahri dates / Jordanian Medjool dates / Reine Claude greengages / Dried fruit – Corsican apricots, Prunes d'Agen / Italian Monk's Beard / Kentish cobnuts / Marron glacé / Wet walnuts / Tomatoes – Italian Vesuvio, Main crop Provence, San Marzano / Chalke Valley watercress, Italian rocket (arugula) / Endives – Escarole, Winter frisée / late Chioggia radicchio / Feuille de chêne (oak leaf lettuce) / Sweet peppers /

Essex sweetcorn / Cauliflower – Boston, Cape, Romanesque / Cime di rapa / Chard – Rainbow, Swiss / Cabbages – Cavolo Nero, Kent Brussels tops, Somerset kale, Kent Hispi, Kent red and white, Normandy Savoy / Cardoon / Jerusalem artichokes / Garlic – French smoked, Lautrec pink, Purple, Turnips' black / Onions – Cevenne, Roscoff / Somerset leeks / Potatoes – Belle de Fontenay, Charlotte, Lincolnshire Agria, Northumberland Yukon Gold, Ratte / Squash – Delica, Italian Turban, Potimarron, Spaghetti / Celeriac / Horseradish / French turnips / Italian chervil root / Parsley root / Parsnips / Red meat radish / Salsify / Somerset heirloom beetroot

Chestnut
The Grain that Grows on a Tree

It might be autumn, but it's still salad season and this week we see some of the best salad leaves on our shopping list. Salanova, which is a new variety of lettuce with flavoursome, crisp, bitesize leaves, and the aptly named Oakleaf both make an appearance, as well as various chicories from Italy.

However, nothing says autumn more than the aroma of fresh, sweet chestnuts roasting over coals. Right now, woodland floors are covered with them. If you're foraging, take care not to confuse them with horse chestnuts (commonly known as conkers), which are toxic and inedible. The shell of the horse chestnut is rounder, smoother and has short spikes; inside, the large, single or double nuts are glossy and round. If you're using bare hands, you'll know if you've tried to pick up sweet chestnuts – they are covered in hedgehog-like spikes. Each shell contains three or four nuts, which are slightly more flattened and triangular in shape than conkers.

Sweet chestnuts grow prolifically all over central and southern Europe – in Spain, Portugal, Corsica, Sicily and Italy. However, it is the Ardèche region in southeast France that gives some of the best.

A hilly, forested region, lying between Marseille to the south and Lyon to the north, the Ardèche has been home to chestnuts for about 800 years and now provides about 50 per cent of the annual French chestnut production – the fruit with the third largest production in the area, after apricots and cherries. Many of its castaneiculturists (chestnut farmers) have been growing chestnuts for generations.

The famous Châtaigne d'Ardèche chestnuts are produced in a specific central area of the region and since 2014 have held an AOC (see page 15) that applies to various chestnut products: fresh, peeled, puréed, dried and flour.

Chestnut trees play an important role in the ecosystem of the area. They are deep-rooted and help limit soil erosion on the hilly slopes and deciduous woodlands (also a good source of wild mushrooms, such as truffles and ceps). They were once referred to as Bread Trees, because whereas wheat and other main grain crops struggle on the rural mountain terrain, the trees produce prolific nuts to make the flour for bread. Chestnut flour is low in starch and naturally gluten free, and is a great alternative for wheat flour in baking and for pasta and noodles. In springtime, the scented white chestnut flowers attract bees, whose honey has a pronounced and unique, almost resiny chestnut flavour. Chestnuts really are generous trees.

Before harvest, beneath the trees the groves are either hand-cleared or sheep-grazed, which not only makes collecting the nuts easier, but also helps to prevent wildfires breaking out. Then, harvesters suspend nets to catch the nuts as they ripen and fall. The fallen chestnuts are either collected by hand (with some pretty thick gloves) or by a giant hand-operated vacuum, then they are graded and processed. The largest, most perfect chestnuts are used to make marron glacé (candied chestnuts), which have been served as a delicacy for at least 300 years – although the debate goes on as to whether they were first made in France or Italy. For these, whole, peeled chestnuts are cooked and steeped in syrup and then dried. The process is repeated multiple times to preserve and coat the nuts in a thin, sugar shell. Any chestnuts that don't make the grade are blended with vanilla and made into a purée – crème de marron.

> "The largest, most perfect chestnuts are used to make marron glacé (candied chestnuts), which have been served as a delicacy for at least 300 years."

From mid-October until mid-November many villages in the Ardèche host Les Castagnades (chestnut festivals) at which the Chestnut Brotherhood takes to the streets in brown robes and green hats, parading between the stalls of chestnut products (marron glacé and crème de marron among them, but also *cousina*, a regional chestnut soup, and chestnut jam, liqueur, cakes, bread and biscuits).

We have to travel to Sicily, though, to find the oldest and largest chestnut tree in the world, known locally as the Hundred Horse Tree. Thought to be between 2,000 and 4,000 years old, it sits only a few miles away from the island's active volcano, Mount Etna.

The simplest way to enjoy fresh chestnuts is to cut a slit or small cross through the brown skin and either roast them in a tray in a hot oven or over hot coals for 15–20 minutes, until they are tender. Peel off the skins and eat the nuts while they are still hot. Roasted, peeled chestnuts bring an earthy flavour when added to stuffings and stews and pair very well with mushrooms and game. You can add marron glacé to desserts and they are particularly delicious combined with chocolate in creamy mousses and cakes.

Chestnut gnocchi

Adding chestnut flour (see page 248) to these potato gnocchi makes them super-tasty. You can serve them simply with the Parmesan cream sauce, or, for a more substantial meal, with roasted butternut squash and a butternut squash sauce. Both options are here.

Serves 4

200g (7oz) fine table salt

4 Agria potatoes, pricked all over

10–12 sweet chestnuts

30g (1oz) Parmesan, grated, plus extra to season the squash and to serve

1 egg

60g (2¼oz) chestnut flour

40g (1½oz) "00" flour, plus extra for rolling out

1–2 tbsp olive oil

salt and freshly ground black pepper

microchickweed, to garnish (optional)

For the Parmesan cream sauce

100ml (3½fl oz) vegetable stock

1 garlic clove, crushed

1 thyme sprig

150ml (5fl oz) double (heavy) cream

60g (2oz) Parmesan, grated

40g (1½oz) butter, cold and diced

For the roasted squash and squash sauce (optional)

1 butternut squash, peeled and deseeded

2–3 tbsp olive oil

2 thyme sprigs, leaves picked

50ml (1¾fl oz) double (heavy) cream

1 banana shallot, finely chopped

2 garlic cloves, finely chopped

Preheat the oven to 200°C/180°C fan/400°F/Gas 6. Scatter the salt on to a small baking tray and place the potatoes on top (this will help to draw out water from the potatoes as they bake). Bake the potatoes on the top shelf for 45–60 minutes, or until they are completely soft inside.

While the potatoes are baking, score the chestnuts and roast them in the oven for about 25 minutes, until they are soft and split open. When they are cool enough to handle, peel and crumble them. Set them aside.

If you are using the squash, cut the top part into chunky dice and the bottom part into 1cm (½in) cubes. Toss the larger pieces with 1 tablespoon of the oil. Add the thyme, season with salt and pepper and roast the pieces in a baking tray on a shelf beneath the potatoes for 30 minutes, until tender. Keep warm. Tip the smaller pieces into a saucepan with the shallot and garlic and the remaining oil. Sweat over a low heat for 10 minutes, until very soft. Add the cream and heat gently for 2 minutes, then blitz it to a smooth sauce. Season with Parmesan and reheat before serving (in place of the Parmesan cream sauce).

Scoop the cooked potato flesh into a fine-mesh sieve and push it through into a bowl. Add the egg, both flours and the 30g (1oz) of Parmesan and combine, but don't overwork. On a floured surface, roll the mixture into a long "rope" as thick as your thumb and cut it into 1.5cm (⅝in) pieces.

Bring a large pan of salted water to a boil. Boil the gnocchi for about 2 minutes, until they float to the surface. Using a slotted spoon, transfer the cooked gnocchi into a bowl of iced water to cool and firm up. Drain, then heat the oil in a large frying pan over a medium heat. Add the gnocchi and pan-fry until golden. Remove from the pan and keep warm.

To make the Parmesan cream sauce, using the gnocchi pan, pour in the stock, add the garlic and thyme and bring to a boil, then reduce by half. Add the cream, bring to a boil and reduce by a third. Remove the thyme sprig, add the Parmesan and stir over a low heat. Gradually add the butter, stirring until smooth and emulsified. Season to taste.

Spoon your chosen sauce into bowls and top with the gnocchi (and roasted squash, if using). Scatter with the chestnuts and extra Parmesan and garnish with microchickweed, if you like.

Chestnut flour

Making your own chestnut flour is possibly a slightly crazy thing to do, but it's quite easy and the results are surprisingly good. Try using the flour to make gluten-free pasta or gnocchi or in gluten-free pancakes or chocolate cake.

Makes about 500g (1lb 2oz)

2kg (4lb 8oz) sweet chestnuts

Preheat the oven to 200°C/180°C fan/400°F/Gas 6.

Using a small, sharp knife, score a cross on the rounded side of each chestnut. Don't be tempted to skip this step otherwise the nuts can and will explode in the oven. Arrange the chestnuts in a large baking tray in a single layer and bake them for about 25 minutes, until they split open.

Remove the chestnuts from the oven and leave them in the tray for a few minutes until they are cool enough to handle. Then, peel the nuts and throw away the skins. If they cool to much and harden so that they are difficult to peel, pop the nuts into the microwave for a few seconds and try again.

Roughly chop the peeled chestnuts, then set about drying them. This is easiest if you have a dehydrator, taking about 2 days. Failing that, finely chop the nuts, tip them on to a baking tray and pop them into the oven on its lowest setting for 6–8 hours.

Tip the dried nuts into a food processor and blitz them until they are very finely ground. Sift the ground nuts to remove any large pieces and whizz these a second time, repeating until you have created some top-level flour.

42

*Chalke Valley **watercress** / Bergamot / Finger limes / Green clementines / Lemons – Cedro, Menton / Cavaillon melon / Prickly pear / Apples – Bramley, French Chantecler Belchard, Hereford Cox Orange Pippin, Hereford Orange Blenheim, Kent Russet / Kent medlars / Pears – French Vassout Comice, Kent Conference / Quince / Muscat grapes / Jordanian Medjool dates / Dried fruit – Corsican apricots, Prunes d'Agen / Italian Monk's Beard / Kentish cobnuts / Marron glacé / Sweet chestnuts / Wet walnuts / Tomatoes – Italian Vesuvio, Main crop Provence, San Marzano / Italian rocket (arugula) / Endives – Escarole, Winter frisée / Radicchios – Castelfranco, late Chioggia, Tardivo / Feuille de chêne (oak leaf lettuce) /*

Sweet peppers / Essex sweetcorn / Cauliflower – Boston, Cape, Romanesque / Cime di rapa / Chard – Rainbow, Swiss / Cabbages – Cavolo Nero, Kent Brussels tops, Kent Hispi, Kent red and white, Normandy Savoy, Somerset kale / Cardoon / Jerusalem artichokes / Garlic – French smoked, Lautrec pink, Purple, Turnips' black / Onion – Cevenne, Roscoff / Somerset leeks / Potatoes – Belle de Fontenay, Charlotte, Lincolnshire Agria, Northumberland Yukon Gold, Ratte / Squash – Delica, Italian Turba, Potimarron, Spaghetti / Celeriac / Beetroot – Somerset heirloom / Crosnes / French turnips / Horseradish / Italian chervil root / Parsley root / Parsnips / Red meat radish / Salsify

Watercress
You Can Lead a Horse to Watercress

This week I have a tale of two foraging experiences – the first an unfortunate slip and the second an unfortunate shot.

It's mid-October, the days are shortening and the sun that has been waking me at 4am is long gone. Now it's 8am in misty Kent. Still, nothing deters this man and his foraging. I have not picked nearly enough blackberries this year and it's getting close to the end of the season, so I'm on a mission to fill the freezer to last us through the winter. I head out with the dog. It all starts swimmingly: I have nearly filled a large bag when I spot a big patch of plump, dark and juicy berries just out of reach. I stamp down the stinging nettles and brambles to get closer. After all, I'm wearing all the proper gear, aren't I? Just as I am at full stretch, those old wellies of mine lose their waning grip on the damp, dewy grass. I fall head first into the hedgerow and get completely tangled up in the sharp thorns. I crawl out of the undergrowth, somewhat noisily extricating myself from the thorny vegetation to find that, thankfully, the only thing I've damaged is my pride.

Two days later I'm playing a round of golf. I start the round off superbly well with a straight drive 250 yards to a rare birdie on the first, followed by a near eagle on the second after driving the green some 265 yards away. I'm flying! Another "screamer" off the tee, not quite on the fairway and slightly buried in the rough, but I'm on a roll. I pull out the eight iron, which should be enough to get the ball over the ditch – it isn't. However, the ball lands in a patch of wild watercress, so I hack the dimpled orb free and pick some leaves, popping them into the bag I always carry with me when I play golf, in the hope of finding such treasure. My love of golf is on a par with my love of food.

Watercress has a long season that starts in spring and ends in November as winter beckons. But, I consider that one season as two. During the warmer summer months, watercress rapidly deteriorates after picking and doesn't taste particularly nice. It loses its peppery flavour and takes on an unpleasant "pee" smell. It's best to stop using it then and bring it back to your dishes when the weather cools down in early autumn.

Chalke Valley watercress

Back when we worked on Tachbrook Street Market in Pimlico, in the summer months we would buy our watercress from the wholesaler at night while it was cooler. The cress was bunched into 12 large handfuls and packed into waxed water-resistant cardboard boxes. As soon as we returned to the stand, we would plunge the boxes into a steel bathtub of ice-cold water at the back of the stall to keep the watercress fresh. We used the same tub to scrub the celery.

The first time I visited our present watercress suppliers in Chalke Valley, some 30-odd years ago, I was with Steve, an agent from Borough Market. I'd assumed we were going to the heart of the watercress world – Alresford in Hampshire, a small, picturesque town that holds an annual watercress festival in May and boasts a heritage steam railway called the Watercress Line. Imagine, then, my surprise when Steve and I arrived in Broad Chalke, in Wiltshire. We've been buying our watercress from the same farmer for over 30 years, but my family's relationship with the Hitchings dates back many more. Forty years before I set up my own business, my dad was buying

> "The ball lands in a patch of wild watercress, so I hack the dimpled orb free and pick some leaves, popping them into the bag I always carry with me when I play golf, in the hope of finding such treasure."

watercress directly from the same farm, from the current farmer's father. The Hitchings family is now in its sixth generation. Our families have a multi-generational connection that looks set to continue, as my own son steps into our business.

Chalke Valley watercress owes its superior flavour to where it's grown. The leaves are darker green, more peppery and with stronger mustard notes than any other cress that is available. Broad Chalke is 16km (10 miles) west of Salisbury and is the source of a natural spring that provides nutrient-rich running water that is perfect for growing this crop. Rain falling on the hills higher up the valley filters down through the Chalke Hills, picking up the natural minerals on its way to the watercress beds.

Watercress production began here in 1889, when the cress was cut by hand. Now a machine does the hard work before the cress is packed and shipped the same day to customers and markets all over the UK.

Chalke Valley watercress soup with garlic croûtons

This easy, vibrant soup will appeal to even the most reluctant greens' eaters. You blanch the watercress before adding it to the soup to preserve its stunning colour.

Serves 4

4 slices of white sourdough bread, cut into 1cm (½in) cubes

4 garlic cloves, crushed

3 tbsp olive oil

300g (10½oz) watercress

2 banana shallots, finely chopped

2 Agria potatoes, peeled and diced

1 litre (35fl oz) vegetable or chicken stock

150ml (5fl oz) double (heavy) cream

salt and freshly ground black pepper

sour cream and freshly grated Parmesan, to serve

Preheat the oven to 180°C/160°C fan/350°F/Gas 4.

Tip the cubes of bread into a bowl, add 1 crushed garlic clove and 2 tablespoons of the olive oil. Season with salt and pepper and mix to combine. Spread the bread cubes out over a baking tray and roast them in the oven for about 10 minutes, stirring from time to time, until they are crunchy and golden brown. Leave them to cool.

Bring a large pan of water to the boil, add the watercress and cook it for 30 seconds. Drain it and transfer the watercress to a bowl of iced water to stop it cooking further and to preserve the beautiful green colour. Then, drain it again, squeezing out any excess water, and roughly chop.

Tip the shallots into the saucepan. Add the remaining olive oil and the remaining crushed garlic and sweat it over a low heat for about 5 minutes, until soft. Add the potatoes to the pan, stir to combine and sweat for a further 4 minutes, to soften the potatoes a little.

Pour the stock into the pan, increase the heat and bring the liquid to a boil, then reduce it again and simmer until the potatoes are tender and completely cooked through. Add the cream and cook gently for a further 5 minutes, until the potatoes are very soft.

Add the watercress and bring the soup back to the boil. Use a stick blender to blend until smooth, then season with salt and freshly ground black pepper.

Ladle the soup into bowls, swirl in a little sour cream and scatter with Parmesan and croûtons to serve.

Chalke Valley watercress salad with preserved peaches

Watercress is a beautiful alternative to rocket, as it is bitter and peppery and pairs superbly with the sweet, preserved peaches that you made earlier, in the height of summer (see page 203). If you like, you can add some crumbled blue cheese or brie to this salad to make it more substantial.

Serves 4

2 bunches of watercress
2 preserved peaches (see page 203)
50g (1¾oz) walnuts, toasted
50g (1¾oz) Parmesan, shaved
5 tbsp olive oil
2 tbsp sherry vinegar
salt and freshly ground black pepper

Wash the watercress under cold running water, drain it and leave it to dry on a clean tea towel. Remove any tough stalks and place the leaves in a large salad bowl.

Drain and slice the peaches and roughly chop the walnuts. Add them to the watercress and then add the Parmesan shavings. Drizzle over the olive oil and sherry vinegar, season with salt and freshly ground black pepper, mix to combine and serve immediately.

43

Celeriac / *Bergamot* / *Finger limes* / *Green clementines* / *Lemons – Cedro, Menton* / *Costa Rican bananas* / *Italian kiwi* / *Mangosteen* / *Queen pineapple* / *Rambutans* / *Réunion bunched lychees* / *Apples – Bramley, French Chantecler Belchard, Hereford Cox Orange Pippin, Hereford Orange Blenheim, Kent Russet* / *Kent medlars* / *Pears – French Vassout Comice, Kent Conference* / *Quince* / *Iranian pomegranate* / *Muscat grapes* / *Jordanian Medjool dates* / *Dried fruit Corsican apricots, Prunes d'Agen* / *Italian Monk's Beard* / *Marron glacé* / *Sweet chestnuts* / *Wet walnuts* / *Tomatoes – Italian Vesuvio* / *Italian rocket (arugula)* / *Endives – Escarole, Winter frisée* / *Radicchios – Castelfranco, late Chioggia, Tardivo* / *Sweet peppers* / *Cauliflower – Boston, Cape, Romanesque* / *Cime di rapa* / *Chard – Rainbow, Swiss* / *Cabbages – Cavolo Nero, Kent Brussels tops, Kent Hispi, Kent red and white, Normandy Savoy, Somerset kale* / *Cardoon* / *Jerusalem artichokes* / *Garlic – French smoked, Lautrec pink, Purple, Turnips' black* / *Onions – Cevenne, Roscoff* / *Somerset leeks* / *Potatoes – Belle de Fontenay, Charlotte, Lincolnshire, Northumberland Yukon Gold, Ratte* / *Squash – Delica, Italian Turban, Potimarron, Spaghetti* / *Celeriac* / *Crosnes* / *Parsnips* / *Horseradish* / *Italian chervil root* / *Parsley root* / *Red meat radish* / *Salsify* / *Somerset heirloom beetroot* / *Turnips – French, Scottish swede*

Celeriac
The Root of the Matter

Around now, the weather is likely to take a turn for the cooler – it's soups, stews and casseroles that are bubbling away on the stove, and we look for comforting root vegetables rather than salads. Hello celeriac!

Hardly the supermodel of the vegetable world, gnarly celeriac is bulbous, with thick, rough skin with little root-type shoots on the underside. But, peel away the pale skin, and the flesh inside is crisp and ivory-coloured with flavour notes of celery and parsley. Celeriac is a type of celery grown for its underground corm rather than its leafy stalks. It is admirably hardworking: shred it to eat raw in salads (famously, remoulade), or boil, steam, mash, roast or bake it for a texture similar to cooked potatoes, just slightly less creamy. With vegan cooking becoming increasingly popular, celeriac has taken on almost cult status – celeriac steaks are wonderful, and a whole baked celeriac makes a great veggie Sunday roast. Blue cheese, nuts, apples, pears and woody herbs are all good partners.

Until relatively recently celeriac was not a commercial crop. Over the 30 years that I've been working, there has been a sea of change in agriculture. For a start, we have lost many farms as sons and daughters have been less keen to follow in their parents' farming footsteps. The rise of the supermarket giants has also had a big impact, with some smaller, independent farmers giving way to large corporate farms. Nonetheless, some forward-thinkers have adopted smaller planting schemes with more profitable crops. They have created co-operatives and retail opportunities with farm shops and farmers' markets.

They've kept an eye on new crops that were already popular in mainland Europe – among them globe and Jerusalem artichokes... and celeriac. About 30 years ago, one Lincolnshire farmer spotted the celeriac gap and took a punt on adding it to his repertoire. The rest is history.

Now, celeriac is grown commercially in the UK, northern France and the Netherlands, with a harvest from October to November. Although British celeriac is good, the best comes from France, from a farm northeast of Paris in Moigneville owned by Monsieur Tremblay, whose growing skills seem to surpass all others. At the start of the season, he and his team lift the vegetables from the ground with their celery-like stems and serrated leaves still attached. As soon as the frosts arrive, these large, beautiful white-fleshed balls lose their leaves.

> "Hardly the supermodel of the vegetable world, gnarly celeriac is bulbous with thick, rough skin... But peel away... and the flesh underneath is crisp and ivory-coloured with flavour notes of celery and parsley."

While the British and Dutch celeriacs deteriorate quickly, the French variety stores superbly well for up to eight months. How Monsieur Tremblay achieves this high standard is a well-guarded secret, and we salute him.

Fenland celery

It would be remiss of me if I didn't mention Fenland celery, a uniquely British vegetable that has a short season starting around now and finishing at the end of December. Grown using specific, labour-intensive and time-honoured growing techniques, it comes from a few protected areas of the Cambridgeshire, Norfolk and Suffolk fens. These are flat, low-lying, marshy agricultural regions, where the climate is cool and dry and the soil is rich, peaty and black.

There are only three permitted varieties of Fenland celery: Hopkins Fenlander, New Dwarf White and Ely White. As the celery grows, four or five times over the growing season, the earth is banked up and over the plants to blanche the stems. Not only does this insulate the celery from overnight frost, but it shields it from sunlight. The celery can be watered using only water from the Fenland waterways or reservoirs. The resulting hand-harvested stems are crisp, crunchy and pale (white at the root and pale green toward the leaves) with a mild, bittersweet, slightly aniseed flavour. The root is cut into a point and the stems are less stringy than regular celery.

"Nutty"

I can't stand it when I read that something has a nutty flavour. The same goes for "earthy". Both are blanket, nondescript terms for vegetables and they drive me crazy. I'm yet to eat a nut that tastes anything like Fenland celery, for example. I'll tell you what is nutty, though: a young lad (yours truly) standing behind his dad's market stall, in the freezing cold, having to break the ice in the steel bath to wash the "soot" off the celery. The only saving grace was dovetailing the job with removing beetroot from the Baby Burco boiler by poking it with a ticket spike, all the while being careful not to burn my fingers.

*Beauty is in the eye of the beholder for this white-fleshed
taste sensation. Celeriac is a famously tricky veg to nurture
– our advice: don't try to grow it at home!*

Celeriac choucroute

This little side dish is a crunchy pickle. It is perfect with red meat, and rich stews or alongside braised sweet cabbage.

Serves 4

1 banana shallot, finely sliced

2 garlic cloves, finely sliced

½ bunch of tarragon

4 thyme sprigs

150ml (5fl oz) white wine vinegar

3 tbsp duck fat

1 small celeriac, peeled and sliced into fine batons (using a mandoline if you have one)

red-stemmed radish, to garnish (optional)

Start by making a vinegar reduction. Tip the shallot and garlic into a saucepan. Add the herbs and pour over the vinegar. Place the pan over a medium heat, bring the liquid to a boil and reduce it by half. Strain the vinegar into a bowl and discard the solids.

Place a large, heavy-based frying pan over a high heat. Add the duck fat and leave it to melt, then add the celeriac juliennes and stir-fry for a matter of seconds until they are just cooked but still have some crunch. Add 4 tablespoons of the vinegar reduction and cook for a further 30 seconds. The whole cooking process should take no longer than 1 minute.

Tip the celeriac into a clean plastic container or bowl and chill it immediately. Once cold, either vacuum pack it or store it in a lidded, sterilized jar in the fridge for up to 1 month. Simply reheat the choucroute in a saucepan when you need it and serve it garnished with red-stemmed radish, if you wish.

Salt-baked celeriac with Parmesan sauce

You could serve this delicious salt-baked celeriac as a main dish for a vegetarian main or as a side to meat. The celeriac gently cooks to melting tenderness inside a crisp salt dough and is then served with a rich, creamy sauce. If you're going for the side-to-meat option, I guarantee that this will be better than the meat! You will need to plan for the celeriac, which will take two to three hours in a domestic oven.

Serves 4

225g (8oz) plain (all-purpose) flour

300g (10½oz) salt

5 egg whites

1 celeriac, scrubbed

50g (1¾oz) hazelnuts, toasted and roughly chopped

1–2 tbsp chopped flat-leaf parsley or chives

2 tbsp hazelnut oil

For the Parmesan sauce

2 banana shallots, sliced

3 garlic cloves, sliced

2 thyme or rosemary sprigs

1–2 tbsp olive oil

150ml (5fl oz) white wine

250ml (9fl oz) vegetable or chicken stock

150ml (5fl oz) double (heavy) cream

75g (2½oz) Parmesan, finely grated, plus extra as shavings to serve

salt and freshly ground black pepper

Preheat the oven to 160°C/140°C fan/315°F/Gas 2–3.

In a bowl combine the flour and salt. Add the egg whites and 150ml (5fl oz) of water and mix into a smooth dough. Completely cover the celeriac in the salt dough, making sure that there are no gaps for steam to escape. Place the celeriac in a lined roasting tin and bake it for 2 hours, until tender to the point of a skewer.

Meanwhile, make the Parmesan sauce. Tip the shallots and garlic into a saucepan with the thyme or rosemary and the olive oil. Place the pan over a low heat and sweat the vegetables for 5 minutes, until soft and translucent. Add the wine, increase the heat and bring the liquid to a boil, then leave it to reduce by half. Add the stock and again reduce by half. By now you will have an intense, flavoursome stock.

Add the cream and leave the sauce to bubble away until it is thick enough to coat the back of a spoon. Add the grated Parmesan, stir to melt and then remove the pan from the heat and, using a stick blender, blitz the sauce until smooth. Taste the sauce and season it accordingly.

Check to see how the crust on the celeriac is looking after 2 hours – it should be golden brown. To test if the celeriac is cooked, pierce the crust with a metal skewer – when the celeriac is cooked the skewer should easily go all the way through.

Remove the celeriac from the oven and leave it to cool for a few minutes, then transfer it to a chopping board and use a meat tenderizer or rolling pin to crack open the crust.

To serve place the cracked-open crust on a serving plate and allow your guests to spoon the soft celeriac out of the crust on to plates. Then, they should pour over the sauce, and scatter the top with chopped hazelnuts, herbs and Parmesan shavings and drizzle with hazelnut oil.

44

Beetroot
Follow the Rainbow

Some years ago, a customer asked me if Rainbow chard was the leaf of the red, yellow and candy-coloured beetroots (beets) I had on display. I told her that they weren't, that Rainbow chard was no relation and beetroot and was simply a colourful chard or spinach. She left happy, but I had a nagging doubt. I'd been selling fruit and vegetables for a very long time, but I realized I knew very little about the many varieties might be related to each other.

Is an apple in the same family as a pear? Are peaches a different variety of nectarine? Are grapefruits a citrus hybrid? Why do the same fruits from different parts of the world or even different regions of the same country vary so much? I knew I had to understand – the result of that need is this book. I have a lot to thank that inquisitive customer for.

Beetroots are the biennial plant from the amaranth family and there are basically two types: one type that is grown for its leaves and another for its bulbous roots. Then, those two types, especially the bulbous beets, can be subdivided into a multitude of colours and sizes. In the red beetroot category, for example, the American heirloom variety Blood Turnip (not a turnip at all) is grown for the root that oozes a deep red juice. Then there's Bull's Blood, which is picked when immature for its stunning, delicate salad leaves with crimson-red stalks and red-and-green variegated leaves.

If you buy bunched beetroot, cut off the leaves, leaving about 5cm (2in) of stalk and the roots still attached. This stops the beetroot bleeding when they cook. Steam the leaves to eat as you would any other leafy green. Beetroot will sit in the fridge for weeks, even months. However, if they start to soften, snip a little off the stalks to reveal a fresh cut and leave the roots to soak in cold water for 24 hours. The beetroot will revive and firm up, but you will have compromised the flavour. This trick works well for other vegetables and salads, too, including turnips, carrots, celery and most salad heads – but not chicory.

Like most root vegetables, beetroots have a long season and thrive in the cold. From March to May, ours come from Spain, with flavoursome Boltardy the most popular; its early season leaves are similar to collard greens and tender chard. In early summer, we move to Essex for brilliant baby beets, whose roots and leaves are great in salads. Come autumn, though, it's the beetroots from Sussex that shine. We see three varieties: deep red Boltardy; Chioggia with its pink-and-white rings; and Burpee's Gold, a beautiful yellow. They look unremarkable until cut to reveal their kaleidoscope of colours.

The colours of autumn

In the autumn our stall is a riot of colour, with produce in red, orange, green, purple, yellow and white. Chard with almost neon pink, yellow and orange stems sits alongside purple, red, green, white and yellow cauliflowers. Potatoes such as the Salad Blue, Red Duke of York and the Shetland Black (from the Carrolls in Northumberland) appear. Red, white, purple and yellow carrots and radishes, and the stunning red and green meat radishes nestle up to white, purple, yellow and green turnips. Pink, white and purple garlic sits alongside purple, mauve, white and striped aubergines (eggplants). Outdoor tomatoes are no longer just orange and red – we see stunning varieties like the crimson and black Noire de Crimée, yellow Pineapple tomatoes, green and orange Tigers and the nearly black Tondo Nero from Italy. This avalanche of colour continues with the deep greens of cabbages and brassicas: Savoy, Hispi, Cavolo Nero, variegate kale and turnip tops. There are piles of purple and red potatoes from the Cambridge Fens. And last, but by no means least, are the stacks of stunning green, yellow, orange and white pumpkins.

> "Beetroots are the biennial plant from the amaranth family and there are basically two types: one type that is grown for its leaves and another for its bulbous roots."

A thank you

This chapter reminds me to thank my wife for putting up with me (and my cooking) while I've been writing, leaving her to captain the Turnips' ship. One October Sunday, we sat down to breakfast. I'd whipped up smoked salmon and scrambled eggs on sourdough toast, with a side order of autumn tomatoes macerated in rock salt, and super-thinly sliced Boltardy beetroot with a drizzle of aged balsamic vinegar. When Caroline finished, she said, "I even toast bread better than you, although you cut the beetroot better." Praise indeed.

Heritage beetroot, such as Golden and Chioggia, have had something of a millennium revival. Somerset is our preferred county for these yellow, red and candy main-crop varieties.

Somerset beetroot tartare with sunflower seeds

This dish brings back memories of the food of my childhood – of deep red beetroot salad and soups. It will convert even the most hardened beetroot sceptics! If you like, you can add some crumbled goat's cheese on top of the tartare and add some little croûtons for extra crunch.

Serves 4

4 large beetroots (beets), scrubbed

10 thyme sprigs

1 rosemary sprig

1 garlic bulb

2 tbsp pomegranate molasses, plus extra to taste if needed

3 tbsp olive oil

1 tbsp Dijon mustard

1 tbsp red wine vinegar

60g (2oz) sunflower seeds, toasted

2 tbsp chopped cornichons or pickles, plus extra to taste if needed

1 tbsp chopped capers

salt and freshly ground black pepper

crumbled goat's cheese, to serve (optional)

a few leaves of microherbs, to garnish

Place the beetroots whole into a large saucepan. Cover them with water and add the herbs, garlic bulb and a good seasoning of salt. Bring the water to a boil, then reduce the heat and simmer the beetroot for about 1 hour, or until tender when tested with the point of a knife.

Remove the beetroots from the heat and leave them to cool in the cooking liquid.

Combine the pomegranate molasses, olive oil, mustard and vinegar, then season and whisk to combine to a dressing.

When the beetroots are cool, peel and cut them into dice no bigger than 5mm (¼in). Tip the beetroot dice into a bowl, add the sunflower seeds, and chopped cornichons and capers and mix to combine. Add the dressing and mix well – the mixture might look wet, but this is perfect because beetroot shouldn't be dry.

Taste and see what's missing – you might want to add a little more molasses for sweetness or cornichons for sourness. Spoon the tartare into a clean bowl, and serve immediately, with crumbled goat's cheese on top, if you wish, and a garnish of microherbs

Pickled golden beetroots

Beetroots are one of my favourite winter vegetables. They are so versatile – we can use them for anything from salads to stews to roasts. Golden beetroots may be hard to find in the shops, but they are worth seeking out, if you can. I suggest preserving them for another time and serving them with roasted fish, in a beautiful salad or even on an antipasto board.

Makes 1 medium jar

4 large golden beetroots (beets), scrubbed but not peeled

good pinch of salt

100ml (3½ fl oz) apple cider vinegar

4 tbsp granulated sugar

2 tbsp clear honey

1 thumb-size piece of fresh ginger, sliced

1 cinnamon stick

1 clove

Place the beetroots in a pan, cover with water and add the salt. Place the pan over a high heat and bring to a boil. Reduce the heat and simmer for about 1 hour, or until the beetroots are just tender when tested with a knife or wooden skewer – they should still be al dente.

Drain and try to peel the beetroots while they are still hot, and the skins should just slide off. Then, leave them to cool slightly and, using a mandoline, thinly slice them 3mm (⅛in) thick or cut them into chunky pieces, whichever you prefer. Pack the beetroot pieces into your sterilized jar.

Pour the vinegar into a pan, add 50ml (1¾ fl oz) of water, and the sugar, honey, ginger and spices. Place the pan over a high heat and bring to a boil to dissolve the sugar. Pour the hot pickling liquid into the jar to cover the beetroot, seal with the lid and leave to cool.

Store the cooled pickles in a cool, dry place for up to 1 year. Once opened, keep them in the fridge and use them within 2 weeks.

Clementines / *Bergamot* / *Finger limes* / *Florida Ruby grapefruit* / *Lemons – Cedro, Menton* / *Pomelo* / *Valencia Navel oranges* / *Costa Rican bananas* / *Italian kiwi* / *Mangosteen* / *Queen pineapple* / *Rambutans* / *Réunion bunched lychees* / *Apples – Bramley, French Chantecler Belchard, Hereford Cox Orange Pippin, Hereford Orange Blenheim, Kent Russet* / *Pears – French Vassout Comice, Kent Conference* / *California cranberries* / *Iranian pomegranate* / *Jordanian Medjool dates* / *Dried fruit – Corsican apricots, Prunes d'Agen* / *Italian Monk's Beard* / *Italian flat parsley* / *Israeli culinary herbs* / *Marron glacé* / *Dried nuts – Almonds, Cashews, Hazelnuts, Macadamia, Peanuts, Pecans, Pistachios, Walnuts* / *Tomatoes – Costoluto, Camone* / *Italian rocket (arugula)* / *Endives – Escarole, Winter frisée* / *Radicchios – Castelfranco, late chioggia, Tardivo* / *Cauliflower – Boston, Cape, Romanesque* / *Cime di rapa* / *Chard – Rainbow, Swiss* / *French Spinach* / *Cabbages – Cavolo Nero, Kent Brussels tops, Kent Hispi, Kent red and white, Normandy Savoy, Somerset kale* / *Cardoon* / *Jerusalem artichokes* / *Garlic – French smoked, Lautrec pink* / *South African cep mushrooms* / *Onions – Cevenne, Roscoff* / *Shallots – Brittany, Thai* / *Somerset leeks* / *Potatoes – Belle de Fontenay, Charlotte, Lincolnshire Agria, Northumberland Yukon Gold, Ratte, Somerset Pink Fir* / *Peruvian oca* / *Squash – Delica, Italian Turban, Potimarron, Spaghetti* / *Carrots – Brittany Sand, Chantenay* / *Celeriac* / *Crosnes* / *Horseradish* / *Italian chervil root* / *Parsley root* / *Parsnips* / *Red meat radish* / *Salsify* / *Somerset heirloom beetroot* / *Turnips – Brittany Golden, French, Scottish swede*

Clementine
Oh, My Darling Clementine!

Sources claim that the clementine's origins trace back to 1892, when the fruit was discovered growing in Algeria, in the citrus groves of a French-run orphanage. Among the mandarins and sweet oranges, Monsieur Trabut, a French botanist and doctor, noticed a tree bearing unusual, small citrus fruit with thin, easy-peeling skin and a juicy, pipless flesh. He named the fruit after Brother Clément, the monk responsible for the gardens.

When I first sold fruit and vegetables, before the UK joined the EU, our citrus imports were dominated by Outspan, a South African company that shipped huge quantities not just from South Africa, but also from India and the USA. Rarely did its produce come from Europe. Outspan didn't promote clementines, focusing instead on satsumas and tangerines, selling the fruit under its own branding and sourcing the produce according to growing seasons across the world to avoid breaks in supply.

When the UK joined the EU in 1973, we began to buy directly from other EU countries, such as Spain and France, countries that favoured the clementine – and so this little citrus fruit began its rise to stardom. Now, once we see clementines in the shops, we know that the run up to Christmas has started. They are by far the most popular fruit of the season.

At Turnips, the clementine season lasts around four months, from October to January. The clementine brand Tout Miel grows on Corsica on the cooler, east side between the sea and the mountains. These are the only clementines growing in France and have PGI status (see page 24), a standard that about 95 per cent of Corsican clementines achieve. Naturally ripened on the trees, the fruit are hand-harvested with their dark green, tapered leaves still attached to the fruit, and have fine, shiny orange skin and juicy, deep-orange flesh.

"Corsica is a haven for incredible flavour when it comes to fruit, and Tout Miel's clementines are one of the island's best exports."

When we hit the New Year, we see a shift from Corsican clementines to those of southern Spain, and the La Soculente brand from the small town of Almenara, Castellón, just north of Valencia, an area famous for growing all manner of citrus fruit. This company is one of Spain's true fruit heroes and produces late clementines that are sweet and juicy and that keep the season going into the New Year.

In his own words: Charlie Foster, Turnips' heir apparent

I consider it a huge privilege to be the next generation of Fosters at Turnips. My parents' business is truly special and I feel it's my job not just to maintain what their blood, sweat and tears have built, but to add something meaningful to their legacy. My ambition, therefore, is to keep taking the business forward into pastures new. I hope that our journey into the world of fine dining will go some way to achieving that goal. Turnips is more than a business, it is my home and I want to do it – and by extension my family – proud.

As a Director of Turnips, I am responsible for the company's day-to-day running. That might mean I'm involved in the catered offering, the raw products, or our hospitality or wholesale trade – there is plenty to keep me busy and no two days are the same. Every day I'm conscious that the main goal is to keep Turnips running well enough to stop my mum sacking me!

Every aspect of our business relies on the quality of our produce, so it goes without saying that buying is a huge and crucial part of my role. Dad has worked hard for over 30 years to find incredible producers, farms and agents, and it's my privilege to continue to bring their products to the public. This brings me on to our beautiful Corsican Tout Miel clementines. In my opinion, these fruit are a fantastic example of our sourcing ethos. Everybody knows what a clementine is, but how many of us know how many different varieties and marques there are available? At Turnips, we strive to find the very best marque for each product we sell. We worry less about the weird and wonderful, and far more about those products and producers that truly excel in their field (no pun intended). Corsica is a haven for incredible flavour when it comes to fruit, and Tout Miel's clementines are one of the island's best exports. The colder, eastern coast of the island limits the accumulation of sugar in the fruit, which means the clementines ripen with a stunning balance of sweetness and delicate acidity. We have worked with Tout Miel for well over 15 years and I can confidently say that their fruit are exactly how clementines really should taste.

Dehydrated clementine skins

You can be certain it's full-steam ahead to Christmas when the clementines arrive. These beautiful, dried clementine skins are simple to make and have so many uses. You can grind them into a powder to use as seasoning or in bakes. Drop a few dried peels into mulled wine, or into a mug or tea pot and pour over freshly boiled water – leave to steep and add a little honey to taste. Or try making homemade tea bags and add some crushed cinnamon, star anise and cloves to the peels for an aromatic brew. They also make a wonderful Christmas gift. As you're preparing them, they will fill your kitchen with wonderful aromas.

10 clementines

Using a vegetable peeler remove the skin from the clementines in strips – try not to remove the pith, which will be bitter. Eat the clementine flesh just as it is or in a seasonal fruit salad, or squeeze the juice.

Place the skins into a dehydrator to dry for about 12 hours. Alternatively, dry the peels on a lined baking sheet in the oven on the lowest setting, checking them every hour or so – they should be dry and crisp and not browned. Leave to cool, then store in screwtop jar at room temperature until you're ready to use them.

Clementine-glazed carrots and parsnips

At Christmas time this twist on roasted vegetables is perfect to serve alongside roasts. I have suggested regular-size veg in this recipe, but you could easily use baby vegetable varieties, if you prefer – you won't need to slice them in that case, just leave them whole. You can prepare this citrussy butter ahead of time and store it in the fridge for up to one week or in an airtight container in the freezer for up to three months.

Serves 4

2 clementines, zest finely grated and juice squeezed

100g (3½oz) butter, diced

3 large Sand carrots, peeled and sliced as you wish

2 parsnips, peeled and sliced as you wish

2 tbsp runny honey

1 tbsp wholegrain mustard

1 thyme sprig

salt and freshly ground black pepper

To serve

2 micro flat-leaf parsley sprigs, leaves picked

1 clementine, zest finely grated and halved

Pour the clementine juice into a small saucepan and place it over a medium heat. Bring the juice to a boil and reduce it until thickened enough to easily coat the back of a spoon (about 3–4 minutes). Add the butter and grated zest, reduce the heat to melt the butter but do not allow the liquid to boil or the acid in the juice might split the sauce.

Pour the butter sauce into an ice-cube tray, a bowl or a small lidded food box, leave it to cool, then chill it until solid.

Boil the carrots and parsnips in salted water until al dente, then drain.

Place a frying pan over a medium heat. Sear the clementine halves to serve, cut side downward, until caramelized. Remove from the pan and set aside, then add the vegetables to the dry pan and sear until golden. Add the honey, mustard and thyme and stir to glaze and lightly caramelize the veggies. Add a good knob of clementine butter and a little splash of water – the glaze will start to bubble and will coat the carrots and parsnips in a beautiful, shiny way.

Season with salt and pepper, remove the thyme sprig, then scatter with the parsley leaves and extra clementine zest, tuck in the seared clementine halves, and serve.

46

White truffles / Bergamot / Clementines / Finger limes / Lemons – Cedro, Menton / Florida Ruby grapefruit / Pomelo / Valencia Navel oranges / Costa Rican bananas / Guadeloupe "Philibon" Charentais melon / Italian kiwi / Mangosteen / Queen pineapple / Rambutans / Réunion bunched lychees / Apples – Bramley, French Chantecler Belchard, Hereford Cox Orange Pippin, Hereford Orange Blenheim, Kent Russet / Pears – French Vassout Comice, Kent Conference / California cranberries / Iranian pomegranate / Jordanian Medjool dates / Dried fruit – Corsican apricots, Prunes d'Agen / Italian flat parsley / Italian Monk's Beard / Israeli culinary herbs / Marron glacé / Dried nuts – Almonds, Cashews, Hazelnuts, Macadamia, Peanuts, Pecans, Pistachios, Walnuts / Tomatoes – Costoluto, Camone / Chicories – French, Italian, Red and white Belgian, Sugar Loaf / Pis-en-lit (dandelion), / Radicchios – Chioggia, Grumalo, Pink Vaneto, Puntarelle, Rose, Tardivo, Treviso / Cauliflower – Boston, Cape, Romanesque / Cime di rapa / Chard – Rainbow, Swiss / French Spinach / Cabbages – Cavolo Nero, Kent Brussels tops, Kent Hispi, Normandy Savoy, Somerset kale, Somerset red / Cardoon / Jerusalem artichokes / Garlic – French smoked, Lautrec pink / South African cep mushrooms / Onions – Cevenne, Roscoff / Shallots – Brittany, Thai / Somerset leeks / Potatoes – Belle de Fontenay, Charlotte, Lincolnshire Agria, Northumberland Yukon Gold, Ratte, Somerset Pink Fir / Peruvian oca / Squash – Delica, Italian Turban, Potimarron, Spaghetti / Carrots – Brittany Sand, Chantenay / Celeriac / Crosnes / Horseradish / Italian chervil root / Parsnip / Parsley root / Red meat radish / Salsify / Somerset heirloom beetroot / Turnips – Brittany Golden, French, Scottish swede

White Truffle
The Whole Truffle…

Highly prized Italian white truffles are the fruiting body of an underground fungus of the Tuberaceae family. We can't cultivate them – they grow wild in specific growing conditions in deciduous woods of oak, beech, poplar and hazel, particularly in northern Italy, where true connoisseurs will find them. They arrive in late September, after the first frosts, are at their best around now and can be available until the end of December, weather permitting.

White truffles should be firm and range in colour from ochre to green-grey. Inside, they are mostly creamy white, marbled with brown tones, but this depends on ripeness, the type of tree they were growing under and the soil they were growing in. Size and shape really do matter: sold by weight (up to £7,000 per kilo in 2021), gram for gram, they are the market's most expensive fresh product. Lobes and folds can harbour decay and excess earth that will "falsely" increase that weight. The surface can be lumpy, but the skin should be smooth.

Pungently aromatic, the white truffle scent is hard to define but is often described as earthy, musky, funky, autumnal, sweaty, like dirty socks, or in the words of Giorgio Locatelli, "humans gone off"! White truffles are not for cooking, which would damage their unique and exquisite flavour. Rather, they are traditionally finely shaved just before serving over simple egg dishes, pasta, risotto, polenta or beef carpaccio. They pair brilliantly with strong cheeses such as Parmesan.

The best white truffles come from Piedmont in Italy and specifically from the area near Alba, a medieval town that lies between Turin and Genoa. The cool, wooded hills and valleys of deciduous trees around the town provide the perfect growing conditions. Historically, truffle hunters used pigs to sniff out buried truffles from underneath the tree roots, but pigs can damage the fragile ecosystem of the forest floor, and in Italy are now banned. Instead, trained sniffer dogs – nimbler, with a love of digging, and far less likely to eat the spoils – have become the humans' partners in this lucrative work.

Wrap your truffles, cleaned and completely dried, in dry kitchen paper and store them in an airtight container in the fridge. Uncooked rice absorbs moisture and egg shells are permeable, so if you put rice or eggs (or both) in the container for up to 24 hours, they will take on some truffle nuances, giving a flavour boost to your risotto, scrambled eggs or freshly made egg pasta.

> "The white truffle scent is hard to define but is often described as earthy, musky, funky, autumnal, sweaty, like dirty socks, or in the words of Giorgio Locatelli, 'humans gone off'!"

In the Foster household, every year we hope that the white truffles will last until Christmas when we invite our children and their partners for a breakfast extravaganza. The highlight is Caroline's creamy scrambled eggs, which she tops with clouds of beautiful, delicate truffle shavings. As a family, we make the most of this decadent ingredient when we come together and celebrate life. It always feels special.

Mary, the "Truffle Lady"

Alba truffles are significantly more expensive than those from regions such as Le Marche, Umbria, Emilia-Romagna and Calabria. In fact, until I met Mary, I was of the opinion that Alba was the only place in Italy for truffles.

Mary popped into the warehouse one chilly November morning some 15 years ago. From her bag, she pulled out a bundle of white truffles wrapped up in a tea cloth. "Are they from Alba?" I asked. "No. But these are just as good, if not better," she replied.

I was interested to compare to see whether Mary's truffles were as good as she claimed. And they were. Mary told me that some unscrupulous people sell white truffles from other countries and regions of Italy pretending they are from Alba in order to capitalize on the higher prices. "My family are five generations of truffle hunters from the region of Matese, not far from Naples." Mary's family had been selling their truffles to agents who would then travel to Alba and sell them there. Fresh out of university and starting in the family business, Mary believed that her white truffles were good enough to rival those from Alba. She impressed me so much, both with her truffles and her sales pitch, that to this day we buy Mary's white truffles from Matese.

White truffle risotto

The beautiful aroma of white truffle is not for everyone, but I'd say 99 per cent of people who try it, love it. Simple dishes, such as this one, show off white truffles at their very best. A little tip – if you can add a dash of sherry vinegar to the finished risotto, it will balance the richness.

Serves 4 as a starter

1 tbsp olive oil

2 banana shallots, finely chopped

2 garlic cloves, crushed

350g (12oz) arborio rice

100ml (3½fl oz) white wine

1 litre (35fl oz) hot (but not boiling) vegetable or chicken stock

4 tbsp full-fat cream cheese

100g (3½oz) Parmesan, finely grated, plus extra to serve

knob of butter

white truffle, as much as you want or can afford!

salt and freshly ground black pepper

Heat the olive oil in a sauté pan over a low heat. Add the shallots and garlic and sweat over a low heat for 5 minutes, until soft and translucent.

Add the rice to the sauté pan, stir to combine and toast the grains in the hot oil for a minute or so. Add the wine and continue to stir until the wine has almost bubbled away. Gradually add the hot stock, a ladleful at a time, stirring continuously until each addition of stock has been absorbed before you add more. After 15–20 minutes, the rice should be cooked and the risotto slightly sticky. Add the cream cheese to loosen the consistency of the rice a little and beat to combine.

Season the risotto with salt and pepper and add the Parmesan. Remove the pan from the heat, add the butter and stir until the risotto is glossy. Spoon the risotto into bowls, scatter with more Parmesan and shave as much truffle on top of each serving as you want.

White truffle honey

Adding white truffle to honey will preserve that unique flavour. This intense honey is wonderful on a cheese board, or you can use it as a glaze for meat or vegetables.

Makes 1 very small jar

30g (1oz) white truffle
100g (3½oz) runny honey

Slice the truffle very thinly and place it in a small jam jar. Pour over the honey and close the lid.

Place a bamboo or metal steamer over a pan of barely simmering water. Place the jar in the steamer and steam for 45 minutes to gently warm the honey and infuse the flavour of the truffle in it. Keep an eye on the water below the steamer and top up, if necessary.

Leave the honey jar to cool, then store it in a cool, dry place for up to 1 year. Once opened, use it within 2 weeks.

47

Brussels sprouts / *Bergamot* / *Clementines* / *Finger limes* / *Florida Ruby grapefruit* / *Lemons – Cedro, Menton, Sicilian* / *Mexican limes* / *Pomelo* / *Valencia Navel oranges* / *Costa Rican bananas* / *Guadeloupe "Philibon'" Charentais melon* / *Italian kiwi* / *Mangosteen* / *Queen pineapple* / *Rambutans* / *Réunion bunched lychees* / *Apples – Bramley, French Chantecler Belchard, Hereford Cox Orange Pippin, Kent Russet* / *Pears – French Vassout Comice, Kent Conference* / *California cranberries* / *Iranian pomegranate* / *Jordanian Medjool dates* / *Dried fruit – Corsican apricots, Prunes d'Agen* / *Bay leaf* / *Italian flat parsley* / *Italian Monk's Beard* / *Rosemary* / *Sage* / *Thyme* / *Marron glacé* / *Nuts – Almonds, Cashews, Hazelnuts, Macadamia, Peanuts, Pecans, Pistachios, Walnuts* / *Tomatoes – Costoluto, Camone* / *Chicories – French, Italian, Red and white Belgian, Sugar Loaf* / *Pis-en-lit (dandelion)* / *Radicchios – Chioggia,* *Grumalo, Pink Vaneto, Puntarelle, Rose, Tardivo, Treviso* / *Cauliflower – Boston, Cape, Romanesque* / *Cime di rapa* / *Chard – Rainbow, Swiss* / *French Spinach* / *Cabbages – Cavolo Nero, Kent Brussels tops, Kent Hispi, Normandy Savoy, Somerset kale, Somerset red* / *Cardoon* / *Jerusalem artichokes* / *Garlic – French smoked Garlic, Lautrec pink* / *South African cep mushrooms* / *White truffles* / *Onions – Cevenne, Roscoff* / *Shallots – Brittany, Thai* / *Somerset leeks* / *Potatoes – Belle de Fontenay, Charlotte, Lincolnshire Agria, Northumberland Yukon Gold, Ratte, Somerset Pink Fir* / *Peruvian oca* / *Squash – Delica, Italian Turban, Potimarron, Spaghetti* / *Carrots – Brittany Sand, Chantenay* / *Celeriac* / *Crosnes* / *Horseradish* / *Parsley root* / *Parsnip* / *Red meat radish* / *Salsify* / *Somerset heirloom beetroot* / *Turnips – Brittany Golden , French, Scottish swede*

Brussels Sprout
As Bold as Brassicas

The Brussels sprout, once a brassica with an identity crisis as an overcooked, soggy and bitter-tasting Christmas veg, has now become rather trendy. While it's true that the cold sweetens the sprout as it grows, back in the day it seemed that no matter how hard the winter, sprouts still tasted bitter. Recently, though, new, less bitter varieties, mainly from Holland, have appeared. But they still adhere to the golden rule: the smaller the sprout, the sweeter the flavour.

Sprouts grow on a large but incdible stalk and produce a cabbage-like leafy floret on top of the stem. Farmers often separate the two, selling them as separate vegetables. In recent years, especially around Christmas time, sprouts have been sold on their stalks with the floret on top. It's a fine sight to behold.

The humble sprout: the epitome of the seasons
Sprouts have no accreditation; they don't have the flavour of asparagus; unlike celeriac, they aren't a great substitute for meat; and you can't buy them all year round. Why do we love them? Well, that's the point: they are truly seasonal, from a time when eating with the seasons really meant something.

Shifting times

In 1997, the Conran Group opened the Bluebird Gastrodome on the King's Road in Chelsea, London. They recruited an Australian head chef who tasked Turnips to source produce for his Australasian cuisine: sucking mangoes, bitter green mango, green papaya, Thai shallots and pea aubergines.

I tracked down a Chinese wholesaler in Barking, East London, and an Indian supplier (remember my mango man?) at Western International Market near Heathrow. It was so exciting to buy fruits and vegetables associated with a particular foreign country or cuisine and to source them directly from people who came from those countries and now lived and traded in London. It was amazing to be part of that diverse new food culture. Snake beans from Thailand, lychees from China, cassava from India, jackfruit from Malaysia... "exotic" produce that catered to our multi-cultural nation and food scene.

Soon the large corporate suppliers realized that they weren't limited to importing exotic produce, but could import produce whose season had ended here, but was still going strong overseas. They bought in bulk to create economies of scale and the British supermarkets gave us our favourite staples all year round. An inevitable result is that now, just as our farmers in Kent are harvesting their beautiful Brussels sprouts, ship-loads of inferior sprouts arrive from Kenya. But I want to talk about Kentish sprouts.

Throughout the festive season, our grower in Kent provides us with "sprout sticks" of the Brodie F1 variety, which produces up to 30 sprouts of varying sizes on the stalk. The sprout leaves are tight and pale green with no hint of bitterness. The cabbage-like top is a beautiful, dark-green bonus and is delicious steamed, then sautéed in garlicky butter. If you can fit the stalk in the fridge, leave the sprouts intact until you need them, sooner rather than later.

A Great British chef

The late Gary Rhodes was a bastion of British cooking and passionate about British produce. I met him three times.

The first time was when he threw me out of his restaurant in Dolphin Square. I'd been invited by Richard, Gary's sous-chef, to join him for drinks and dinner. I'm not sure if it was the alcohol or that I'd been awake for 22 hours, but when Richard brought Gary out of the kitchen to meet me, they found me face down in my main course. I was duly escorted out.

The second was on the sideline of a rugby pitch watching our sons play a school match on opposing teams. Gary's trademark spiky hair made him unmistakable. I apologized for my previous misdemeanour, and we spent the whole rugby game putting the food world to rights.

"The sprout leaves are tight and pale green with no hint of bitterness."

A few years later we met again at the Glenfiddich Food & Drink Awards. Gary congratulated me on my success (I'd won the best radio series prize with Sybil Kapoor and Anna McNamee) and asked how my son was doing with his rugby.

Fish-sauce-glazed Brussels sprouts

At this time of the year Brussels sprouts are everywhere. Like Marmite, the world seems divided into those who love them and others who hate them. And, to be honest, I'm not that crazy for sprouts, but when you glaze them in fish sauce, they become something really stunning to serve alongside your roast meat or fish.

Serves 4

750g (1lb 10oz) Brussels sprouts
1–2 tbsp olive oil
4 tbsp fish sauce
knob of butter
salt

Start by prepping the sprouts. Trim the base of each sprout and remove any damaged outer leaves. You can cut a cross into the bottom of the sprouts so that they will cook quicker, but it's not necessary and entirely optional.

Bring a large pan of salted water to the boil, add the sprouts and cook until just tender – the timing will depend on the size of the sprouts and whether you have cut a cross on the underside.

Drain and either refresh under cold running water or plunge the sprouts into a bowl of iced water to stop them cooking further. Drain and leave to dry on a clean tea towel for a few minutes.

Heat the oil in a large frying pan over a medium–high heat and turn the extractor fan on to full speed, or open a window. Add the sprouts to the hot pan and cook, shaking the pan, until the sprouts start to take on some colour. Add the fish sauce and continue shaking the pan for 10 seconds. Add the butter and a splash of water and shake the pan again so that the butter melts and you coat the sprouts in a beautiful, glossy glaze. Serve immediately.

Pickled sprout tops

I'm quite sure not everyone has tasted sprout tops, and if you haven't you are missing out. With a similar flavour to spring greens, they are the leaves on top of a sprout stick and are sometimes sold as a separate vegetable. They are perfect for stir-fries or sautéed in a pan with butter – or, you can preserve them as a pickle. Serve the pickled sprout tops in salads, as a side dish or in a sandwich as a replacement for cucumber pickles or gherkins.

Makes 1 medium–large jar

500g (1lb 2oz) sprout tops
200ml (7fl oz) rice wine vinegar
100g (3 ½ oz) caster (superfine) sugar
pinch of salt

Separate the sprout tops into leaves, wash them in cold water and pat them dry on kitchen paper. Taking a couple of leaves at a time, roll them up and cut them into shreds (or chiffonade) and pack the shredded leaves into the sterilized jar.

Pour 300ml (10 ½ fl oz) of water into a small saucepan, add the vinegar, sugar and salt and place the pan over a medium heat. Bring the liquid to a boil, stirring to dissolve the sugar, then reduce the heat and simmer for 1 minute. Pour the pickling liquor into the jar over the shredded sprout tops, seal with the lid and turn the jar upside down. Leave the contents of the jar to cool.

Turn the jar the right way up and store the pickles in a cool, dry place for up to 1 year. When opened, store in the fridge and use within 1 week.

48

Costa Rican bananas / Bergamot /
Clementines / Finger limes / Florida
Ruby grapefruit / Lemons – Cedro,
Menton, Sicilian / Mexican limes /
Pomelo / Valencia Navel oranges /
Guadeloupe "Philibon" Charentais
melon / Queen pineapple / Réunion
bunched lychees / Apples – Bramley,
French Chantecler Belchard, Hereford
Cox Orange Pippin, Kent Russet / Pears
– French Vassout Comice, Kent
Conference / California cranberries /
Iranian pomegranate / Jordanian
Medjool dates / Dried fruit – Alphonso
mango slices, Corsican apricots, Prunes
d'Agen / Bay leaf / Italian flat parsley /
Italian Monk's Beard / Rosemary / Sage
/ Thyme / Nuts – Almonds, Cashews,
Hazelnuts, Macadamia, Peanuts, Pecans,
Pistachios, Walnuts / Tomatoes –
Costoluto, Camone / Chicories –
French, Italian, Red and white Belgian,
Sugar Loaf / Pis-en-lit (dandelion) /
Radicchios – Chioggia, Grumalo, Pink
Vaneto, Puntarelle, Rose, Tardivo,

Treviso / Cauliflower – Boston, Cape,
Romanesque / Brussels sprouts / Cime
di rapa / Chard – Rainbow, Swiss /
French Spinach / Cabbages – Cavolo
Nero, Kent Brussel tops, Kent Hispi,
Normandy Savoy, Somerset kale,
Somerset red / Cardoon / Jerusalem
artichokes / Lautrec pink garlic / South
African cep mushrooms / White truffles
/ Onions – Cevenne, Roscoff / Shallots
– Brittany, Thai / Somerset leeks /
French potatoes – Belle de Fontenay,
Charlotte, Lincolnshire Agria,
Northumberland Yukon Gold, Ratte,
Somerset Pink Fir / Peruvian oca /
Squash – Delica, Italian Turban,
Potimarron, Spaghetti / Carrots –
Brittany Sand, Chantenay / Celeriac /
Crosnes / Horseradish / Parsley root /
Parsnips / Red meat radish / Salsify /
Somerset heirloom beetroot / Turnips –
Brittany Golden, French, Scottish swede

Banana and Lychee
Driving Me Bananas

Here we are at the start of December and talking about seasonality with exotic fruit that comes from opposite sides of the world: bananas from Costa Rica and lychees from the island of Réunion in the Indian Ocean.

The small island of Costa Rica in Central America produces around 13 per cent of the world's banana supply. There are hundreds of varieties of bananas grown across the world and Costa Rica exports only a small fraction of those banana varieties to the UK, but one of them is the Grand Nain. This banana has more flavour than the Cavendish variety – which is popularly grown for its ability to withstand travel without bruising. Another from Costa Rica is Gran Enano (meaning "large dwarf"), which at only 10–12cm (4–4¼in) long is smaller than other varieties and it has a very distinctive sweet flavour. An American businessman called Minor Cooper Keith planted the first banana plantations on the island in the late 1880s. The Costa Rican government contracted him to build part of the island's railway infrastructure, but with his keen eye for opportunity, he also planted bananas trees on the vast tracts of land that the government granted him. With transport at his

Of all banana varieties (there are over 1,000), the Cavendish has a superior yield – which is why it makes up more than 47 per cent of the world's exports.

fingertips, he was soon selling huge shipments of bananas to the USA. He went on to found the United Fruit Company, which later became the Chiquita brand that we know today.

Throughout the 20th century, bananas from Costa Rica made up the majority of UK banana imports, but in recent years producers there have struggled to compete with new plantations in Cameroon, Ecuador, the Philippines and Guatemala. Modern farming methods and cheaper labour in these countries have resulted in less emphasis on producing flavoursome fruit.

> "The Costa Rican banana growers decided to focus on sustainability and lobbied the EU for PGI status for their fruit."

The Costa Rican banana growers decided to focus on sustainability and lobbied the EU for PGI status (see page 24). Success came in in 2015 and the accolade (one of only two issued outside the EU) has regenerated the banana business in the country.

Cavendish bananas can trace their roots back to Derbyshire in around 1830. At the time, Joseph Paxton was the head gardener at Chatsworth House, home of the Duke of Devonshire. Paxton built a vast conservatory at Chatsworth, some 91m (300 feet) long, where he grew all manner of exotic plants and fruit, including bananas from a plant from Mauritius. Years later, the Duke sent boxes of banana plants to Samoa and beyond. Paxton named his bananas after William Cavendish, the 6th Duke of Devonshire. Although Cavendish bananas are now the most widely commercially grown variety, they are possibly the least flavoursome. Like many supermarket fruits, the banana has the looks, a price point and a shelf life that take precedence over flavour.

For another seasonal fix of tropical fruit, we head back to the French island of Réunion, from where we also source Queen Victoria pineapples (see page 54). Here, the lychees are juicy, fragrant and sweet, and were introduced by French colonists in the 1760s (lychees have been grown in China for over 4,000 years). The island produces around 8,000 tonnes of lychees per year. They ripen in December for eating before their deep pink, slightly prickly skin dries and becomes brittle – having the leaves still attached is a good indication of freshness. They deteriorate quickly, which means airfreighting them to the UK – this might increase their cost, but it is definitely a price worth paying.

I love to think that there is some great celestial game plan that means that the best of our tropical fruits, including these wonderful lychees, are available when there's little that's growing closer to home, filling an important gap in the British and European fruit calendar.

And one thing that the outstanding Costa Rican bananas and Réunion's wonderful lychees really have in common is the volcanic soil in which they grow. Piton de la Fournaise in Réunion and Irazú in Costa Rica are both volcanic, mountainous areas producing world-class fruit. But that's not all: it's one thing to have incredible soil and the perfect climate – but neither of these means anything without the care and farming prowess of those who are cultivating that abundant land.

Caramelized banana jam

I'm sure we've all been in the situation of having some blackened bananas left in the fruit bowl. This amazing, unusual and very easy preserve will use up those bananas and give you a delicious jam for your breakfast toast. It is also good with pancakes or to spread on top of a cake.

Makes 1 medium jar

600g (1lb 5oz) very ripe bananas, peeled and cut into 1cm (½ in) slices

finely grated zest and juice of 1 lemon

160g (5 ¾ oz) caster (superfine) sugar

1 tsp pectin

50ml (1 ¾ fl oz) spiced rum

Tip the banana slices into a bowl and add the lemon zest and juice and 200ml (9fl oz) water.

Tip 140g (5oz) of the sugar into a dry, medium pan set over a low heat. Leave to melt, but do not stir. Continue to cook until the sugar becomes a rich golden caramel, swirling the pan to ensure that it cooks evenly. Slide the pan off the heat and carefully add the banana mixture, the caramel will splutter and harden. Return the pan to the heat to melt the caramel.

In a small bowl combine the remaining sugar and the pectin, add to the pan, mix to combine and continue to cook for a further 10 minutes, until the mixture has thickened and become jammy.

Leave the jam to cool and then stir in the spiced rum. Spoon the jam into a sterilized jar and store it in the fridge for up to 1 month, or 2 weeks once opened.

Banoffee pie   *Recipe by Jamie Oliver*

Jamie Oliver first came to Borough Market to film an episode of his original TV series *The Naked Chef*. "How's the baby turnips?" he asked. "Growing," I said. He was talking about the vegetables – I was talking about my children! He was blown away by the array of stunning produce on the stand and has been a fan of the market for a long time. He shares his love of bananas in his book *Jamie's Kitchen* and here's his recipe.

Serves 12

Perfect pastry recipe (makes 2 x 28cm/11in tart cases)

250g (9oz) butter

200g (7oz) icing (confectioner's) sugar

500g (just over 1lb) plain (all-purpose) flour, plus extra for dusting

1 vanilla pod, halved, seeds scraped out

1 lemon

4 egg yolks

2–4 tbsp cold milk

Continued overleaf...

Pastry: I like to have a pie case rolled, blind baked and in the freezer, ready to use when needed. Cream the butter, icing sugar and a pinch of sea salt together, then rub or pulse in the flour, followed by the vanilla seeds, finely grated lemon zest and the egg yolks. When it's looking like coarse breadcrumbs, add the cold milk (or use water). Pat together to form a ball of dough, then lightly flour. The idea is to get the ingredients to form a dough with the minimum amount of movement to keep the pastry short and flaky (the more you work it the more elastic it will get, causing it to shrink in the oven and be chewy, and you don't want that to happen).

On a clean, floured surface, roll the pastry into a large, short and fat sausage shape, wrap it in clingfilm and put it in the fridge to rest for at least 1 hour.

Cut the pastry roll in half. Working lengthways, carefully slice off very thin slivers of one pastry roll. Place the slivers all around a 28cm/11in tart mould, fitting them together like a jigsaw. Push the pieces together and tidy up the sides by trimming off any excess pastry. Repeat for the other roll in a second tart mould. Place the pastry cases in the freezer for at least 1 hour.

Blind bake both cases for around 15 minutes at 180°C/350°F/Gas 4 – this will cook them all the way through, colouring them slightly.

Once your tart shells have been baked blind, brush the inside of them with a little egg white and then put them back in the oven for 30 seconds – no longer. This will give them a nice waterproof layer which will protect them from the wetter banoffee filling. The pastry will stay crumbly and crisp for longer instead of going all soggy. Freeze one tart case for another day; allow the other to cool, then use it to make the pie.

Continued overleaf...

Filling for 1 pie

200g (7oz) blanched, whole almonds

280g (10oz) icing (confectioner's) sugar

1 jar of dulce de leche; or 2 x 397g (14oz) tins of condensed milk, boiled

6 ripe bananas

450ml (15fl oz) double (heavy) cream

1 tablespoon Camp coffee

1 vanilla pod, halved, seeds scraped out

Pie: Preheat the oven to 180°C/350°F/Gas 4. Give the almonds a quick rinse in cold water, drain, then mix with the icing sugar in a bowl until sticky. Place on a baking tray and toast in the oven for 15 minutes, or until golden and crisp, turning every 2 minutes. Allow to cool.

Spread the dulce de leche as thick as you like across the base of the pastry, then slice the bananas and place on top. Whip the cream, then add the Camp coffee – add a little less if you'd like a more subtle coffee flavour – and the vanilla seeds. Dollop the cream on top of the bananas, as high and as rough as you like. Sprinkle the almonds over the top and serve immediately.

49

*Golden turnips / Bergamot /
Clementines / Finger limes / Lemons –
Cedro, Menton, Sicilian / Mexican
limes / Pomelo / Valencia Navel oranges
/ Australian "Kent" mangoes / Brazilian
Jumbo pawpaw / Costa Rican bananas
/ Queen pineapple / Réunion bunched
lychees / Apples – Bramley, French
Chantecler Belchard, Hereford Cox
Orange Pippin, Kent Russet / Pears –
French Vassout Comice, Kent
Conference / California cranberries /
Chilean Muscat grapes / Iranian
pomegranate / Jordanian Medjool dates
/ Dried fruit – Alphonso mango slices,
Corsican apricots, Prunes d'Agen /
Italian Monk's Beard / Bay leaf / Italian
flat parsley / Rosemary / Sage / Thyme /
Nuts – Almonds, Cashews, Hazelnuts,
Macadamia, Peanuts, Pecans, Pistachios,
Walnuts / Tomatoes – Costoluto,
Camone / Chicories – French, Italian,*

*Red and white Belgian, Sugar Loaf /
Pis-en-Lit (dandelion) / Radicchios –
Chioggia, Grumolo, Pink Vaneto,
Puntarelle, Rose, Tardivo, Treviso /
Cauliflowers – Boston, Cape,
Romanesque / Cime di rapa / French
spinach / Cabbages – Cavolo Nero,
Kent Brussels tops, Kent sprout sticks
with tops, Normandy Savoy, Somerset
kale, Somerset red / Cardoon /
Jerusalem artichokes / Lautrec pink
garlic / White truffles / Onions –
Cevenne, Roscoff / Shallots – Brittany,
Thai / Somerset leek / Potatoes – Agria,
Belle de Fontenay, Charlotte, Ratte,
Somerset Pink Fir / Peruvian oca / Delica
squash / Carrots – Brittany Sand,
Chantenay / Celeriac / Crosnes /
Horseradish / Parsley root / Parsnips /
Red meat radish / Salsify / Somerset
heirloom beetroot / Turnips – Brittany
Golden, Scottish swede*

Turnip
All That Glisters is Not Gold

From Poland to Ireland, the turnip is one of the most popular root vegetables all around the world. The turnip family is large and varied – producing veg that not only vary in size, shape and flavour, but in colour, too. There is a veritable turnip rainbow – from white Tokyo turnips to green kohlrabi, purple York, yellow Boule D'or and Orange Jelly. All are grown for both their edible bulbous root and, in early season, their tender leafy tops.

Flavours within the varieties differ immensely. Kohlrabi are curious-looking, pale, jade-green turnips with tendril-like roots and leafy stalks. They have crisp, crunchy white flesh, which is slightly watery with a fresh, mildly bitter taste reminiscent of water chestnuts or radishes. You can eat them raw or cooked and they make excellent salads and pickles. Orange-fleshed swedes have a far sweeter taste and are well-suited to being mashed – if you celebrate Burns' Night you will be familiar with the notion of Neeps and Tatties, which are an integral part of the traditional Scottish meal. The familiar and humble white and purple turnips can be quite bitter and peppery. They are considered a rather old-fashioned vegetable nowadays and compete for our attentions with the more beautiful golden turnips, for example.

Turnips also vary in size. On one of my many trips to the Rungis market outside Paris, I stumbled across a small crowd that had gathered around a table. Curious to see what the commotion was about, I ventured forth to behold a table covered with myriad turnips in all shapes and sizes. It was an auction – the members of the crowd were haggling over the price of each turnip. I couldn't believe that what we perceive to be a modest vegetable could, in Paris, create the kind of energy you'd see if you were buying sought-after fresh truffles. The French take their *navets* very seriously.

And it's for this reason that, even though we can get turnips in the UK and they grow easily here, at Turnips we get our turnips from Brittany, where much like celeriac, this root veg is rather more prized.

Baby turnips, though, are a different story. Early in the season, around May, we buy those from a grower in Essex. These little beauties often sit alongside other diminutive vegetables such as carrot, beetroot, fennel and courgettes and feature in stunning dishes at fancy restaurants.

The golden turnip

Golden turnips – Golden Globe, Golden Ball and Boule D'or, among other names – are a European heirloom variety that was first cultivated in France in the 1800s. As the name suggests, they are golden in colour both inside and out, with a firm and crunchy flesh. They have a mellow, sweet, earthy and peppery flavour that is reminiscent of red or green meat radishes. Like kohlrabi, they do not store as well as the purple-and-white varieties, but what they lack in shelf life, they make up for in flavour. In springtime, young, golf-ball-size golden turnips are delicious in salads. You'll buy them with their tender, peppery leaves still attached, and you can use these as salad leaves. Baked, mashed or roasted, these varieties will guarantee you a sweeter and creamier finish than other turnips on the market.

We've been selling golden turnips at Borough for about ten years, but they are still relatively unknown, and we like it that way. Unusual varieties are the ones that excite us the most and our customers are always interested in learning about them.

Our head chef Tomas recalls his impressions of the many different products he saw at our market throughout his first year working with us: "Working at Turnips gives me the opportunity to experiment with products I would otherwise not know even exist. As a chef you are confined to the kitchen and your free time is very limited – you very rarely venture out to markets like Borough. For me there is now an abundance of exciting new fruit and vegetables to experiment with. It is like going back to childhood and standing in the sweet shop!"

> "We have been selling golden turnips at Borough for about ten years, but they are still relatively unknown, and we like it that way."

Kohlrabi fritters with chive and sour-cream dip

Ever since I was a kid, I've been a massive fan of fritters. My mum used to cook them for us using pretty much any vegetable that she had available and was in season. These sweet and buttery fritters with sour-cream dip are a stunning start to a meal or are delicious served alongside a pint of cold beer.

Serves 4

2 large kohlrabi, peeled and coarsely grated

1 egg, lightly beaten

3 tbsp plain (all-purpose) flour

½ tsp smoked paprika

sunflower oil, for frying

salt and freshly ground black pepper

For the dip

120ml (4fl oz) sour cream

80g (2¾oz) mayonnaise

3 garlic cloves, crushed

½ tsp onion powder

finely grated zest and juice of 1 lime

½ bunch of chives, finely chopped

Tip the kohlrabi on to a clean tea towel, gather up the edges and squeeze tightly to draw out the excess water. Tip the kohlrabi into a bowl, add the egg, flour and smoked paprika and mix well to combine.

Heat 2–3 tablespoons of sunflower oil in a frying pan over a medium heat. In batches, drop spoonfuls of the kohlrabi mixture into the pan to make mini pancakes and fry them until golden on the underside (about 2 minutes), then flip and cook the other side. (Take care not to overcrowd the pan.) Remove the cooked fritters from the pan, and set them aside to drain on kitchen paper. Continue cooking the fritters, adding more oil to the pan as needed, until you've used all the mixture. Season with salt and pepper.

To make the dip, combine the sour cream, mayonnaise, crushed garlic and onion powder. Add the finely grated zest of the lime, season with salt and pepper and mix well. Add the chives, then stir in the lime juice to taste. Spoon the sauce into a bowl and serve with the hot fritters.

Kohlrabi gratin with smoked bacon and garlic crumb

I'm quite sure that all kids love pasta bake – maybe fewer like cauliflower cheese, but I doubt that many have tried kohlrabi gratin. This creamy gratin with flavours of cabbage, smoked bacon and crunchy garlic crumble will really shine at suppertime and is perfect for family dinners. I love adding potatoes to this gratin to give a little texture to the kohlrabi, which can be very soft if over-cooked.

I like to use Alsace bacon – this bacon is one of the best I have ever tasted. It's really smoky with a stunning flavour, but you can use any good-quality bacon; or use pancetta, if you prefer.

Serves 4

200ml (7fl oz) double (heavy) cream

3 garlic cloves, crushed

5 thyme sprigs

3 large Agria potatoes, peeled and thinly sliced with a mandoline

4 large kohlrabi, peeled and thinly sliced with a mandoline

150g (5½oz) Alsace bacon, thinly sliced

100g (3½oz) butter

salt and freshly ground black pepper

2 tbsp combined chopped flat-leaf parsley and chives, to serve

2–3 tbsp freshly grated Parmesan, to serve

For the garlic crumbs

2 tbsp olive oil

100g (3½oz) panko breadcrumbs

75g (2½oz) butter

1 tsp garlic granules

½ tsp onion powder

Preheat the oven to 180°C/160°C fan/350°F/Gas 4. Line an ovenproof baking dish with baking paper.

Pour the cream into a small saucepan. Add the garlic and thyme, place the pan over a medium heat and bring the cream to a boil. Reduce the heat to stop the cream scorching, but continue to cook until the liquid has reduced by half (about 7–8 minutes). Remove the thyme sprigs.

Layer the potatoes, kohlrabi, thinly sliced bacon and dots of the butter with the reduced cream and season with salt and pepper in between the layers. Bake for 35–45 minutes, until the vegetables are tender when tested with a wooden skewer or point of a knife.

Meanwhile make the garlic crumbs. Heat the olive oil in a large frying pan over a medium heat. Add the breadcrumbs and cook, stirring continuously, until they start to turn golden. Add the butter and continue cooking until the crumbs are golden brown. Tip the crumbs on to a tray, stir through the garlic granules and onion powder and season with salt and pepper.

To serve, scatter the hot gratin with the garlicky crumbs, then the chopped herbs and grated Parmesan.

50

Agria potatoes / Bergamot / Clementines / Finger limes / Lemons – Cedro, Menton, Sicilian / Mexican limes / Valencia Navel oranges / Australian "Kent" mangoes / Brazilian Jumbo pawpaw / Costa Rican bananas / Queen pineapple / Réunion bunched lychees / Apples – French Chantecler Belchard, Hereford Cox Orange Pippin, Kent Russet / Pears – French Vassout Comice, Kent Conference / California cranberries / Chilean cherries / Chilean Muscat grapes / Iranian pomegranate / Jordanian Medjool dates / Dried fruit – Alphonso mango slices, Corsican apricots, Prunes d'Agen / French pâte de fruits / Bay leaf / Italian flat parsley / Italian Monk's Beard / Rosemary / Sage / Thyme / Nuts – Almonds, Cashews, Hazelnuts, Macadamia, Peanuts, Pecans, Pistachios, Walnuts / Tomatoes – Costoluto, Camone / Chicories – French, Italian, Red and white Belgian / Pis-en-lit (dandelion) /Radicchios – Chioggia, Grumolo, Pink Vaneto, Puntarelle, Rose, Tardivo, Treviso / Mexican asparagus / Cauliflowers – Boston, Cape, Romanesque / Cime di rapa / French spinach / Cabbages – Cavolo Nero, Kent Brussels tops, Kent sprout sticks with tops, Normandy Savoy, Somerset kale, Somerset red / Jerusalem artichokes / Lautrec pink garlic / White truffles / Cevenne onions / Shallots – Brittany, Thai / Somerset leeks / Potatoes – Belle de Fontenay, Charlotte, Ratte, Somerset Pink Fir / Peruvian oca / Delica squash / Carrots – Brittany Sand, Chantenay / Cardoon / Celeriac / Crosnes / Horseradish / Parsley root / Parsnips / Red meat radish / Salsify / Somerset heirloom beetroot / Turnips – Brittany Golden, Scottish swede

Fenland Agria Potato
A Good Roasting

With the winter well under way, the great British roast dinner is surely a weekend fixture up and down our country. Of course, no self-respecting Sunday roast, at home or in the pub, is complete without a great big bowl of crisp, golden roast potatoes.

To cook perfect roasties, you must start with the right potato. Flavour and texture are most important – roast potatoes should be fluffy and tender inside, and crisp on the outside. And colour: aesthetically those roasties have to look right... they should cook to an enticing golden brown. The sugar and starch content in potatoes varies, and this will determine the cooked texture and whether a potato is best suited to mash, chips or roast. The final consideration is size: if the potatoes are too big, they become stodgy and chewy; but if they're small, the insides will not have that all-important fluffy texture. Firm potatoes with soil still on their skins will store better (in a cool, dark place) than those that are scrubbed clean, as the soil stops the skins being exposed to light and turning green.

In Northern Ireland, the most popular potato for roasting is the Golden Wonder; in Wales (for its *tatws rhost*) it's the Red Rudolph; and in Scotland cooks prefer Markies. In England, it's the Agria from Cambridgeshire that comes out top. But it wasn't always so.

*The Agria potato is the perfect roasting potato at this time
of year. Grown in the UK, it is harvested and then stored
from mid-July to late April the following year.*

When I was a child growing up in London, my mother would buy King Edward potatoes for roasting. These are pale-skinned with red speckles around the "eyes". When cooked they become fluffy, making them especially good when roasted, baked or chipped. However, while they may have a great flavour, they don't store well over the winter months. For years, our farmers and botanists have been hybridizing potatoes to create new varieties that not only taste delicious but store well from one season to the next.

A roll call of the nation's favourite roasting spuds starts in the 1940s with Red Duke of Yorks, a good all-rounder. Fast forward a few years and Desirée became the favourite. Large red tubers with a waxy yellow flesh, these are especially good for mash. Then, in the late 1970s along came Caras, from Ireland, which are a white potato with a red blush on parts of the skin. In the early 1990s we started to see yet more new varieties, such as Yukon Gold, originally from Canada, with its pale golden-coloured skin and yellow flesh. The Maris Piper was developed in Cambridgeshire in the late 1960s but took some 40 years to become the most widely used variety in the UK. This white potato with creamy, yellow flesh tastes fantastic and stores well into early March, leaving a couple of months in between the old and new season crop.

Now it's the turn of Agrias, which were developed in Germany in 1985. They have a very similar appearance to Maris Pipers and are often sold as such (I think it's so as not to confuse us). However, Agrias not only have a better flavour, they are also richer and creamier, and store better. Harvested in late autumn, they will keep until the following May. They have a pale golden skin and a deep yellow flesh that is very floury and fluffy when cooked. They are not only fabulous for roasting, but also make excellent chips and crisps.

Most cooks have an opinion about which fat you should use to make the best roast potatoes. Many use olive or sunflower oil or butter – or a combination of those. Chefs proclaim that goose fat is the only option. My wife's choice is classic: "You can choose whatever fat or oil you wish for – as long as it is heavily salted, golden butter." There are those who feel the need to add flavourings to roast potatoes, too – garlic, herbs, spices and even citrus – but, to me, if you have the right potato, all you need is a simple seasoning of sea salt. I think it's best to keep to Gary Rhodes' mantra: "Get the basics right first, then move on!"

"To cook perfect roasties, you must start with the right potato. Flavour and texture are most important – roast potatoes should be fluffy and tender inside, and crisp on the outside."

This time of the year is one for family and friends. The office-party season is nearly over, and we can start to concentrate on matters closer to home, with thoughts turning to festive cooking. My wife doesn't see herself as a cook. Indeed, she's so modest that she doesn't like me or our children to talk about her impressive culinary skills at all. To us, Caroline's Sunday roasts are legendary, and her Christmas dinner is completely unsurpassed. To that end, I've persuaded her to share her family recipe (from her grandmother) for the best roast potatoes (see page 295).

Agria potato crumble

This little jar of crispy potatoes will come to your rescue when you need to add some texture and crunch to salads or gratins, or to scatter over steak and grilled fish. They are so simple to make, taste amazing and add next-level crunch to your food!

Makes 1 medium jar

5 Agria potatoes, peeled and chopped into 2cm (¾ in) chunks

1 litre (35fl oz) sunflower oil, for deep-frying

1 tsp garlic powder

1 tsp onion powder

½ tsp smoked paprika

salt

Place the potato pieces in a food processor and whizz until they are the size of a grain of rice. Tip them into a sieve and wash the potatoes under cold running water to remove the starch. Once the water runs clear, leave the potatoes to drain and then tip them into a clean tea towel. Gather up the edges of the towel and squeeze the potatoes tightly to dry them out as much as possible.

Heat the oil in a deep-sided pan or deep-fat fryer to 180°C/350°F. In batches, carefully add a handful of the potatoes to the hot oil, stirring with a whisk, and cook until golden brown. Remove the potatoes from the hot oil using a slotted spoon and set them aside to drain on kitchen paper. Continue cooking the potatoes in this way, but make sure that the oil comes back up to temperature in between each batch.

Season the potato crumbs with the garlic and onion powder, smoked paprika and salt. Leave to cool, then store in an airtight jar or box for up to 3 months.

Roast potatoes *Recipe by Polly McCarthy*

Polly McCarthy was Fred's wife Caroline's grandmother, who lived on the King's Road in Chelsea, London. This is her recipe for roast potatoes, which she passed down to her children and, by extension, beyond. Agria would be the best choice of potatoes to use here, but you can also use Maris Piper or any floury yellow-flesh ones.

Serves 4–6

3kg (6lb 8oz) Agria potatoes, peeled and cut into your preferred size
250g (9oz) salty golden butter
salt

Preheat the oven to 180°C/160°C fan/350°F/Gas 4.

Put the potatoes into a saucepan, cover with water and add a good pinch of salt. Bring to a boil over a high heat, then reduce the heat and simmer for 5–10 minutes – how long varies depending on the size of your potato pieces, but your aim is to get the edges of the potatoes a little softened, just not too much. Drain well.

Cut the butter into 4 equal pieces. Add this to a large roasting tin and place it into the oven for about 3–5 minutes to let the butter melt, but without burning – it should look creamy.

Add the potatoes to the pan, coat them in the butter and return the roasting tin to the oven. Roast the potatoes for 1–1 ½ hours (depending on the size of the potatoes). I turn them only once they've been cooking for 1 hour, and sometimes not at all.

The potatoes should be golden and crispy. If they are not crisp after 1 hour, you may have too much butter, so drain some of it from the roasting tin and return the tin to the oven. Continue cooking until crisp and deep golden.

51

Boston cauliflower / *Bergamot* / *Clementines* / *Lemons – Cedro, Menton, Sicilian* / *Mexican limes* / *Valencia Navel oranges* / *Australian "Kent" mangoes* / *Brazilian Jumbo pawpaw* / *Costa Rican bananas* / *Queen pineapple* / *Réunion bunched lychees* / *Apples – French Chantecler Belchard, Hereford Cox Orange Pippin, Kent Russet* / *Pears – French Vassout Comice, Kent Conference* / *California cranberries* / *Chilean cherry* / *Chilean Muscat grapes* / *Iranian pomegranate* / *Jordanian Medjool dates* / *Dried fruit – Alphonso mango slices, Corsican apricots, Prunes d'Agen* / *French pâte de fruits* / *Quince jelly* / *Bay leaf* / *Italian flat parsley* / *Rosemary* / *Sage* / *Thyme* / *Cinnamon* / *Cloves* / *Galangal* / *Ginger* / *Star anise* / *Tahitian vanilla pods* / *Nuts – Almonds, Cashews, Hazelnuts, Macadamia, Peanuts, Pecans, Pistachios, Walnuts* / *Tomatoes – Costoluto,* *Camone* / *Chicories – French, Italian, Red and white Belgian* / *Pis-en-lit (dandelion)* / *Radicchios – Chioggia, Grumolo, Pink Vaneto, Puntarelle, Rose, Tardivo, Treviso* / *Mexican asparagus* / *Cauliflowers – Boston Lincs, Cape, Romanesque* / *Cabbages – Kent Brussels tops, Kent sprout sticks with tops, Normandy Savoy, Somerset kale, Somerset red* / *Jerusalem artichokes* / *Lautrec pink garlic* / *Truffles – Perigord black, white* / *Onions – Cevenne, Roscoff* / *Brittany shallot* / *Somerset leeks* / *Potatoes – Agria, Belle de Fontenay, Charlotte, Ratte, Somerset Pink Fir* / *Peruvian oca* / *Delica squash* / *Carrots – Brittany Sand, Chantenay* / *Celeriac* / *Crosnes* / *Horseradish* / *Parsley root* / *Red meat radish* / *Salsify* / *Somerset heirloom beetroot* / *Turnips – Brittany Golden, Scottish swede*

Boston Cauliflower
I Wish it Could be Christmas Every Day...

Christmas isn't until next week, but now is the time to procure your fruit and vegetables for the festive feast. You'll be needing Corsican clementines to put into Christmas stockings and, for your table, Agria potatoes; Brussels sprouts, Tenderstem broccoli and Hispi cabbage from Kent; leeks and red cabbage from Somerset; and garlic, shallots and carrots from Brittany. Last but not least, you'll need a cauliflower from Lincolnshire – for the cauliflower cheese.

Cauliflowers from Boston, Lincolnshire, have bright white heads, beautiful tight, crisp florets, deep green leaves, and a sweet taste. There are other colourful cauliflower varieties around at this time of year – such as the vivid green Romanesque and the Purple Cape – but it is the white variety that is my focus for this week. I have been sourcing cauliflower, or "white jewels", from Boston for nearly 40 years.

Even though cauliflower and broccoli are both flowering brassicas, the best varieties of each come from different counties. Stunning Tenderstem broccoli is best from Kent – and although farmers there also produce great cauliflowers, they cannot compete with those grown further north by the Lincolnshire farmers. Boston cauliflowers have tighter and whiter florets, which equates to a superior and sweeter flavour.

Although it's possible to use glasshouses to grow cauliflowers throughout the year, the quality is not as good as you'll find in caulis grown outdoors true to the seasons – summer and winter. The winter harvest in November and December being the best caulis of all: dark green leaves envelop the white florets, or "curds", and the tighter the leaves the whiter the heart. Cold winter temperatures mean that the cauliflower grows more slowly, giving a sweeter taste than those from the summer. When it comes to harvesting, cauliflowers can be fickle – fluctuations in air temperature can slow or hasten growth. The late summer and early autumn varieties are famously unpredictable – farmers wait with bated breath to see if their veg will be ready in time for the festive rush. If it's not, farmers across the Channel in Brittany step in for us and can provide what we need in time for Christmas.

> "When it comes to harvesting, cauliflowers can be fickle – fluctuations in air temperature can slow or hasten growth."

With the rise of vegetarian or plant-based cooking, caulis have had something of renaissance, becoming the poster child for veggie roast dinners. Smothered in spices and herbs, they are delicious baked whole or cut into thick slices and pan-fried much like a prime steak. Or, you can eat cauliflower raw, whizzed into "rice" or "cous cous", or steamed or deep-fried; or, of course, coated in cheese sauce and baked to a blistering golden crust of pure comfort. And with the Turnips' mantra of "All taste, no waste" in mind, the stalk and leaves are equally delicious.

Dawn chorus in the fields

Have you ever heard of the Cauliflower Creak? In June, when the nighttime temperatures increase following the cooler weeks of early summer, cauliflowers put on a growth spurt. Very early in the morning, they push and jostle as they grow, rubbing together to create an eerie squeaking sound that drifts over the fields. It is the equivalent of a cauliflower dawn chorus, or the vegetable audio version of the Northern Lights. Pure magic.

And they say it's me who's cheesy!

Most professional chefs will happily take a back seat and let their mum, dad or gran take to the kitchen when it comes to cooking a roast dinner. And what is the Christmas feast, other than a revved-up roast with extra trimmings? In our diverse, modern society, our national cuisine has become a wonderful melting pot of multi-cultural tastes and flavours and the traditional roast dinner is on the decline. But if had to pick one dish or meal that epitomizes British food heritage, it would have to be the roast. For many people a roast dinner is a comforting celebration of family and home. Behind every one, there is usually one hero in the kitchen: in my house, that person is my wonderful wife, Caroline. In the previous chapter she shared her roast potato recipe. This week, we have the joy that is her cauliflower cheese (see page 300).

Sweet 'n' sour cauliflower

This dish of spicy, fried cauliflower has been on the menu since the first day we opened our restaurant and I'm not sure if we'll ever take it off – our customers absolutely love it. Like many of my recipes, it is super-easy and super-tasty, and works just as well with broccoli, if you fancy that instead (or as well!). The glaze will keep for weeks in a jar in the fridge, so it's worth making a double batch so that you always have it on hand to fulfil your desire for sweet-and-sour deep-fried vegetables.

Serves 4

1 litre (35fl oz) sunflower or vegetable oil, for frying

8 garlic cloves, finely chopped

150ml (5fl oz) rice wine vinegar

100g (3½oz) granulated sugar

1 tbsp sesame oil

2–3 tbsp gochujang paste, to taste

1 large cauliflower, trimmed and cut into thumb-size florets

1 tbsp plain (all-purpose) flour

salt

2 tbsp snipped chives, to serve

For the tempura batter

100g (3½oz) plain (all-purpose) flour

100g (3½oz) cornflour (cornstarch)

1 tsp bicarbonate of soda (baking soda)

1 tsp salt

½ tsp ground coriander

½ tsp curry powder

250ml (9fl oz) sparkling water

Heat 1–2 tablespoons of the oil in a frying pan over a low–medium heat. Add the garlic and fry for about 3–5 minutes, until soft but not coloured. Add the vinegar, sugar and sesame oil, mix to combine and continue cooking until reduced by half. The mixture will be sticky and the consistency of runny honey. Add 2 tablespoons of the gochujang, taste and add more if you like extra heat. Strain the mixture into a clean bowl and leave to cool.

Heat the remaining oil to 180°C/350°F either in a deep-sided saucepan or deep-fat fryer.

Meanwhile, tip the cauliflower into a bowl and dust it with the tablespoon of plain flour to lightly coat.

To make the tempura batter, mix the plain flour, cornflour, bicarbonate of soda, salt, ground coriander and curry powder in a bowl. Add the sparkling water, whisk to combine to a thick-ish paste that will coat the cauliflower without running off.

Working in batches, dip the cauliflower florets into the tempura batter to coat, then drop them into the hot oil and deep-fry until crisp and golden brown all over (about 2–3 minutes). Remove each batch of the cauliflower from the oil using a slotted spoon and set it aside to drain on kitchen paper. Season with salt. Once you've fried and seasoned all the cauliflower, transfer it to a serving bowl and pour over the sweet and sour sauce to coat. Scatter with the chives and serve.

Cauliflower cheese   *Recipe by Caroline Foster*

To really honour the Boston cauliflower, you could use a Lincolnshire poacher cheese for this dish, but every great cook or chef adapts the recipe and puts their own twist on it, and a good cheddar would work, too. Make a hearty cauliflower cheese and you are everyone's friend – they will all be begging for an invitation to Sunday lunch!

Serves 4–6

1–2 litres (35–70fl oz) full-fat milk (depending on how much you need to cover the cauliflower)

1 Boston cauliflower, trimmed and cut into florets

50g (1¼oz) butter

50g (1¼oz) plain (all-purpose) flour

350g (12oz) Lincolnshire poacher or strong cheddar cheese, grated

1–2 heaped tsp English mustard, to taste

salt and freshly ground black pepper

Preheat the oven to 180°C/160°C fan/350°F/Gas 4.

In a large saucepan, bring the milk to a boil, add the cauliflower and cook until just tender (about 10 minutes). Drain the florets through a colander set over a bowl to catch the milk. Pour the milk into a jug and keep warm.

Melt the butter in a medium saucepan over a low heat. Add the flour, mix to combine to a roux, then cook for 3–5 minutes over a low heat so that you cook out the flour taste and have a thick paste.

A little at a time, add the reserved warm milk to the paste, stirring continuously to avoid lumps. Once the sauce is smooth and will thickly coat the back of a spoon (you'll probably need only about 500ml/17fl oz of the milk), start to gradually add the cheese.

Consistency can be a little tricky here – when the sauce is piping hot from the oven it will become slightly thinner so allow for this in the mixture at this stage and think about making the sauce a little thicker than you might ordinarily. That said, I always keep some of the remaining hot milk back to add to the sauce once I've added the cheese, in case it is looking too thick and needs letting down again.

Add the mustard to your liking and season to taste. Put the cooked cauliflower in an ovenproof dish, pour over the cheese sauce and bake for 30 minutes until bubbling and golden brown.

52

Sicilian lemons / *Bergamot* / *Clementines* / *Lemons – Cedro, Menton* / *Mexican lime* / *Valencia Navel oranges* / *Brazilian Jumbo pawpaw* / *Costa Rican bananas* / *Queen pineapple* / *Réunion bunched lychee* / *Apples – French Chantecler Belchard, Hereford Cox Orange Pippin, Kent Russet* / *Pears – French Vassout Comice, Kent Conference* / *Chilean Muscat grape* / *Iranian pomegranate* / *Jordanian Medjool dates* / *Dried fruit – Alphonso mango slices, Corsican apricots, Prunes d'Agen* / *French pâte de fruits* / *Quince jelly* / *Bay leaf* / *Italian flat parsley* / *Rosemary* / *Sage* / *Thyme* / *Cinnamon* / *Cloves* / *Galangal* / *Ginger* / *Star anise* / *Tahitian vanilla pod* / *Nuts – Almonds, Cashews, Hazelnuts, Macadamia, Peanuts, Pecans, Pistachios, Walnuts* / *Tomatoes – Costoluto, Italian Camone* / *Chicories – French, Italian, Red and white Belgian* / *Endives – Pis-en-lit (dandelion)* / *Italian radicchios – Chioggia, Grumolo, Pink Vaneto, Puntarelle, Rose, Tardivo, Treviso* / *Cauliflowers – Boston, Cape, Romanesque* / *Cabbages – Kent Brussels tops, Kent sprouts, Normandy Savoy, Somerset kale* / *Jerusalem artichokes* / *Lautrec pink garlic* / *Perigord black truffles* / *Onions – Cevenne, Roscoff* / *Brittany shallots* / *Somerset leeks* / *Potatoes – Agria, Belle de Fontenay, Charlotte, Ratte, Somerset Pink Fir* / *Peruvian oca* / *Delica squash* / *Carrots – Brittany Sand, Chantenay* / *Celeriac* / *Crosnes* / *Horseradish* / *Parsnips* / *Parsley root* / *Red meat radish* / *Salsify* / *Somerset heirloom beetroot* / *Turnips – Brittany Golden, Scottish swede*

Sicilian Lemon
The Fruit That Just Keeps Giving

My foraging at this time of year is limited to my larder rather than the woods and hedgerows in the surrounding countryside. The larder is now full of preserves that either I or the chefs at the restaurant have made throughout the year to make the most of each season. Jars of pickled vegetables are on the bottom shelf in a cozy, dark spot. Moving up, there are flavoured vinegars and sauces, there's some of Tomas's fermented blackened Lautrec garlic, Caroline's Bing cherries in kirsch and my attempt at a tricolour of peaches in syrup. We finish with the *pièce de resistance*, Oana's Vassout Comice pear compôte (see page 229). I don't need any special hat, gloves or protective clothing for this kind of foraging and Sapphire can have a snooze in her basket, safe in the knowledge that she's not going on a dawn mission for a few weeks yet.

We're at the end of the calendar year and it was hard for me to know what wonderful produce to end with. However, after much deliberation I have settled on the Sicilian lemon – more of that over the page. In general, though, the humble lemon is one of the most versatile fruits we have. I'd go so far as to say that chefs and cooks all over the world think of it as a vital ingredient in cooking. From salads to desserts to drinks, in sweet and in savoury dishes, we can all use it in myriad ways. But I'm also convinced that, so often, we put a squeeze here or a zest there without really thinking about the origins of this fruit, and the season in which it grows.

Sometimes I think of a lemon as two fruits in one – the different parts provide distinctive flavours and we use them for different purposes. The zesty rind gives a hit of fresh citrus and pop of colour; the acidic juice adds a sharp tang. In fact, lemon juice is perfect for cutting through oily, fatty or fried foods, for adding freshness to grilled meats and fish, and for giving a lift in sweet dishes. It's wonderful to balance or enhance flavour. We rarely think about the variety or flavour of a lemon when we're using it for its juice – we tend to place more importance on actual juiciness. However, every lemon variety, influenced by the soil and climate in which it's grown, offers something different when it comes to acidity and sourness.

At Turnips, we travel the globe to source many different varieties of lemon, each with their own subtle identities. Sought-after yuzu lemons (ask a chef) are imported directly from Japan and command a very high price. Thought to be a hybrid of satsuma and Ichang Papeda (a variety of slow-growing citrus from tropical Asia), yuzu have an intense aroma that retains its sourness even when cooked at high temperatures. Often used in drinks, this rare lemon is one for using sparingly. The Meyer lemon, from North America, has a similar cult status, is also rare and also demands high prices. It is a small, thin-skinned variety of lemon growing on trees that mostly fell foul to a crippling disease. Now, though, it is being reintroduced in the USA. The fruit is thought to be a cross between Eureka and Lisbon lemons and mandarin oranges. The lemons have a striking, vibrant yellow skin encasing an extremely sweet and juice yellow-orange flesh. This is an extremely versatile fruit that is edible in its entirety and is often used raw in salads, as well as many cooked savoury and sweet dishes. Bergamot are a hybrid of lemon and orange and have a unique and aromatic flavour that is more bitter than sour. These fruit are mostly used to flavour Earl Grey tea and for their essential oils.

> "Sometimes I think of a lemon as two fruits in one – the different parts provide distinctive flavours and we use them for different purposes."

Wax on, wax off

If you are using any citrus fruit for zest, or are using the rind to make marmalade or confit, it's very important to use organic, or at the very least unwaxed fruit. After being harvested, some citrus fruit is sprayed with a fine wax coating to give it shine, slow down its deterioration and prolong its shelf life, and limit damage from pests. Food-grade wax is made from a number of different things, but mostly from carnauba wax, which is sourced from the leaves of a South American palm tree. Petroleum-based waxes are also used and even those made from shellac, which is made from the secretion of lac insects and therefore not vegetarian. Waxes are non-toxic and apparently edible, but all waxed fruit should be thoroughly washed in hot water before using. Organic citrus is never waxed.

"The mineral-rich soil around Mount Etna and the peculiar
climate of our geographic area... give our citrus, including
the Sicilian lemon, their success," Melo Laudani, grower.

Sicilian lemons

You will know by now that I place huge importance on the provenance of all fruit and vegetables. When it comes to lemons, I head back to my trusted citrus growers in Sicily, the Laudani family. The Laudanis have been running their citrus groves, in the fertile Sicilian soil, for generations. Now under the guardianship of Melo, the business continues to operate without the use of pesticides and waxes, and is as close to fully organic as possible. The Laudanis grow varieties of lemon that bloom and fruit at three times over the year, and provide us with their beautiful lemons throughout.

Melo explains "*We have a winter production called 'Primo Fiore', or first flower, the spring lemon production called 'Bianchetto', or white, which has a lighter-coloured skin that is less strong yellow and more whitish, but has the same qualities of Primo Fiore, and last we have a summer production of lemons called 'Verdello'.*

Verdello lemons are different from the previous varieties; they have a green skin and a medium size. Their harvest starts around July and their production is significantly less abundant. The juice content is lower, but the aroma is stronger. This is a peculiar lemon that allow us to extend our season to summer. We can say the season for our lemons goes from November to September, but the season of our yellow lemons goes from November to June.

We have mainly two varieties of lemons: Femminello Siracusano and Femminello Nostrale. They are pretty similar in many things, but are different in appearance. The Femminello Siracusano is preferred for its good looks and smooth skin, and Femminello Nostrale for its stronger aroma. One is grown in the Syracuse area, the other one in the volcanic seaside of Catania."

The Laudani family takes great pride in knowing that their exceptional citrus fruit are highly regarded by chefs and cooks in London, and indeed across the UK. This humble family produces what I believe to be the very best citrus all the world's groves have to offer, and we are grateful to them for letting us into their world to experience their work and produce.

To end this book, I could have chosen any one of over a hundred fantastic products that are on our stand at Borough Market at the end of December, but I chose lemons. In December, we stock six different lemons: Meyer, the giant Cedro, Etrog or finger lemon, Menton (which is an IGP-accredited lemon from the Cote d'Azure), Bergamot and, of course, Melo's Primo Fiore. I could happily have chosen any one of these brilliant citrus fruits to highlight in this chapter, and that is why this wonderful journey – through the weeks and seasons of the year – never really ends.

Preserved Sicilian lemons

Preserved lemons are such a useful ingredient to have in the kitchen. Use them whenever you need a little lemon kick in your salad dressing, or a sauce such as a hollandaise.

Makes 1 large jar

6 Sicilian lemons

6 tbsp Maldon salt

juice of 6 large Sicilian lemons

3 thyme sprigs

1 large red chilli, deseeded and chopped

Wash the six regular-size lemons. From the top, pointed end, cut each lemon into quarters, but not all the way down to the bottom – the lemons should still hold together. Slightly open up each lemon and spoon 1 tablespoon of salt into the middle of each. Press the lemon back together and pack each one into the sterilized jar. Pour over the lemon juice, seal the jar with the lid and refrigerate for 1 week.

Open the jar and, using a spoon, press the salted lemons as hard as you can to release the salty juices. Add the thyme and chilli, replace the lid and refrigerate for at least a further 1 month (the longer you wait, the better the flavour).

You can now use the lemons, chopped or sliced to add a pop of salty, lemon kick to salads, stews or sauces. You can also blitz the lemons until smooth to add to sauces or for glazing fish. They will keep in the fridge for up to 1 year.

Lemon pie

When lemons are at their peak, we should use them to make stunning desserts! This tart is so simple but with an unbelievable flavour thanks to the amazing lemons that are available at this time of year.

Serves 4–6

For the pastry

180g (6¼oz/1⅓ cups) plain (all-purpose) flour, plus extra for rolling out

55g (2oz) icing (confectioner's) sugar

pinch of salt

120g (4¼oz) unsalted butter, chilled and diced

finely grated zest of 1 lemon

1 egg, lightly beaten

For the filling

2 eggs

2 egg yolks (save the whites for the meringue, below)

150g (5½oz) caster (superfine) sugar

finely grated zest of 2 lemons

120ml (4fl oz) lemon juice

120g (4¼oz) unsalted butter, chilled and diced

For the meringue

250g (9oz) caster (superfine) sugar

4 egg whites

finely grated zest of 1 lemon

Make the pastry. Sift the flour, icing sugar and salt into a large mixing bowl. Add the butter and, using your hands, rub the butter into the dry ingredients until the mixture resembles crumble and there are no pieces of butter still visible. Add the lemon zest and mix to combine. Gradually add the egg and mix using a palette knife until the dough clumps together. Knead the dough briefly until smooth, then flatten it into a disk, cover it and chill it for 30 minutes. Roll out the chilled pastry on a floured work surface into a disk large enough to line an 18cm (7in) tart tin. Transfer the pastry to the tin and trim off any excess. Prick the base with a fork and chill the tart case while you preheat the oven to 180°C/160°C fan/350°F/Gas 4.

Line the pastry case with foil, fill it with baking beans and bake it for 15–20 minutes, until golden brown. Remove the beans and foil and cook the pastry for a further 2–3 minutes to dry out. Leave to cool.

Make the filling. Combine the eggs, yolks, caster sugar, zest and juice in a heatproof bowl and set the bowl over a pan of simmering water. Whisk for 15–20 minutes, until the mixture thickly coats the back of a spoon. Gradually whisk in the butter, then strain through a fine-mesh sieve into the cooled pastry case. Chill for 2 hours, until set.

Meanwhile, make the meringue. Tip 225g (8oz) of the sugar into a small saucepan. Add 100ml (3½fl oz) of water and set the pan over a low heat to dissolve the sugar. Bring to a boil and cook until the syrup reaches 120°C/235°F on a sugar thermometer.

Meanwhile, whisk the egg whites in a stand mixer with the remaining 25g (1oz) of sugar until they hold soft peaks. Whisking continuously on a slow speed, slowly pour the hot syrup into the egg whites. Once you've added all the syrup, increase the speed to high and whisk until the meringue is cold, thick and glossy. Spoon the meringue into a piping bag fitted with a ribbon nozzle and pipe the meringue in ruffles all over the top of the set lemon tart. Use a blow-torch to lightly caramelize and brown the meringue, scatter with extra finely grated lemon zest and serve in slices.

Lemon tart *Recipe by Jeff Galvin*

Here is Jeff Galvin's take on the classic French lemon tart. He learned how to cook it while working for the three-Michelin-starred chef Nico Ladenis and has adapted it in his own inimitable style. Be careful of the blowtorch when caramelizing the icing sugar.

**Makes a 30cm (12in) tart
(serves 10)**

For the pastry

100g (3½oz) unsalted butter, at room temperature

75g (2½oz) icing (confectioner's) sugar

seeds from ½ Madagascan vanilla pod

1 egg, beaten

200g (7oz) plain (all-purpose) flour, plus extra for rolling out

small pinch of sea salt

For the filling

375ml (13fl oz) double (heavy) cream

finely grated zest of 5 lemons

375ml (13fl oz) lemon juice

400g (14oz) caster (superfine) sugar

15 eggs

You will need one 30cm-diameter (12in), deep tart ring set on a large baking sheet lined with baking paper.

Cream the butter, icing sugar and vanilla seeds until pale and light using a free-standing mixer fitted with the paddle attachment. Little by little, add half of the beaten egg, mixing well between each addition. Sift over half of the flour and the salt and mix until nearly combined. Add the remaining egg, mix to combine and then mix in the rest of the flour.

Turn the dough out of the bowl on to the work surface and knead lightly until smooth but do not overwork or the pastry will be tough. Gather the dough into a ball, flatten it into a disk, wrap it in cling film and chill it for 2 hours before using.

Meanwhile, start the filling. Pour the cream into a saucepan, add the grated lemon zest and bring to the boil over a medium heat. Remove the pan from the heat and leave the cream to infuse for 30 minutes.

Lightly dust the work surface with flour and roll out the dough into a neat 40cm (16in) disk and use to create a pastry case inside the tart ring on the lined baking sheet. Press the pastry neatly into the corner and trim off any excess at the rim. Prick the base with a fork and chill the case for 20 minutes. Preheat the oven to 170°C/150°C fan/325°F/Gas 3.

Line the pastry case with foil, fill it with baking beans and bake blind for about 20 minutes, until the edges are just starting to turn golden. Remove the foil and beans and cook for a further 3–4 minutes to dry out the base.

Reduce the oven temperature to 110°C/90°C fan/225°F/Gas ½.

In a saucepan combine the lemon juice and sugar. Bring to the boil, stirring to dissolve the sugar. Whisk the eggs together in a large mixing bowl and pour over the lemon juice and sugar, whisking continuously. Add the infused cream, whisk until smooth and thoroughly combined and then strain into a clean bowl or large jug.

Pour the mixture into the tart case and bake for 60–65 minutes, until the filling has set. Leave to cool, then chill the tart before serving.

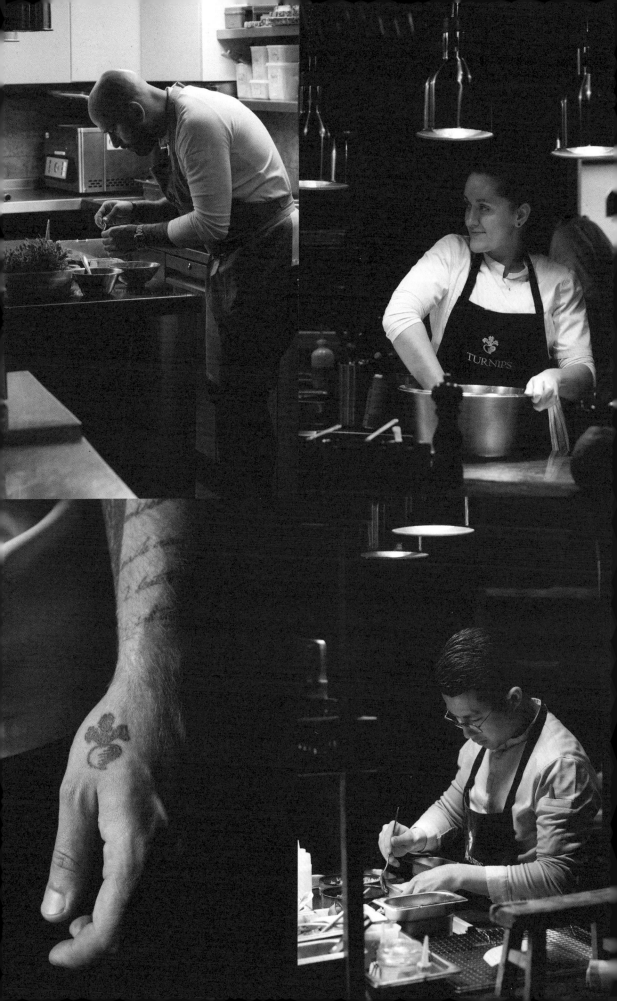

Index

About Fred Foster

Fred Foster is the Co-founder of Turnips, a fruit and vegetable wholesale and retail company with an emphasis on quality and seasonality in the heart of London. As a greengrocer, Turnips has built strong ties with independent farmers across the UK and Europe and has been supplying restaurants with the finest ingredients for more than 30 years. As well as being a core fixture at Borough Market, where the beloved Turnips retail unit caters to the market's 4.5 million yearly visitors, in 2020 Turnips set up its own critically acclaimed restaurant.

You can find out more about Turnips online at turnipsboroughmarket.com.

Acknowledgments

Wow, where do I start? Let's reverse the journey, the culmination of which is this beautiful book. A huge thanks to my Editor at DK Books Stephanie Milner in believing in me and this project. Her effortless professionalism and ability to bring together a phenomenal team of people whom I could not be more thankful for was inspiring. That team are: Maxine Pedliham, Art Director at DK Books; Matt Cox, Art Direction and Graphic Design at Newman+Eastwood Ltd – Matt, thank you for patiently listening to my many stories, something only my mum would normally do! The artwork and photography are incredible, and your calmness was contagious. Matt Russell, photographer, whose true passion in the beauty of food is something we shared right from the start. The amazing recipes, fruits and vegetables in your pictures encapsulates our stand at Borough Market and the feel of the market itself. Alexander Breeze and Kitty Coles, prop stylists for the food photography – thank you. Lucy Philpott, Editor, your nudging us to keep on track was polite-fully subtle, but brutally persistent and we loved it. And thanks to Judy Barratt, who has done an amazing job and put in some serious hours to get the text 100 per cent perfect.

To my co-conspirator and major player in the book, *chef extraordinaire* Tomas Lidakevicius. Who, along with my son Charlie, has created a restaurant from the devastation of the Covid pandemic when all seemed lost, from a pop-up to a permanent and outstanding fine-dining experience.

Tomas along with his brigade led by his two deputies, Susan (part-time chef and full-time sound man and DJ) and Oana Florentina Ciobanu (*The Pudding Lady*) have helped create most of the recipes in the book. Victoria Glass for helping me initiate the process, and Jemima Forrester at my agents David Higham Associates, who helped me compose my initial writings and is always on call if needed. Big thank you to Annie Rigg who helped hugely in the writing of this book – her infectious enthusiasm kept me going when the storm clouds moved in. I guess the sun always shines on the righteous.

It has always been my policy that business does not mix with pleasure; I have never wantonly gained favour through business. But I have made great friends through my business, through serving chefs and restaurateurs. Too many to name them all, but I think they know who they are. Nonetheless, I must single out a few: Nico Ladenis, for giving me an opportunity to shine against all the odds; Jeff Galvin, my thought-provoker who constantly challenges my expertise and who has been a friend for over 25 years. Sean Davies, who along with his wife Karen has been a true friend for 20 years and whose daughters Maggie and Lillie have both worked on the retail stand at Borough Market. Lillie has been a member of the Turnips team since she was 16, working part-time when she was at school, and now beyond. I am sure Lillie wouldn't like me to reveal her age, so let's just say she has worked with us for over ten years! Sean, who was Executive Chef at Tate Modern and various other roles was firm but fair and taught me that work is work and family life is a separate entity. *The Florida Chefs*, Nick, Tim and Jeff for being my guinea pigs in testing recipe combinations while travelling to our golf destinations back in 2019.

Thanks to all the agents who are providers of this beautiful fresh produce – Marc at Rungis, Tess in Milan, Tim and Nathan in Covent Garden Market, Cliff and Benny in Spitalfields Market. Mr Khan in Western International Market, the Jolly Family in Norfolk, the Laudani family in Sicily and the Hitchens in Wiltshire. All the great farmers in the Brittany Cooperatives and the people at Speciality Produce in San Diego: Bob Harrington, Angela, Joe and Cathy.

The fresh produce team, which is the foundation of Turnips, whether they are the office team led by Adnaan Merchant, or the wholesale night gang, with Gino at the helm, or the retail boys and girls with MJ giving the orders... they have all played a magnificent part in this wonderful family.

...And family is where it all began. Thanks to Charlie's partner Emma-Jayne or EJ, for reminding me of my pledge at Christmas 2018 to put pen to paper, which led to creating this book. My beautiful daughter Frederica, who helps to organize my time – she's my PA, PR, secretary, agony aunt and confidante, which is so invaluable for me. Tom, Freddy's husband, for listening patiently about my journey through the chapters in the book. Thank goodness he has a passion for food. My son Charlie, who has helped me throughout the process, organizing products for photo shoots, creating shopping lists, liaising with the farmers and suppliers who contributed to the book and the day-to-day running of Turnips. I am so proud of this man. He has taken the business to new highs, including wholesale, retail, catering, home delivery, restaurant, street food and juice offers. One moment he is on the phone to Jean-Philippe at Alain Ducasse, the next he is talking to Tomas about the new dishes going on our restaurant menu. Before you know it he is back on the phone and talking to Melo in Sicily about our shipment of blood oranges. Moments later you see him on the wild mushroom stall waxing lyrical about the Scottish Girolles to the market customers. But he never refused any of my demands while creating this book. Thank you, son.

Finally, my wife Caroline. My woman of the year, decade, lifetime. The true leader of our company Turnips. This lady is the glue that holds everything together. She inspires people and energizes the whole team in our workplace. She encouraged me to write this book, gave me the confidence to put it all down and then constantly pushed me to finish it. A great cook, whose dishes inspired me to include a wonderful mix of restaurant-standard food together with simple, beautiful home-cooked offerings. Caroline my love for you and all you do has no limits. Thank you for making this book a reality.

DK | Penguin Random House

Editor Lucy Philpott
Senior Designer Glenda Fisher
Senior Acquisitions Editor Stephanie Milner
Design Manager Marianne Markham
Production Editor Tony Phipps
Production Controller Rebecca Parton
Jacket Coordinator Jasmin Lennie
Art Director Maxine Pedliham
Publishing Director Katie Cowan

Consultant Writer Annie Rigg
Editor Judy Barratt
Book and Jacket Designer Matt Cox at
Newman+Eastwood
Photographer Matt Russell

First published in Great Britain in 2022 by
Dorling Kindersley Limited
DK, One Embassy Gardens, 8 Viaduct Gardens,
London, SW11 7BW

The authorised representative in the EEA is
Dorling Kindersley Verlag GmbH. Arnulfstr. 124,
80636 Munich, Germany

Text copyright © 2022 Fred Foster
Fred Foster has asserted his right to
be identified as the author of this work.

Photography copyright © 2022 Matt Russell

A CIP catalogue record for this book
is available from the British Library.
ISBN: 978-0-2415-5564-4

Printed and bound in Latvia

For the curious
www.dk.com

MIX
Paper | Supporting
responsible forestry
FSC™ C018179
www.fsc.org

This book was made with Forest
Stewardship Council™ certified
paper - one small step in DK's
commitment to a sustainable future.
For more information go to
www.dk.com/our-green-pledge

CREDITS

**DK and Fred Foster would like to thank
the following authors and publishers
for the right to include their recipes:**

• Apple tarte Tatin with crème
Normande, page 21; Salad of heirloom
tomatoes, goat's cheese and basil,
page 154: copyright © Chris and Jeff
Galvin, 22nd November 2011, *Galvin:
A Cookbook de Luxe,* Bloomsbury
Publishing Plc
• Beef wellingtons, pages 51–52;
New potato piccalilli salad, page 63:
copyright © Gordon Ramsay, 30th
August 2012, *Gordon Ramsay's
Ultimate Cookery Course*, Hodder &
Stoughton Limited (reproduced with
permission of the Licensor through
PLSclear)
• Potatoes and ceps, page 221: copyright
© Antonio Carluccio, originally
published 17th October 2003,
Complete Mushroom Book, with kind
permission of Quadrille
• Green artichoke salad, page 126;
Gratin of pumpkin, page 238:
copyright © Jennifer Paterson, 26th
September 1997, *Jennifer's Diary by
One Fat Lady*, The Oldie magazine
• Banoffee pie, pages 283–284:
copyright © Jamie Oliver 2002, 2019
• Jeff Galvin for his Lemon tart,
page 308
• Jennifer Paterson for her Pesto,
page 153; Passata, page 154

DK would also like to thank Sarah Epton
and Elizabeth Dowsett for proofreading,
Hilary Bird for indexing, Alexander
Breeze for prop styling, and Tomas
Lidakevicius and Loïc Parisot for
food styling.

Monthly shopping lists

JULY

Mangoes – Alphonso, King Kesar / French Charentais melon / Italian Cantaloupe melon / Italian Torpedo watermelon / Blueberries – Dorset, Panach' / Currants from Kent – black, red, white / French Tulameen raspberries / Italian green figs / Kent gooseberries / Loganberries / Panach' blackberries / Strawberries – Gariguette, Kent Christine, Mara des Bois / Bing cherries / French apricots / Peaches – Doughnut, Italian Flat, Pêche blanche, pêche jaune, Pêche de Vigne / Plums – French Mirabelle, Italian Drago Sanguine, Pershore / Nectavigne / Kentish wild strawberries / Wild bilberries / Curry leaves / Kentish mint – many varieties / Norfolk herbs / Norfolk marsh samphire / Methi leaves / Purple basil / Sea purslane / Edible flowers from Surrey / Sussex courgette (zucchini) flowers / Pumpkin flowers / Fresh almonds / Hazelnuts / Tomatoes – Italian summer varieties, Main crop Provence, Outdoor varieties / Baby mixed leaves Campania / Chalke Valley watercress / Italian wild rocket (arugula) / Mizuna and Tatsoi leaf / Surrey salad leaves / Endives – Pis-en-lit (dandelion), Summer fine frisée / Feuille de chêne (oak leaf lettuce) / Italian Cos / Red and green Butterhead / Salanova salad / Surrey Little Gems / Breakfast radish / Sussex celery / Cucumbers – Italian round Caroselli, Surrey / Surrey Downs spring onions / Bell peppers / Italian Friggitelli peppers / Jalapeño peppers / Padrón peppers / Pimiento Asado del Bierzo / Beans – Broad (fava) from Worcester, Coco de Paimpol, Extra fine French, Kent Bobby, Runner from Worcester / Yorkshire peas / Asparagus – Les Landes white, Norfolk / Kent broccoli / Cauliflower – Boston, Brittany / Rainbow chard / Natural vine spinach / Young Italian spinach / Chinese bok choy / Somerset Savoy cabbage / Artichokes – Brittany baby, Camus globe, Jerusalem, Violet baby artichokes from Apuli / Tiger aubergine (eggplant) / Courgettes – Brittany round, Sussex, Trombetta / Mushrooms – Cauliflower, Chicken of the Woods, Horse, Puffball, Scottish Girolle, Summer cep / Onions – Cevenne, Roscoff / Somerset leeks / Young French leeks / Potatoes – Belle de Fontenay, Charlotte, Ile de Ré, Maris Bard "earlies", Noirmoutier / Squash – Italian Turban, Potimarron / Celeriac / Baby veg – Essex beetroot, fennel, turnips / Italian fennel / Kohlrabi / Nantes carrots / Radishes – Kent, Red and white long French / Somerset bunched carrots

AUGUST

Mangoes – King Kesar, Sucking / Finger limes / Cavaillon melon / French Charentais melon / Italian Cantaloupe melon / Italian Torpedo watermelon / Plantain / Apples – Bramley, Discovery, Scrumptious, Worcester Pearmain / Pears – Bartlett, Clapp's Favourite / French figs / Italian green figs / Quince / Blackberries – Kentish, Panach' / Currants from Kent – black, red, white / Dorset blueberries / French Marquette strawberries / French Tulameen raspberries / Kent gooseberries / Muscat grapes / Bing cherries / Damsons / Nectavigne / Peaches – Doughnut, Italian Flat, Pêche de Vigne / Plums – French Mirabelle, Pershore / Reine Claude Greengages / Curry leaves / Kentish mint – many varieties / Methi leaves / Norfolk herbs / Norfolk marsh samphire / Pea aubergines (eggplants) / Purple basil / Thai basil / Edible flowers from Surrey / Pumpkin flowers / Kentish cobnuts / Hazelnuts / Tomatoes – Ailsa Craig and Red Alert from Essex, Italian summer varieties, Italian Vesuvio, Main crop Provence, San Marzano / Chalke Valley watercress / Surrey salad leaves / Endives – Pis-en-lit (dandelion), Summer fine frisée / Feuille de chêne (oak leaf lettuce) / Red and green Butterhead / Surrey Little Gems / UK Cos / Breakfast radish / Cucumbers – Italian round Caroselli, Surrey / Italian Friggitelli peppers / Jalapeño peppers / Pimiento Asado del Bierzo / Beans – Coco de Paimpol, Snake / Essex sweetcorn / Kent broccoli / Cauliflowers – Cape, Boston, Romanesque / Rainbow chard / Cabbages – Kent red and white, Somerset kale / Camus globe artichokes / Tiger aubergine / Courgettes (zucchini) – Brittany round, Sussex, Trombetta / Lautrec pink garlic / Mushrooms – Bay Bolete, Cauliflower, Chestnut, Chicken of the Woods, Hen of the Woods, Judas Ear, Penny Bun, Scottish Girolle, Slippery Jack / Onions – Cevenne, Roscoff / Somerset leeks / Potatoes – Belle de Fontenay, Charlotte, Cyprus Nicola (for mashing), Javelin "earlies", Italian Spunta (for chipping), Maris Bard "earlies", Noirmoutier, Ratte / Squash – Italian Turban, Potimarron, Spaghetti / Casava / Celeriac / Italian fennel / Kent radishes / Somerset bunched carrots / Somerset heirloom beetroot / Turnips – French, Kohlrabi / Yams

SEPTEMBER

Finger limes / Cavaillon melon / French Charentais melon / Plantain / Prickly pear / Sharon fruit / Apples – Bramley, Hereford Cox Orange Pippin, Kent Russet / Kent medlars / Pears – French Vassout Comice pear, Kent Conference, Kent Victoria / Quince / Currants – black, red, white / Kentish blackberries / Muscat grapes / Damsons / Reine Claude greengages / Plums – French Mirabelle, Kent Victoria, Pershore / Kentish mint – many varieties / Italian Monk's Beard / Norfolk herbs / Norfolk marsh samphire / Pea aubergines (eggplants) / Purple basil / Thai basil / Chestnuts / Kentish cobnuts / Tomatoes – Ailsa Craig and Red Alert from Essex, Italian Vesuvio, Main crop Provence, San Marzano / Chalke Valley watercress / Italian rocket (arugula) / Surrey salad leaves / Endives – Escarole, Summer fine frisée, Winter frisée / Late chioggia radicchio / Feuille de chêne (oak leaf lettuce) / Red and green Butterhead / Surrey Little Gems / UK Cos / Breakfast radish / Italian Friggitelli peppers / Jalapeño peppers / Pimiento Asado del Bierzo / Snake beans / Essex sweetcorn / Kent broccoli / Cauliflower – Boston, Cape, Romanesque / Cime di rapa / Chard – Rainbow, Swiss / Cabbages – Cavolo Nero, Kent Brussels tops, Kent Hispi, Kent red and white, Normandy Savoy, Somerset kale / Tiger aubergine / Courgettes (zucchini) – Brittany round, Sussex / Garlic – Lautrec pink, French smoked, Turnips' black / Mushrooms – Bay Bolete, Beefsteak Fungus, Chanterelle, Chestnut, Common Puffball, Hen of the Woods, Horse, Penny Bun, Scottish Girolle, Trumpet / Onions – Cevenne, Roscoff / Somerset leeks / Potatoes – Belle de Fontenay, Charlotte, Italian Spunta (for chipping), Lancashire Agria, Northumberland Yukon Gold, Ratte / Squash – Delica, Italian Turban, Potimarron, Spaghetti / Casava / Celeriac / Italian chervil root / Parsley root / Red Meat radish / Somerset bunched carrots / Somerset heirloom beetroot / Turnips – French, Kohlrabi / Yams– Agria, Jersey Royal "earlies", Italian Spunta / Beetroots – Candy, Cheltenham, Golden / Italian fennel / Nantes carrots / Radishes – Red Meat, Red mooli / Salsify / Turnips – Golden, Tokyo